BETTER TO BE FEARED

BETTER TO BE FEARED
Jail Life in the Raw

SEAN BRIDGES

MAINSTREAM
PUBLISHING

EDINBURGH AND LONDON

First published in Great Britain in 2008 by
MAINSTREAM PUBLISHING COMPANY
(EDINBURGH) LTD
7 Albany Street
Edinburgh EH1 3UG

ISBN 9781845963316

This book is a work of non-fiction based on the life, experiences
and recollections of the author. In some instances, names of people,
places, dates, sequences or the detail of events have been changed to
protect the privacy of others. The author has stated to the publishers
that, except in such respects, not affecting the substantial
accuracy of the work, the contents of this book are true.

Copyright permissions cleared by the author. The author has tried to trace
all copyright details but where this has not been possible the publisher will
be pleased to make the necessary arrangements at the earliest opportunity.

A catalogue record for this book is available
from the British Library

Typeset in Caslon and Gill Sans

Printed in Great Britain by
Clays Ltd, St Ives plc

AUTHOR'S NOTE AND ACKNOWLEDGEMENTS

Sean Bridges is a pseudonym. I was very tempted to write this book in my own name; however, after discussing it with my family and friends and receiving up-to-date information about one of those depicted in my story, I decided to write it under this pseudonym.

My heartfelt and grateful thanks go to my agent Mark Stanton (Stan) at Jenny Brown Associates, and to Bill, Peter and all the staff at Mainstream Publishing. I couldn't have written this book without the guidance and encouragement of a good friend, who was the inspiration required for me to write it in the first instance.

My mum, dad, brother and sister have all been very supportive of this project, as have my parents-in-law and all of our extended family. The unflinching support they gave me in the build-up to and during the term of my sentence is something I will never forget or be able to repay. To all the friends who stood by me and us as a family, thank you.

My wife and daughters have been through so much because of my actions. They have never shown anything other than understanding towards me and my situation and the commitment to all of us getting through the pain – what doesn't kill you can only make you stronger. All of my love and total respect goes to them.

May 2008

THE PSYCHOLOGY OF PRISON

Hell, as Sartre once famously remarked, is being in the company of other people; and other people are never more hellish than when they are forced upon you and their company is inescapable. That is why prison, no matter how physically comfortable it is made, will always be, for the vast majority of prisoners, utter torment.

The participants/competitors in reality TV concepts such as *Big Brother* are, in effect, imprisoned with one another. Unlike prisoners, however, they have volunteered for their incarceration in the hope of becoming very suddenly rich and famous. They have no control whatsoever over who their fellow participants/competitors might be. Like any other prisoner, they must adapt quickly to their new and very different surroundings and circumstances. It is always the case that people will assimilate change at different rates. In any given situation in which a number of people are enclosed together, there will be an immediate struggle to establish social rank. Fear of others is almost universal: fear of exploitation, of assault, of the new and of the unknown. Distrust, in these circumstances, leads to mild and not-so-mild paranoia and a feeling that everyone is, or might be, a real threat.

People differ as to how they assert themselves in such a situation. The more outgoing often react by using boastfulness, by telling tall tales about themselves in order to inflate their own importance, prowess, strength and ruthlessness. If you actually listen to prisoners talking to one another, you will hear many such stories, each man making himself out to be a criminal mastermind and enjoying oligarchic rule over the criminal underworld. Far from expressing low self-esteem, they glorify themselves; without exception, they have always outwitted the police (though their presence in jail completely defeats this premise) and many have in the past got away (sometimes literally) with murder. While most are poor, they have nonetheless made large amounts of money from undetected crime. As for physical violence, they have never hesitated to use it and they have long been feared in their respective domains.

The reason behind such boasting is clear: it is like the mimicry of species in the natural world – they fool potential predators into not preying on them. 'Don't touch me!' is the implicit message and as there is nothing criminals admire more than a crime that is both lucrative and undetected, the telling of Baron Münchausen-like tales establishes the reputation of the narrator. But since the purpose of such stories is to establish standing in the group, a sort of competition ensues as to who can tell the tallest and most impressive tale. Confrontation often results and therefore truth is the first casualty of imprisonment.

Not everyone is boastful. Some follow the 'Sinatra Doctrine', which involves getting the head down and doing time 'My Way'. These prisoners cope by making themselves as unobtrusive as possible and apparently accepting everything, no matter how unacceptable in other circumstances. Far from boasting about what they have done, or indeed complaining to other prisoners about their plight, they tell no one. Just as importantly, neither do they exhibit any curiosity about others. They play the 'Grey Man'.

These tactics have several distinct advantages. The silent remain unknown quantities whom it is dangerous to provoke or underestimate. In a general atmosphere of boastfulness in which those who lie suspect everyone else lies too, silence might seem like wisdom and strength, but it is always a mark of singular difference. The silent also do not have to live up to reputations they have falsely established for themselves. By contrast, when two men meet who have declared themselves to be fearless, a duel of some sort, mental or physical, is inevitable. The loser will then have to plot his revenge and so a vicious circle is set in motion. Men who have 'No Fear' tattooed somewhere on their bodies almost always get involved in fights.

The silent prisoner plays his cards close to his chest and is in a good position for double-dealing. Silence is one way for the coward to disguise his cowardice; for, in prison, whilst everyone is afraid and vulnerable to varying degrees, the greatest fear is appearing to be afraid or vulnerable. The very first sign of weakness invites exploitation. True friendship is almost impossible; friendliness is but a ruse, a seeking of temporary advantage and a prelude to betrayal. Tactical alliance is the nearest to friendship that is possible when people are forcibly enclosed together with no common purpose.

The enclosed world of the imprisoned is a zero-sum world – one man's advantage is another's disadvantage. Going into prison is akin to entering another world or parallel universe. You leave virtually all control at the gates, along with some of your dignity and most of your self-respect. Small – or tiny – as this world or universe might be, the horizons of those inside become limited to it. The outside world loses not only its importance but also its very existence, and a minor event inside the enclosed world is of vastly more importance to the imprisoned than anything that could be happening on the outside. Petty day-to-day events take on a level of significance for prisoners that appears absurd to the outsider, a manifestation of small-mindedness. Minor irritations become the focus of deep resentments and can even provoke extreme violence.

One of the consequences of closed, maximum-security imprisonment is a permanently inflamed sense of injustice, which leads to irritation, bitterness and anger. Although each man is himself manoeuvring for position and advantage and knows it, he is outraged when others behave in a similar fashion. The thief is outraged when others thieve, the liar when others lie, the bully when others bully.

Everyone, prisoners and staff alike, wears a mask to disguise his true character and feelings. The thickness of this mask depends entirely on the character traits inherent within the individual. No matter, it ensures the entire day-to-day operation of each prison is, in effect, a masquerade, with falsehoods aplenty, and totally devoid of genuine care and concern within its entire population.

Whilst the vast majority seek to break the rules to secure advantage for themselves, a prisoner is embittered when he is not afforded every privilege detailed under those very rules he is prepared to break without a moment's hesitation. Selfish small-mindedness comes to prevail and the bigger picture is not so much lost sight of as never exists. Outside observers of prison life are astonished – that is until they become familiar with the prevailing culture. Murderers, rapists and robbers genuinely feel bitterly aggrieved if some minor privilege has temporarily been withdrawn when under the rules it should not have been. On the face of it, this scenario sounds bizarre in the extreme; however, the prison rules are there to protect vulnerable people at the most vulnerable times of their lives.

The lack of control goes hand in hand with the paucity of influence and sits alongside the real problems attached to communicating in any meaningful manner. Telephone calls are recorded, visits are monitored.

To judge prisoners by their emotionally charged, impulsive responses, a late delivery of tobacco into prison is to them a far worse thing, morally speaking, than slashing a face from ear to ear. Indeed, the injustice suffered goes some way to justifying retrospectively their own crimes. A society that lets tobacco be delivered late into jail is not in any position to point the finger at anyone who has offended against it. That's how cons think. That's why it is absolutely vital that prison staff always play the game according to the rules – the problem is, they don't.

An almost incredible pettiness married to a total absorption in minutiae and irrelevancies results from enforced enclosure with others. It is the tiniest things that count and also provoke the deepest bitterness: words that are interpreted as insults, the most minor delays and actions that are perceived as slights or threats. Almost everything is seen in the worst possible light, for to see it otherwise is to render oneself deeply vulnerable. In the circumstances, naivety is the most dangerous of traits; cynicism is essential for survival, and the most cynical prisoner is likely to come out on top.

It is infinitely better to be feared than loved in prison; rather, it is impossible to be loved, so the only real question is how much you need to be feared.

The prison universe is a distorting mirror of 'normal' human life. Those who spend too long in it apply its principles to the whole of their earthly existence. They see all human relationships as instrumental, as a means to an end rather than as ends in themselves. All questions are for them questions of power and control: who can get away with what? If you want an idea of what Hell is all about, lock yourself up with others – they will be your Hell . . . but in return *you will be theirs*!

Anonymous

PROLOGUE: JULY 2005

I'VE NEVER BEEN LUCKY WITH BUSES

Normal service was in operation on that beautiful summer's day as I walked up towards Edinburgh's busy St John's Road, the main route into Scotland's capital city from the west. About 50 metres from the junction, you can see a bus stop on the other side of the road. It's tantalising, as inevitably the traffic is heavy and you must walk in the opposite direction to get to the pedestrian crossing rather than take a chance dodging cars. Each time I walk up towards that bus stop, I get the correct change out of my pocket in anticipation. Those last 50 metres or so are filled with trepidation, although you'd think I would be well used to it by now.

There goes one bus, and there's another right behind it. I start to walk a bit faster. Surely, there can't be another one, but, sure as fate, there is. What am I getting worked up about? It's a lovely, warm summer's day, I'm going into town to meet my brother for a bite of lunch, my iPod is blasting away in my ears and I've been out of prison for almost a year.

Needless to say, I'm on my own at the bus stop – everyone else has been picked up by one of the three buses I've missed. I lean against the wall, confident that the wait will be short and I'll make the meet time OK. Michael McDonald is sounding fantastic and his 'Sweet Freedom' has never sounded so ironic but so good.

One of the many great things about living in Edinburgh is that the bus services are generally excellent and on this particular route into the city centre I probably have a choice of eight buses or more. The wait will be short, I'm sure – but no less eventful, as it turns out.

After about a minute or so, and just as the sun is beginning to make me sweat through my new linen shirt, along comes a skinny guy of indeterminate age, with a Staffordshire bull-terrier trudging along behind him, trailing a shabby lead along the pavement. You know the type of guy I'm talking about: could be anywhere between 30 and 50, probably at least 14 pounds underweight for his height, which was around six foot. He is wearing a tweed-type jacket that is way too big for him, and in spite of the heat he looks fairly cool. I take in all of these details in a matter of two seconds whilst the guy is walking towards me. Without looking him in the eye, I am able to assess the threat level posed by this man.

What threat? The guy is out for a walk with his dog! He poses no threat to me whatsoever. I am over six feet tall and weigh around 210 pounds. Get that prison mentality out of your head – you're no longer in jail, I tell myself, as Robert Palmer fills my head with 'She Makes My Day'. I hadn't solved this particular jail problem just yet, even though there had been a couple of occasions during the previous few months when the violence and anger in me had reared their ugly heads.

The guy and his dog walk slowly past. I keep my gaze to the west until I'm certain he's past me and then slowly turn my head to look ahead. In my peripheral vision, I can see that he is scouring the ground in and around the bus shelter. His dog is standing close to him, looking underfed and pissed off with the heat, its long tongue dangling out of its mouth. This takes me back, and how! This guy's looking for cigarette butts. It's just like I'm back in the jail again, with the cons who don't have a bolt searching for a discarded butt so that they can get a last couple of drags out of it, or can squeeze the last few strands of tobacco out into a cigarette paper, or skin, for a poor man's roll-up.

Bingo! As I turn my head slightly towards him, he picks up a butt and fishes a disposable from his pocket and lights it. Next, he does something I just can't do. He squats, his back against the wall of the bus shelter and his knees in full flex, with his heels right up against his backside. His dog shuffles closer, but he only blows a lungful of smoke in its direction and it backs away, sniffing and snuffling. Robert Palmer is still chanting away and I look again towards the west in my forlorn search for that distinctive shape and colouring of Edinburgh buses.

Another guy is walking towards the stop now. He looks around 40, maybe a bit younger, and is wearing a white cotton, long-sleeved shirt. He has on smart slacks and black dress shoes. His trousers seem a bit too high on the waist. He is carrying a small rucksack which is swung over his right shoulder as he removes his glasses to read the timetable posted on the inside of the shelter. I'm still listening to Palmer and enjoying the heat of the sun as it beats down.

My attention is then grabbed by some movement to my left and, as I look round slowly, Scumbag is standing close to Whiteshirt and is talking to him. I can't hear a word of what is being said, as the beats are still pounding in my ears. I slowly reach into my pocket, unlock the iPod and immediately pause the play function but leave the earphones in place. At the same time, Whiteshirt looks at me with fear in his face, pleading for help.

As my hearing adjusts to the lack of beats and the new sounds of traffic, I strain to catch what is being said. Whiteshirt is looking ever more fearful. Scumbag is standing very close to him now and has glanced at me a couple of times, but his movements are too deliberate, so I'm able to anticipate them and look away in time. I clearly hear: 'Give me it or I'll kick your fuckin' head in.' Here it comes, and as that familiar cold feeling washes over me, everything seems in focus but distant with zero perspective, like I'm looking through the wrong end of a telescope. Time to move.

'Hey, pal,' I shout. 'What's your name?' There's nothing more disarming in a situation in which you think you are in control than to have someone ask your name – all of a sudden, it's personal.

'Fuck off, big man. This's got fuck all to dae wi' you!'

I remove my iPod from my pocket and start to wrap the earphones' flex around it for safety's sake – no point in damaging my prized possession. 'Go on, tell me your name. I tell you what, I'll tell you mine first and then we can both get to know each other a wee bit better.'

'I told you to fuck off, big man. This is nane o' yir business!'

The dog has this mystified but attentive look on its face. It looks half-starved but could pose a threat if I give it half a chance. Whilst Scumbag is getting clammier with Whiteshirt, I instantly work out a strategy to deal with Muttley. At the same time, I say, 'Hey, fuckwit, go and bother someone else, that is unless this guy here in this beautifully clean white shirt tells me that it's OK for you to be bothering him today. Well, is it, pal?'

He both shakes his head and in some kind of accented English says that he'd never met this man until a couple of minutes ago and he *is* bothered by his presence – at least that's what I think he says, it's definitely English as you would learn it from a textbook. Regardless, he's in trouble and beginning to look more and more frantic.

Scumbag then decides to get even fresher by threatening me with the dog just as I take one giant step towards Muttley with my left foot and stand about halfway down the lead so that it's trapped between my foot and the ground. The dog doesn't even get a chance to work out what the fuck's happening to it before my size-nine right peg crashes into its skull and knocks it spark out – I was always handy with the old right peg. I hear it take a long sighing breath and know that the potential problem of the dog is just that – potential.

Scumbag is about to start complaining about the fact that I've just laid his dog out cold when I grip him by the throat with my right hand and grab his trouser waistband with my left. One of the things I got into in jail was gym work and I'm strong enough to lift this fuckwit right off his feet, which I manage to do. His head comes into contact with the bus shelter, accompanied by a dull thud. Very quietly, and desperately trying not to gag with the stench of very ripe body odour, I explain to Scumbag that I want him to take himself and his dog for a nice long walk, well away from this bus stop, so that me and Whiteshirt can go back to enjoying what was, until three minutes earlier, a wonderful day. I then realise that he can't take the dog for a walk because it's still snoozing from the kick. This thought makes me smile.

I let Scumbag down from his elevated position and he picks up Muttley, then proceeds to walk away towards the city centre. Whiteshirt is, in fact, a Norwegian tourist who loves the city and is gushing in his thanks for my intervention.

This is what jail has made me. I am frightened of nobody and yet wary of everybody. No situation scares me and yet I never feel relaxed except when I'm at home. I'm ready and willing to have a go at anyone, any time, if I think they've got it coming – all of this despite being known as a white-collar criminal.

CHAPTER ONE

My crime was fraud, a business fraud – a ridiculous one at that. My treatment at the hands of the Scottish Criminal Justice System and the Scottish Prison Service was beyond ridiculous and ended up being just plain cruel. Another whining criminal, I hear you shout. No, just someone who pled guilty at the first opportunity, was hit with a shocker of a sentence and then had that sentence managed in a way that defies belief.

A thought: Lord Jeffrey Archer was sentenced to four years' imprisonment for another crime of dishonesty – perjury. I was sentenced to four years for an attempted fraud involving a business contract. Lord Archer spent three weeks in HMP Belmarsh, which is a maximum-security facility in London, before moving to less secure conditions. I spent almost 14 months in maximum security, and it is precisely that experience that has made me what I am today.

My story is a simple one. A basically decent, well-educated family man stupidly gets himself into bother with the law and ends up in jail. My intentions for my jail time were to use it productively. I had known for some considerable time that I was to receive a custodial sentence; the police investigation started in February 2000 and I was sentenced in September 2002 – more than two and a half years. It was a sentence on its own. The waiting was hellish.

Anyway, back to my intentions. I was going to use the time inside to better myself, get more education, read more, study new subjects, all the usual stuff – oh, and also to reflect on my guilt and sob through long dark, very noisy nights at the plight of my wife and daughters, who were suffering just as much as me and who were guilty of precisely zero. I did plenty of sobbing, especially in those very dark early days.

I expected to enter a system that was 'fit for purpose', with the right people in the right positions, all of whom would be focused on ensuring that care, rehabilitation and reducing the potential for re-offending were their top priorities. I was in for a massive shock.

■ ■ ■

The shit hit the fan for me on the last Friday of February 2000. It was on that day that I confessed to my fellow directors that I had engineered a fraud involving a business contract. The police were informed that day and so began the slow, tortuous process of getting me to court so that I could be sentenced. I met with a criminal solicitor later that afternoon, who advised me to say nothing to anyone and explained how the process would pan out.

Telling my wife and daughters was and still is the most difficult thing I've ever done in my life. Their looks of incredulity and incomprehension, sliding into anger and then realisation that this was very, very serious will never be forgotten by me. I felt like a complete fucking idiot. I was head of the household, a larger-than-life character who was always there to help them – all of a sudden, sitting on the sofa, I'd turned into a shell of a man, with tears running down his face, muttering 'sorry' every four or five seconds. None of them moved to console me by hugging or touching me in any way. I needed that but understood why they were sitting still. After a long silence, my elder daughter asked if there was anything else that they should know – I asked if what I'd told them wasn't enough for now and tried a half-hearted laugh. She didn't laugh and merely stared straight back at me until I shook my head to confirm that there was nothing else. I started shaking a bit and was crying again. I felt totally alone, and insecurity washed over me in ever-greater waves. Most of all I felt ashamed that I'd caused so much grief and unhappiness for the three people I love more than anything or anyone else on this planet.

I needed to develop a plan, a strategy for coping with this total upheaval in my life, all of it self-inflicted. I decided that I had to tell the rest of my family – my parents, brother and sister – as well as a few close friends. Over the course of the weekend, I visited my parents and brother along with my wife and told them the gory story. They reacted with astonishment, similar to my wife and kids, but stated that they would be right behind me all the way. I never expected anything less. For all of our faults as a family, loyalty has never been a question. My mum and dad asked if it would help me if they told my sister. I needed that offer then, as I was beginning to wilt under the constant telling and re-telling.

I also visited and spoke with three close friends, guys whom I trusted implicitly and who knew us very well as a family; guys who I considered would be supportive of me and, more importantly, of my wife and kids. Was I wrong about them being friends whom I could trust! One of the things my solicitor told me as part of her throwaway stuff at our first meeting – a bit like the terms and conditions at the foot of a credit agreement – was that I'd soon find out exactly who my friends were. I remember thinking, I know exactly who my friends are, thanks. What an arrogant arse! Those three friends turned out to be so-called friends, fairweather friends – people whose lack of support caused me and my family so much additional grief over such a long time that I now have feelings of total disdain for them. I seriously hope that nothing happens in their lives that shakes the monotonous, straightforward nature of their existence – they just would not be able to cope with it. To all of them, and they know who they are, thanks for fuck all. Oh, and by the way, don't try crossing the road in front of my car. I might not be able to find the brake.

On the Monday following my various confessions, it was just as if nothing had happened. My wife went to work and our younger daughter went off to attend her lectures at university, leaving me at home – jobless. Our elder daughter was sharing a flat at that time. It was like this for the next couple of weeks – more and more of precisely nothing, all the time waiting for that fateful knock on the door. I spent some days over at my parents' house talking, crying, getting angry with myself and feeling the guilt and responsibility ripping out of every pore in my body. They were great. In spite of a few bits of advice, which showed me they just had to say it out loud to hear it for themselves, their support was a major plank in rebuilding the platform that would allow me to start to find myself again. I needed to get a job – one for which the application form didn't ask too many questions and which would require attendance and not much else. We didn't need the cash at that time, but I needed to get back on the bike.

Two weeks later, I spotted that the local pizza place was advertising in their window for delivery drivers. Here goes. Went in, filled in a single-sided application form and went away with a uniform comprising a multicoloured polo shirt and an equally bright baseball cap. I've got a head the size of a football, so there was no way that cap was going to make it onto my bonce. 'Start tomorrow at midday and we'll work the rest of your hours out from there,' said the midget of a manager. All I needed to bring with me, other than the uniform, was my car to deliver the pizzas. Big problem was that I was driving a 5-Series BMW at the time and somehow just couldn't see myself delivering Pepperoni Paradises in that. My old man had a Ford Fiesta, so a quick call to him was all that was needed and I was set. The thought that someone actually needed me again was unbelievable. Even if all I did was walk through the back door of the shop and sign on to deliver the next couple of pizzas off the conveyor, fuck me, it felt fantastic. I began to kid myself on that I'd bottomed out and was on the up again.

It's amazing how your brain, mind, call it what you like, works in stressful situations. I was only two weeks into the biggest fucking nightmare of my life at age forty-eight and I was beginning to think I'd cracked it. The realisation that I would still have to go through the grinder of the Scottish Criminal Justice System brought me back to my senses. That, along with the fact that the Fairweathers had started to signal their intentions by not returning calls and gradually moving away, sent me on a downward spiral emotionally. The only positive thing I had to hold on to was the job.

In the beginning, I was doing evenings, starting at 5 p.m. and working through until around 10.30/11 p.m., Monday to Saturday. It meant that I hardly saw my wife, as she was coming in the door as I was going out. Curiously, it sort of worked for both of us during those first few weeks as we came to terms with the situation.

The police called unannounced one Thursday afternoon in late March 2000. Our younger daughter was at home at the time, as she didn't have lectures that day. Five of them arrived and announced that they had a warrant and intended to search our house and remove whatever they felt would provide them with evidence of my fraud. They arrived around 2.30 p.m. and the only question I asked them was how long they thought they might take. I didn't want my wife arriving back to find some cop going through her underwear drawer. It took them about two hours to complete their search and they removed some papers and the family computer, which had precisely nothing on it. The head man said that they would be in touch when they had something to tell me, but he couldn't tell me when that would be – it turned out to be months later, when I was detained and interviewed under caution.

I went to work that night and it dawned on me that I needed to start working to repair my relationship with my wife. We'd been married for twenty-five years; it was our silver wedding anniversary two days after the police search of the house. We'd planned a trip to Venice on the Orient Express but obviously cancelled it when the shit hit the fan. I asked the pizza boss, who was about five feet tall and just as wide – too many pizzas methinks – if he could change my hours to daytime, Monday to Friday. He said he would look into it and let me know. The only thing was that there weren't lots of pizzas ordered during the day; however, the cardboard boxes for pizzas and garlic breads needed to be folded from flat packs in preparation for the busy evening shift. If that's what it would take to get me back into my marriage, then stack them up and let's get folding. By the end of that job, some four months later, I was known as 'The Boxman' – I set some sort of record for the amount of boxes folded in one hour. Wow!

During the next couple of years, I worked as a postman with the Royal Mail, a mini-cab driver and lastly as an enforcement officer with TV Licensing, at that time part of the Post Office. Looking back on it, all I was was a delivery man: started with pizzas, moved on to letters, then on to people in the taxi, and finally on to delivering 'bad news' with TV Licensing.

CHAPTER TWO

I was arrested by appointment on a Tuesday in April 2001 – I was very grateful for that. I was called the previous Thursday to set a time and date for my arrest. Couldn't be the Friday – that might mean a weekend in police cells. Mondays are too busy, so Tuesday it was. The arrangements were that if I consented to be arrested before 5 a.m. the police would guarantee that I would be put before the sheriff that day, where I would be guaranteed to get bail. Any later than 5 a.m. and there was the possibility that I would miss that day's court diet, meaning a night in police cells. A total no-brainer. The two principal detectives picked me up from home at 4.30 a.m. and I was taken to a local police station for processing, which included fingerprinting, photographing, etc., before being moved to the main police station, which serves the Sheriff Court in Edinburgh's city centre. I arrived there around 5.30 a.m. and was told that I'd be getting moved to the court at around 8.30 a.m. Nothing in the cell other than a concrete bench and a very thin plastic mattress, so I tried to get my head down, tried to snooze, but thoughts of not getting bail were battering around my brain. What happens in court? Will my solicitor be there? How do I contact my wife if I don't get bail? Fuck's sake, don't panic, I kept telling myself.

I'd just started to nod off when the peephole shifted at around half-seven and I was asked what kind of hot roll I fancied. For a moment, I didn't know where I was. A couple of nanoseconds later,

I'd got my head back in gear and chose the black-pudding roll. The door was then opened far enough to pass me the roll and a very sweet, milky tea in a Styrofoam cup. I don't take sugar in tea or coffee but wolfed the roll washed down by the tea. Some time passed and then I heard the round-up of the various guys who were occupying the other cells in that fairly long corridor before they arrived at my cell. I was cuffed by my right hand to another guy's left hand and told to follow on. It was the first time I'd been in handcuffs – I never, ever, got used to it. There were about nine or ten of us. Come to think of it, it had to be an odd number, as one guy had his very own personal pair of cuffs.

We were loaded into a Transit van with smoked windows. There weren't enough seats for all of us, so there was a minute or so of sorting ourselves out – not much chat, just general manoeuvring to get comfortable. One guy ended up squatting on the floor with his right hand held high, connected to his cuffmate, who was seated. The journey to Edinburgh's Sheriff Court took about ten minutes, if that. No one spoke during that time. There was something strange about being able to hear the chat between the driver and his mate, and also listen to the van radio, which was tuned to the local station, Forth One. It was as if everything in the world was OK, but how could it be? I was in the back of a police van being taken to court, having been arrested and charged with a serious fraud. It was almost as if no one really cared. A sense of isolation started to grip me – crazy, I know, but it was as if I was on my own in this mess and I would just have to get on with it. That, of course, wasn't the case, but it was probably the first of my coping strategies coming to the fore: this is me, I'm to blame for all of this shit, so get a fucking grip and get through it. Sounded great for the couple of seconds it took me to start having doubts again. It was to be that way after sentence was passed on me and throughout my time inside – a continual questioning of my capability to get through, cope and come out the other side, whilst at the same time battering myself with guilt and feelings of responsibility, particularly in relation to what I'd put my wife and daughters, wider family and real friends through.

Arriving in the bowels of the Sheriff Court, we were all shuffled off the van and awkwardly walked and were guided towards some heavy double doors, which were unlocked by the driver's mate. A narrow fluorescent corridor stretched in front of us. As we walked along it, towards yet another locked door, that, too, was opened and we were led into a larger space with cells on either side. The guy who was cuffed to himself and partner-less was unceremoniously shoved into the first cell on the right. He shouted some unintelligible abuse at the police escorts. One particularly big screw stood up against the cell bars and laughed, as if trying to encourage the guy to keep going. Sensibly, the guy backed off and sat down on the steel bench at the back of the cell. One by one the remaining cell doors were opened along the right-hand side of the holding area. Some cells already had occupants. I was loaded into the third cell up on the right and uncuffed before being invited to enter.

I'd had to give up my watch and belt at the police station and was trying to estimate the time. It had to be around 9 a.m. If I was close to the time estimate, then I was sure the court opened for business at 10 a.m. and so there was not too long to wait. There were another five guys of varying ages and states of dress in the same cell as me. Two of them knew each other and were chatting away about a mutual friend in terms that I didn't understand, using language that was alien to me, filled with slang and guttural, sometimes coughed words that although whispered between the two of them could probably be heard yards away – heard, but not understood. Suddenly, one of the two chatterers jumped up, went over to the bars and kicked one of them whilst shouting at the top of his voice that he needed a smoke and that would be 'right fucking now', wouldn't it?

'Shut the fuck up!' was the response that wafted along from the desk, which was a further ten yards or so into the cell area. There then followed a game of ping-pong as shouts of 'I know my rights' were followed by further abuse from the desk, and then someone in a white shirt with some fancy epaulettes arrived to try and placate the nicotine addict. The unusual thing was that the person in the white shirt was a female. She instantly quietened the guy down, handed him a fag and lit it with her click lighter. An air of calm was restored until the others in the cells either side also piped up about needing a fag, desperate for a drag at the weed. She made sure that everyone was sorted out. I could have kissed her. It wouldn't be the only time I was to see female staff deal with a problem in a fashion that male colleagues would have struggled with, although I did see one female screw take a hellish beating at Glenochil before other staff got to her. Mind you, it wasn't her fault, she was dealing with a fucking psycho.

We waited in the holding cell for about 30 or 40 minutes, I'd guess, before various solicitors were escorted along in front of the cells to identify their clients to staff, who opened up and let them out for the pre-appearance chat. I just had to be the last of my group, but eventually my solicitor arrived and nodded at me and I was told to come out of the holding cell. I followed her along to the desk area and into a small room just off it, where she immediately started talking very quickly, explaining what was about to happen. Never even got a 'How are you doing?' or 'Are you OK?' before I was forced to concentrate on her instructions. Then followed the details of what to say and what not to say when ushered into the dock. Confirm my name, address and date of birth only. No plea would be entered and the sheriff would be asked to decide on bail. 'Nothing is certain' – I'm sure I heard her say that. The rest was lost to me as my brain started reeling and effectively shut down my ability to listen. What if I was remanded? What would Saughton be like? What about my wife and girls? They all thought this was just part of the procedure, as did I.

I was fourth up from my cell. Two of the previous three had been returned to the cell, one awaiting remand transfer and the other for various bail documents to be prepared. I had no idea who the sheriff was – was he a 'hanging judge' type, or more of a liberal? These thoughts flashed through my brain for the next hour or so. Finally, it was my turn and I was summoned by the screw to walk through the rabbit warren and then up into the bright sunlight of the court.

You enter the dock by walking upstairs straight into it. I was told to face the sheriff by the guy who'd escorted me up. I glanced right to see my solicitor and another guy in black gowns facing each other over a large rectangular table. I was asked by the clerk to confirm my name, address and date of birth, and then we were into it. Here goes, I thought, shit or bust. But then the whole thing was over in less than 30 seconds. The other guy said something about the charges against me, my solicitor said that I would be pleading not guilty to them and requested that I be granted bail. The other guy said that he had no objections to bail and the sheriff said OK and that was it. I actually didn't realise that the whole thing was over until the screw tapped me on the shoulder to take me back downstairs again.

A few seconds later, I was back in the holding cell being asked by the chatterers what had happened. 'I got bail,' I responded. Nothing came back. That was great with me; I wasn't up for conversation, at least not with that pair. The desk screw had said it would take a few minutes to complete the paperwork and then I could be on my way. It took a good 30 minutes and then I was summoned to the cell door and allowed out to walk along to the desk to sign a few forms and collect my personal stuff – watch, cash, belt, etc. From there, it was just a short walk to the exit door, which threw me out onto the road that stretches below the court. Old Edinburgh is full of criss-cross streets and I followed this one down to the Grassmarket, feeling as if everyone who was walking and driving in the area would know that I'd just appeared in court and been released on bail – ridiculous, yeah, but real feelings nonetheless.

CHAPTER THREE

Almost 16 months passed before I was back in the system and it was to be a completely different experience from the one I'd gone through in April 2001. During the intervening period, I was answering bail calls on a semi-regular basis, all of them dependent on public holidays, judges' holidays and admin problems within the Scottish Court Service. I was also having meetings with my defence team, comprising my solicitor and a QC who, according to the *Scotsman* newspaper, was 'a celebrated criminal practitioner'. He would be a lot less celebrated in my eyes when my case actually came to court.

Criminal law is a mystery to most of us, me included. We all think we know a bit about it by following news stories that take our interest and watching documentaries and the like, but the one thing that no one realises is the inordinate amount of time it takes to get to court. I stupidly thought that when the shit hit the fan I was going to hold up my hands, admit my guilt for exactly what I'd done and get the crappy part out of the way as soon as possible. Madness!

First, my solicitor told me to admit to nothing. 'But I've told you what happened and I'm guilty,' I said.

'That's not the point,' I was told. 'We can't control things if you admit to your guilt at this stage – you'll be crucified.' What? Surely I couldn't be crucified for anything other than what I was admitting to. Wrong! My experience of the system is the same as that of many others: that the Crown attempt to shoot at you with a sawn-off shotgun, hoping that at least some of the pellets are going to hit you and do as much damage as possible. The search for the truth starts to fail at that very early point.

During the long months between my appearance at the Sheriff Court and eventually getting to the High Court in Glasgow, I was continually amazed by some of the stuff that was going back and forwards between the Crown Office and my solicitor. It was as if the Crown were trying to ensure that I was 'done', regardless of whether their allegations were true and could be proved or not. It was like being forced into a corner, so that I would realise that it was useless to try and defend the charges because all they would do was produce more and more of them. Drowned in a mountain of paper – what a way to go. For every new allegation they came up with, I was called into the solicitor's office to explain. I wanted to plead guilty, for fuck's sake. Surely it couldn't be that difficult.

I was warned by a close family friend who had experienced 'the system' some years earlier that I wasn't to plead guilty and was asked by him to promise that I wouldn't. I looked him in the eye and gave him my word. If I had my chance again, knowing what I know now, I wouldn't have, but with the advice and guidance given by my solicitor and QC and the way in which the Crown Office were levelling more and more ridiculous allegations against me, it seemed the only possible route to go down was to plead guilty and get on with serving whatever time was handed down to me. That was the only certainty – that I was going to do time.

Just before I went to court in July 2002, I sat for a whole morning at the solicitor's office in a large, stuffy room on my own, wading through the copy evidence file, which was over three feet high, turning various shades of red as I scanned over the police interviews with the others involved. You see others were unwittingly involved in ensuring that my fraud was 'successful' in the first instance. Only one of them was able to tell the truth in their police statements.

Put it this way, if I had my time again I'd plead not guilty. The system fucked me anyway. The judge did not announce any discount for my pleading guilty, one of a number of mistakes made during the case, and it would have been worth it to see the others involved in my case in the witness box. They really didn't know that in their statements they all contradicted one another – even my QC would surely have had a field day, but then again maybe not. The judge did say at the end of my court appearance that perhaps the Crown Office should consider looking at other prosecutions – none materialised.

I appeared at the High Court in Glasgow on 29 July 2002 on petition. I was charged with five heads of indictment, (a) to (e), and the deal 'hammered' out with the Crown over a period of sixteen months or so was that I would plead guilty to (a), (d) and (e), and that as a result (b) and (c) would be 'considered delete'. The fact that (b) and (c) were absolute garbage meant nothing to me other than the fact that they were no longer worth worrying about. I couldn't have been more wrong. Another fuck-up was to come to light a month or so into my sentence in relation to this so-called plea bargain.

I travelled through to Glasgow by train on that sunny Monday morning with all my family, apart from our younger daughter, who was on a working holiday in the States, and we all connected via a couple of taxis to the High Court. We got there early, as advised by the solicitor, and I was shown to one room, while my wife, elder daughter, parents, brother and sister and her husband were shown to another. Why Glasgow when the High Court sits in Edinburgh? Well, it's like this. My case was allocated to a particular judge, as are all other cases coming before the High Court. These judges travel a circuit and so, regardless of the inconvenience to anyone and everyone and the associated expense involved, the location of the judge decides where the case will be heard. We had all turned up at the High Court in Edinburgh ten days previously and spent the whole day there, doing precisely nothing other than sitting looking at one another before being told that the judge was going to be delayed on a murder trial as the jury was taking longer than anticipated in reaching a verdict. Glasgow it was, then.

The solicitor arrived first and asked me how I was and we exchanged inane pleasantries. She explained that the way the hearing would work was that the heads of indictment would be read out and I would be asked to sign the plea book, pleading guilty to (a), (d) and (e). The Crown would then detail its case against me and my QC would probably decide not to offer a plea in mitigation at this time and rather wait until the sentencing hearing to proffer my pleas, such as they were. The intervening time would be spent having a social inquiry report prepared on me – normally three weeks, but at that summer holiday time of year no one knew exactly how long it might take. Thoughts of being remanded in custody should be 'swept from my mind', as I'd already been on bail for over 15 months and so obviously did not present as a flight risk and could be relied upon to attend on any future date for sentencing.

My QC arrived in a swirl of black winged collar, white shirt and long straggly grey hair tied in a ponytail – I kid you not. He took me outside into the very grand corridor that encircles the High Court; others were already meeting with their advisers in the main waiting room for accused persons. QCs have to be accomplished actors to be in any way successful in their profession, and so I always felt that I was on the receiving end of a performance. It continued with the classic assurance that we wouldn't even talk about me being remanded in custody, as the chances of that happening were so insignificant as to preclude any discussion! I remember that conversation as if we had it ten seconds ago. I reminded him of it *ad verbum* in the cells under the High Court after the judge had decided that I was far too dangerous a criminal to be allowed bail pending sentencing. I don't blame her for making that decision. Sounds crazy, I know, but I remember virtually every word spoken by the Advocate Depute on behalf of the Crown that fateful day and I can understand entirely why she remanded me in custody. I was told by my QC that it would be more beneficial if my pleas were heard before sentencing, so they were fresh in the judge's mind. But the result was that he just sat there and let a load of utter shit be said about me and how and why I'd committed the crime. Some of it was complete fiction, some of it had a basis in fact and some of it was true. The judge wasn't to know that, however, and after I'd signed the plea book, pleading guilty to heads (a), (d) and (e), she stated that she felt she had no option but to remand me in custody.

Ever been in a situation that is so stressful, strange, unexpected and new that you hear a humming in your ears allied to a sense of utter disbelief that what has just happened has actually happened and it isn't just a bad dream? I heard her say, 'Take him down!' and, as I turned to look at my family to try and mouth that I was OK and to force a smile, I was shoved by the police officer on my left and pulled at the same time by the one on my right. The next minute I was walking down steps into the brightly lit and stale-smelling bowels of the court.

I had managed to catch just a fleeting glimpse of my wife, elder daughter and the rest of my family as I was rapidly disappearing from their sight. They looked shell-shocked – the QC had told them exactly the same as he'd told me: my being remanded was virtually impossible. Yeah, that will be shining bright! I must admit that my primary concerns were for them, but all that changed when I was taken before the desk in the cell area under the court. I had seen, read and heard so much about the drills of removing tie, shoelaces, belt and anything else that might be used to do damage to yourself or others. Here I was going through it myself.

'Empty your pockets,' the desk guy said.

That was when it really hit me that I wasn't going home that day. I had the return train ticket in my suit jacket pocket. I laid it on the desk in front of the guy. He took a look at it and said, 'Ye'll no' be needin' that the day.' He glanced at it again and said, 'Pity it was a *day* return, eh?' The two policemen either side of me started to suppress giggles. I said precisely fuck all and started to take my belt off and untie my laces, having already emptied my pockets onto the desk. I think it was at that exact moment that my total disdain for most of the guys in white shirts was germinated. That disdain was to grow like crazy over the next couple of years or so and develop into almost total contempt.

The desk guy started to go through the formalities: 'You've been remanded in custody, blah, blah, blah' – I didn't hear very much of it, my head was spinning almost beyond my control. I was on the point of screaming, '*This is a big mistake! I was told by my brief . . .*' but fortunately I thought better of it and kept totally schtum.

'Normally, your brief comes down to see you with your solicitor,' said the desk guy. 'We'll stick you in a room to wait for them. What kind of sandwich would you like for lunch? You see, you've missed the morning bus to Barlinnie, so you're here for a wee while.'

Lunch! Was he fucking joking? The last thing I needed to do at that time was make a decision between corned beef or tuna. Looking back, it's hilarious. At the time, it was launching me towards screaming out loud at a fucking rate.

I was shuffled into a brightly lit room with a half-glass door and no windows – no surprise there, as we must have been below ground level. A bit of consolation: my brain was still working, although obviously not at the same level as normal.

I must have waited about 15 minutes, sitting in the one position with my elbows resting on my thighs and my head in my hands. A policeman opened the door and said that my brief was on the way down. The QC and my solicitor came in, or should that be breezed in, and sat behind the cheap table that dominated the centre of the room – bolted down, of course. I was on the other side and waited with bated breath to hear what was going to be said by either of them, but particularly what Catweazle's take on this was going to be.

Then it came. 'You'll be going to Barlinnie.'

'Are you having a fucking laugh?' I responded, trying desperately to keep seated. I could feel my blood pressure rising. Thoughts of strangling my QC were rapidly developing in my mind. 'I know I'm going to Barlinnie – I've just been remanded in custody. That's where they take you from this court!' Neither of them said anything in response. 'What the fuck happened in there?' I asked. 'Some of the shit that was put before the court was just that – shit – and you never moved to say anything that might have in some way contradicted what was being said, despite the fact that you know all the facts.'

'The time for me to say what we want said is during the plea in mitigation, which will be in Edinburgh in five weeks' time. It wasn't the right time today,' responded the QC.

'Oh no?' I said. 'By not saying anything, you sealed my fate. If I'd been the judge and heard all of that shit, I would have remanded me in custody as well.'

The solicitor spoke next. 'We'll try to get you High Court bail, which will get you out, but we're not very hopeful.'

Catweazle pipes up that he thinks, given my background, social class and the fact that I come from Edinburgh, that I should ask to be put into 'protection', as I might become a target for 'less savoury types'.

'You've got to be fuckin' kidding, eh? I'm not going into protection. You both know fuck all about me. Is that it?'

They looked at each other and then back at me and started to get up from the table. That was it! I can't remember if anything was actually said by way of goodbyes, but they left the room and my choice of a tuna sandwich and a can of Coke was brought in by a white shirt after they had vanished from my view. He said that the van would be at least another hour or so and that I'd get moved to the jail in plenty of time for the tea meal. I didn't appreciate the importance of food and mealtimes in prison at that stage – I had no thoughts of food – but it wasn't very long into my time inside that I became aware of its significance and all things related to it.

The time between my 'legal team' leaving and the van arriving seemed to pass very quickly. I picked at the tuna sandwich and drank about half of the Coke. I couldn't get rid of my thoughts of my wife, daughter and the rest of my family travelling back through to Edinburgh without me. How would I make contact with them? When could I phone them?

I deliberately hadn't taken any money with me just in case of that one-in-a-million chance I was remanded. What a clanger that was. Here's a tip – if you know you're going to be locked up, then make sure you have a few quid in your pocket. The cash goes immediately into your own PPC account for use in making purchases through the canteen and paying for phone calls, etc. (PPC stands for Personal

Property and Cash.) I had fuck all on me and it meant that I had to make an emergency call to my dad (courtesy of the only decent screw in Bar-L), who fired through from Edinburgh in his car the next day and deposited some money into my PPC account.

I was cuffed and led into the van for transfer to Barlinnie. These vans are divided into minute cubicles, called sweat boxes, where I found that my knees were up against the facing divide whilst I was sitting as bolt upright as I could. The act of sitting down without being able to put my hands down first was bad enough, and the metal seat, all metal fittings, made for an uncomfortable ride. The small window was opaque and scratched to hell on my side, making it even more difficult to distinguish shapes outside. There were seven other guys in the van, none of whom I could see during the journey. A couple of them started to 'noise up' after a couple of minutes, shouting unintelligible shit backwards and forwards to each other. The sound of the engine inside the van meant that I was unable to hear anything, even when we'd stopped at traffic lights.

Glasgow High Court to Barlinnie meant about 25 minutes in that van. I could hear the sound of the engine dumbing down as we moved inside the jail. There was some chat between the driver or his mate and some guy operating the gates and then we inched forward into the prison.

CHAPTER FOUR

The Reception facility at Bar-L is something to behold. It is a sprawling mess of a space that takes in a desk area, two facing rows of cubicles, known as dog boxes, with half-swing doors either side of a raised platform, where a screw sits and watches as you strip off. There is also a small room where everyone gets a pep talk before transfer to one of the Halls. The dog boxes are effectively holding cells but are only marginally bigger than the sweat boxes in the van. When I stood up in mine, my shoulders touched both sides. If I sat down on the narrow wooden bench, my knees touched the door, which, thankfully, opened outwards. There was a small wire mesh at eye level in the door for ventilation, but after being in there for a few minutes the temperature rose dramatically. I was still wearing my suit.

My cuffs had been removed before I was stuck in one of the dog boxes and I was told to wait my turn for processing. A small guy in a green polo shirt and jeans was scuttling about in the area outside the dog boxes. There were some twenty boxes facing one another in two rows of ten. This guy was the Reception 'passman'. Passmen in jails perform numerous tasks, mainly cleaning and making tea and coffee for the screws and other staff, and are generally considered to be the more trusted prisoners, who have earned the right to their elevated position. The original meaning of the term is fairly self-explanatory: he is one who 'passes'. This meant that passmen were allowed to be unlocked when other prisoners were locked up and

were used to pass things from one con to another. I first experienced
a passman when he was doing precisely that, in this case satisfying
the nicotine dependency of the majority of the six other guys who
had arrived in the same van as me.

'Here pal, goat any skins?' he asked me through the wire mesh.
Having absolutely no fucking idea what he meant by 'skins', I tried a
simple, 'No, thanks,' and quickly sat down, thinking he'd move on.

He was still there, and came back with, 'What ye in fur?' Here's
my first test – what the fuck do I say? I stalled for thinking time
by way of, 'What d'you say, mate?'

'By the way, big man, 'am no' your fuckin' mate, and wh . . .' He
drifted away from the door as he got a shout from one of the screws
to go and get 'passing'. I later found out that skins are cigarette
papers used for making roll-ups.

The incident gave me the opportunity to decide on how I was going
to respond to questions about my crime. I resolved fairly quickly
that I would just tell the truth: I was awaiting sentence on a large
business fraud. Sounded good – short and sweet. Get in and get out.
No need for further clarification. Wrong! Cons are invariably nosy
bastards who find it impossible to ask just one question even if the
answer to that one question is comprehensive. What kind of fraud?
How much? Would it work again? Who did you fuck – hopefully
a bank? How much have you got out there waiting for you?

My dog box was unlocked after about half an hour, I guessed, and
by then my shirt was soaking with sweat. I was told to follow the
screw who had opened me up. I was led through the dog-box area
and into a larger room towards a desk, behind which a big screw
was standing.

'Name?' he shouted.

I told him who I was and answered his other questions, all of
which I'd answered under the High Court about two hours earlier.

'Is there any reason you know of which could mean that you are
under threat of any kind?'

'No,' was my super-quick response.

I was desperately trying to maintain control and patience and also take everything in through my eyes and ears and say as little as possible. This seemed to me to be the best strategy at the time and, looking back, I wouldn't change anything, even knowing what I know now about how the system works.

After I had answered all of his questions, the screw ushered me over to a raised desk sitting on a kind of plinth with an older, grey-haired screw behind it. On either side of him was a swing door, which would have cut across me between my chest and my knees, leading into a cubicle. He was effectively sitting with a grandstand view into each of the cubicles either side of him. He said nothing, but merely pointed to the door on my left, his right. I walked in, still wearing my suit, no tie, white shirt, underpants, socks and shoes with no laces.

One thing I wanted to keep was my hankie. Sounds soft, eh, but surely they'd let me keep it as a form of physical reminder of home and my family. No chance. The hankie had made it past the 'Empty your pockets' procedure under the court but had no chance of getting by this gnarled old bastard who looked as if he'd been sucking a lemon all day. I tried to object when it was taken with the rest of my gear but was given a look that could have shrivelled me up into a slimy mess if I'd let it.

Don't look as if it worries you, I kept trying to tell myself, as I rapidly got out of my clothes. Surely, not my pants as well – but they went the same way as the hankie. I hung all of my clothes, as instructed, over the swing door and sat on the wooden bench naked. I'd been naked plenty of times in front of other guys during my rugby-playing days, but this was different. All the other guys in the room bar one were fully clothed. The old screw was talking to the con in the other cubicle on his other side. I kept my head down and got a fright when he moved closer to the partition and said in a deep voice, 'Nice suit and shoes.' I said fuck all. What can you say? 'Yeah, the suit cost me a few quid, as did the shoes.' No, keep quiet.

Whilst I was letting all of these thoughts fester in my mind, he came back with, 'Pity you'll no' be seeing them for a while,' and he sniggered for a second or two. I could feel my anger rising as I considered the number of cons who had been through this procedure and had been on the receiving end of the type of shit that this old bastard was dishing out. All of it when you are at your most vulnerable, at the start of something which you'd definitely not choose for your worst enemy – well, not all of them anyway – sitting bollock naked and feeling as shit as you'll ever feel.

As I became more and more angry, another of the Reception passmen came over and started to stuff, and I mean stuff, my gear into a plastic bag until he realised it was a suit and vanished out of sight for a couple of seconds, returning with a coat-hanger. He carefully draped the suit trousers over the rail of the hanger, followed by the shirt and then the jacket. He slotted my tie in over the trousers and then stuffed my pants, hankie and socks, shoes and laces into a plastic bag with string ties. He pulled the strings to close the bag and tied them around one end of the hanger rail, so that all of my gear was together. He handed me a white all-in-one suit that was made of some sort of man-made material and buttoned up from the crutch. I was also given a pair of size-nine shoes. They were ultra-cheap versions of the Doc Martens famous brand.

First thing I did was to start putting the suit on, even before the grizzled old screw told me to. Try and keep communication with the old shit to an absolute minimum, I told myself. The legs went on fine and I started to pull the body part up and over my arms and chest. Problem was that when I got it over my shoulders the pressure on my crutch was almost unbearable. It seemed to cut my cock and balls in two. I must have a longer body than standard, I thought. Hopefully, I wouldn't be in this fucking thing for too long – I might just end up impotent. Certainly my sperm count would be adversely affected for a while, but that wouldn't be a major problem for me where I was going, would it? Would I have a legal case for compensation? Could I get Viagra on the NHS? For fuck's sake, move on! I was shouting silently to myself.

The shoes were next and presented a bigger problem than the white suit – they were used and stank. You've got to be joking! The nugget that had been wearing these might have had all sorts of problems with his plates of meat! Even worse, the fabric sole-lining on the right shoe was missing, meaning that the bare inner sole was going to be against my bare foot. I need to get hold of this passman, I thought. I caught his eye as he was walking about in the general area and was in the process of showing him the dodgy right shoe when the old grumpy bastard of a screw wanted to know what was going on. In a firm and businesslike manner, I started to try and explain exactly what the problem was but had got no further than holding up the shoe when he laughed and said, 'Welcome to Barlinnie. Get your fuckin' shoes on and get out of my fuckin' Reception.'

I put the shoes on, the right one first, and realised that the inner sole was covered in tiny spikes of the composite rubbery-type material that made up the sole. When I put my weight on my right foot, it was like walking on a bed of drawing pins with every step, causing me to try and reduce the weight I was putting on my right side. I was told to go into a small room off the main area, where another screw went through some health questions with me and allocated me my prison number. He fired a five-digit number at me and told me to make sure that I remembered it as it allowed me to make purchases from the canteen; in fact, for virtually every aspect of jail life, before anything happened for me, I would need that number. He seemed a decent type of guy and I'd noticed a slight shiver in his body language when I'd told him that I'd never been inside before.

'Any tips?' I said.

'Yeah,' he replied, 'keep your mouth shut and your eyes and ears wide open, and I mean *wide* open.' His choice of emphasis shook me a bit, but I thanked him and was then told that I was going to be housed in A Hall, complete with 'slopping out'. 'Pray for a decent co-pilot,' was his closing aside. Co-pilot? I quickly got what he meant. Keep everything crossed, I thought. Christ, the only things that were crossed at that moment were my balls.

I walked out of the Reception area, following another screw, who had been detailed to take me over to the Hall. I was slightly stooped, bent forward at the waist as the white boiler suit was cutting me in half from head to crutch, with a severe limp on my right side, clutching a form of sorts containing all my personal details. I must have been some sight. Self-pity and real fear and apprehension were definite other factors in my forlorn attempt to appear invisible. I was then outside, still following the screw, who was disappearing into the distance, having locked the back door to the Reception behind me.

'Keep up,' he shouted back at me, as he started to slow down so that I could catch up. As I limped alongside, he said, 'Don't worry, mate. It doesn't get any worse than this. This is the fuckin' pits. It only gets better from here.' Having a zero benchmark to compare 'this' with only made me even more apprehensive.

I was aware of other prisoners passing me, going in the other direction, dressed in a variety of different coloured polo shirts, with screws at the front and rear of the group and a bit of chat and comment directed at me. They were swaggering along and appeared to be laughing and joking. I made no eye contact with any of them and continued to limp alongside the screw. On my left-hand side were various nondescript buildings, whilst on the right were these massive red-sandstone structures, dating from Victorian times. I could hear noise coming from each of them as I passed. Noise was to become a significant player in my time in prison.

After walking/limping about 120 yards or so, we came to the front of A Hall, where the screw walked into the doorway and started to unlock the massive wooden door. It opened with a sustained horror-movie-type squeak and I could see the bars of another door right behind it. He wasn't able to open that door, so he shouted to the desk and a Hall screw came over and unlocked it for the two of us to enter.

The first thing that hit me was the noise. Every surface in the place was hard metal, plastic or some composite or other. The acoustics were fantastic for singing or music, or any other audio-based form of entertainment, but there were people shouting, both screws and prisoners, and the noise was constant. There were doors banging and loud music was blaring out from an open cell door further along the ground floor. I tried to keep my eyes facing forward but just had to look upwards. There were three further storeys in the Hall and the walkways encircled each of the Flats. The cells were around the outside of the building. Strung across the middle of each Flat was a steel net on which there were a number of pieces of paper and other bits of debris. I wondered how many guys had been saved from plummeting to their deaths by these steel nets.

I followed the screw over to the desk. The Hall screw had a badge with his name and 'Residential Officer' printed underneath. Some fucking residence this, I thought. He just stuck his hand out, which meant that I was supposed to pass over the form I'd been told to bring from Reception. I duly gave it to him, but the look he gave me as I did so told me that I hadn't handed it over just quickly enough for his liking. It was the first of many instances where Hall screws re-emphasised their control over every part of life inside.

The Hall screw said it was OK for the Reception screw to leave me in his capable hands. I was asked to confirm my name again and told that I had been remanded to HMP Barlinnie as I was awaiting sentence on a charge to which I had pled guilty. He looked up at me and seemed to be expecting me to say something. I said nothing. This appeared to make him even more pissed off because he sighed deeply and muttered something I couldn't hear whilst bending down behind the desk. He came back up after a couple of seconds, holding a plastic box about the size of a picnic hamper. He placed the box on the desk and lifted the lid off to reveal the goodies.

'There you go,' he said. 'Toothbrush, toothpaste, towel, plastic bowl, some plastic cutlery, piss-pot and pot for the other. Oh, and there's a plastic comb in there for your hairdo. Grab it and let's get you kitted out.'

I followed him with the noise seeming to build in my ears. Surely, it wasn't like this all the time? He walked and I limped (the pain in my right foot was getting worse) over to a room on the right-hand side of the ground floor of A Hall. The converted cell had a half-door, on which sat a narrow shelf, and a con with a red shirt was hanging out, leaning on the shelf.

'Awright, Mr Bain,' the con said. 'Another customer looking for some threads?' The screw sniggered and told him that he needed to get jeans, pants, socks and a shirt for me.

'What waist are ye, big man?' said the con.

'Thirty-eight,' I replied.

He vanished into the back of the room and came back with a pair of jeans, saying, 'Sorry, pal, nae 38s. There's a pair of 40s.'

'You look like a 44 chest,' he continued, as he was scurrying away to bring back a blue-and-white thinly striped shirt that had definitely seen better days. A pair of pants – charcoal grey – and a pair of light-grey socks were dumped into my plastic box, along with the jeans and the shirt. The socks looked decidedly thin but would surely help my right foot withstand the treatment it was suffering from the lack of an insole. The pants – well, let's just say that I was in for a surprise when I looked closely at them; maybe not as much of a surprise as the guy who had worn them before me.

Barlinnie is unlike any other prison in its treatment of remand prisoners. When on remand, prisoners are technically untried, whether they are awaiting sentence or their first proper court appearance. All other jails permit remand prisoners to wear their own clothing and footwear, as they are not convicted men or women. Not Bar-L – you wear what they tell you to wear. Control in its most basic form.

CHAPTER FIVE

Carrying my plastic box, I was told to follow the screw up the iron stairway, which took us up to the first floor, where we turned a sharp left and went along the walkway towards cell number four. He unlocked the door, and held on to the handle as he ushered me in and then said as I passed him in the doorway, 'Someone will be in with you shortly.' I was still facing the window wall as the door slammed behind me. Fuck's sake, that's it. Holed up in this shithole. Ten feet by eight, stinking, with double bunks and a four-foot-high piece of chipboard that I supposed I was meant to shit and piss behind. That is, shit and piss into the pot and plastic bottle I'd just been supplied with. I frantically looked round for the one thing that all of a sudden I realised was missing from my box of essentials – toilet paper, none anywhere. Not that I was needing to go, but you know what it's like, there's nothing more likely to make you need than the knowledge that you can't go. I quickly solved the problem by consigning the pants to a terrible fate if push came to squeeze. Though it looked as if someone had already beaten me to that particular use for them.

There was one plastic chair in the cell and a shelf, which was screwed to the middle of the wall opposite the bunks. The shelf was about 18 inches wide, no more. Two large pipes ran through the cell along the back wall, which also housed the only window, which comprised four panes, two fixed at the outside and two hinged at the middle, and all about two feet deep. Each pane was about four inches wide, giving a maximum of eight inches of ventilation when both panes were opened. The main problem with the window was that it was about seven foot off the ground. I'm just over six feet tall and the top pipe was about a foot off the deck, so by standing on the pipe I was able to see out.

I wished I hadn't stepped onto that top pipe, the reason being that I had to grab onto the windowsill in order to keep my balance. I then squinted out of the open window, which only looked on to the next Hall; B, I supposed. It only took a couple of seconds for the stench to hit me. It was coming from the sill. My fingers were in it – the shit, the food debris and fuck knows what else. I jumped down from the pipe, looking to get rid of the fucking stuff that was causing the problem on my hands. No water! Nothing, zilch, zero. My hands automatically came back up to my nose to confirm the stench; it was still there. No escape. No remedy. Well, maybe. There was an alarm button on the wall. Given the fact that this stuff could cause all sorts of problems for my health, I thought that it might just be considered an emergency. I jumped up from the plastic chair and pressed the button. A light went on above the button and I just sat there and waited, and waited. No idea how long it took, no watch, but it must have been at least 20 minutes – some emergency. The screw who came opened the door and looked round and asked me what the problem was. I never even got as far as waving my stinking fingers in the air before the door was slammed shut with the shouted threat, 'Don't press that fuckin' alarm again if you know what's good for you. I'm havin' ma tea.'

The door immediately re-opened and my hopes soared again, as I got ready to wave my stinky fingers, only for him to say, 'Get out of that windae licker's outfit and get your gear on. I'll be coming back for that fuckin' white suit soon!' I'm sure he laughed as he left the doorway.

'Welcome to Bar-L.' The words from the grizzled old bastard on the Reception platform were battering about in my head as I slowly started to squeeze the suit off my shoulders, which immediately relieved the pressure on my groin. It's amazing how you become used to discomfort when your brain is whirling with loads of other shit. I'd forgotten about how constricting the whole thing had been until I shrugged the shoulders off and started to slip it down and off my legs. I tried to keep the shoes on, but the legs wouldn't go over them, so I was forced to sit down and take the shoes off first. There was no way I was putting my bare feet down on that floor – it was bogging. It seemed to have a slime on it. It was a composite-type material in a ruddy brown colour. Whether it started out that colour, I wouldn't know. What made it that colour now I was even less interested in finding out. I used the 'windae licker's outfit' to stand on. Pulled the box over towards me, pulled out the pants and dropped them back in – go commando, done it before, no great problem. The socks seemed clean, if a bit thin, slipped them on. Picked up the jeans, which were about two sizes too big in the waist and at least one size too long in the leg. No belt to keep them up. Well, I'd just have to keep my hands in my pockets. Picked up the shirt and – bingo! – it fitted me and was clean and relatively new, although it was short of a couple of buttons.

More tedium followed, only punctuated by sniffs at my stinky pinkies. Checked out the bunks – short and narrow and the mattress couldn't be called one. One sheet, a thin blanket and a pillow that was as thick as a wrapped-up tea towel. The frame of the bunks squeaked like crazy – could be fun.

It must have been an hour or so later that the door opened and the same screw came in, followed by a young guy wearing a white suit and carrying another plastic picnic hamper. The guy shuffled in and immediately dumped his plastic hamper on the top bunk – mine was still on the floor. That's the sleeping arrangements settled then – bottom bunk for me. His name was Raymond Minto – 'Call me Mints!' He was in his early 20s and had been remanded after being arrested and charged for possession of class-A drugs – heroin, to be precise. He was skinny, dark-haired and stood at about five foot ten. My threat analysis was that everything should be OK, even though you should never, ever, underestimate your potential attacker/opponent.

Mints immediately started to unpack his hamper and it quickly became apparent to me that he had done all of this shit before. I asked him the question.

'Yeah, I've been in here before on remand but managed to get a fine at court, so I've no' really done any hardcore time. What about you?' I tried to explain my situation to him, but then the door opened and my first thought was that the system had eventually realised that it had made a mistake by putting me in custody and after a curt apology they would send me home. The screw ducked his head around the door and said, 'Minto!' followed by 'Doctor!' Mints quickly scooted out the door, which was slammed and the key turned in the lock.

I was on my own again and decided that I had better start getting my head around the fact that I was staying. I finally managed it about four days later, but I started the process at that moment.

I looked around the cell again, but this time in more detail. I took my piss-pot and the other pot out of the hamper and put them in the area behind the chipboard screen ready for use. I looked at the toothbrush – the mere action of picking it up was sufficient to loosen around half-a-dozen bristles. I wondered how many would be left after a vigorous brushing. I was squeezing a small amount of toothpaste out of the small tube when the door opened again and Mints blew in.

'Not so bad, got on a detox, so should be OK in three weeks or so.' He was talking a language that was alien to me. I had never been around the drugs scene. Never smoked in my life, never touched any type of drug other than alcohol at a social level. I could guess what a detox was, but what exactly did it entail and why was three weeks significant? I explained to Mints that this was my first time inside and asked if I could depend on him to show me the ropes. 'Nae bother, big man. Ah'll keep you right.' He seemed to blow out his chest a bit, as if his new responsibility was a badge he could wear with pride.

He started to describe how his detox would work, explaining it was a gradual reduction in medication over the course of 21 days, involving diffs, blues and other weird-sounding tablets. He went on to say that a load of guys, including him, used the jail system to 'clean themselves up'.

'You've got to be joking,' I responded.

'Naw, man, it's the only way sometimes.' He then started telling me what we needed in the cell that wasn't already there: toilet paper, water . . . could I get a radio in, 'cause he couldn't? 'The fucking screws give ye fuck all here, so don't ask for anything. Are ye clean?' he asked.

Clean? It took me a second or two, and then I replied, 'Yeah!'

'You'll get moved on then,' he said.

What did he mean? Get moved on to where? How long would that take? So many questions and a reticence to ask them all at one time for fear of appearing to be exactly what I was, an FNG – Fucking New Guy. Worse than that, an FNG who was so wet behind the ears it was running down his back and soaking the crease in his arse.

We chatted for the next, well, fuck knows how long, but were abruptly stopped by the door opening again and the screw shouting, 'Slop out!' Mints jumped up and flew out the door. I struggled to keep up with him, stupidly thinking he must be desperate to go to the loo. No, he was off down the walkway to the right and towards what I later found out was called 'the Head'.

The Head was an open area that could be locked up by closing two massive barred doors, which slid along rails to either side. I saw a row of sinks and daylight coming in from above via some high windows. Mints had managed to get hold of a plastic juice bottle from who knows where, which he was busy sluicing with water coming from a huge brass tap that was running at an incredible rate into a massive porcelain sink that was chipped and dirty-looking. I had all my questions answered about that huge sink as a con breezed by me to empty his piss-pot just as Mints was finishing rinsing our newly acquired bottle. Nothing was said. The other guy merely drained the last few drops of piss from his pot, placed it into the flow a couple of times to complete the process and then turned and left the Head. Mints filled our bottle and then told me to piss, shit or wash my hands right now, as this was the only chance for a while. I'd grown used to the stench on my fingers but remembered to wash my hands, at which the attendant screw looked on bemused.

I was desperately trying to take everything in. There were other cons dressed in red polo shirts and jail jeans. I asked Mints why that was and he told me that this Hall was split from stem to stern, with remand prisoners on one side and convicted prisoners on the other side. Fuck's sake, you could be convicted and doing your time slopping out! I thought this regime was only a temporary one – wrong again.

We both got shouted at to get back into our cell and hurried up about it. Mints explained that the tea meal was next up, but as we were fresh in the door we would have to take what was left. Choices were available, but only to those who had filled in menu sheets the previous week.

Food distribution throughout my time inside was haphazard, due to the vagaries of the various passmen who dished it out. Bar-L was no different, with some decent guys and some complete arseholes who took great pleasure in winding you up and looking, waiting and hoping for a reaction. No way was I getting into any sort of caper when I was just in the door – self-preservation was the only thing on my mind. That, and how my family were coping with the shock of me being locked up.

We were all ushered out along the landing towards the other end of the Hall, where we picked up a plastic tray with portion indents and walked along a line of five or six passmen, who put various bits of the meal on the tray. I was to see a lot more of these trays later in my time at Barlinnie. The main course was some sort of pasta dish; bread was next to be picked up. Then I heard: 'Duff?'

'Eh, yeah, thanks.' Duff is jail-speak for pudding, or dessert, if you want to be ultra-posh, which this duff certainly wasn't. It comprised a chunk of layered sponge covered in what was yellow water passing for custard. No worries, I thought, bread will be enough for me. Remember to pick up a couple of spread portions before I go back to the cell.

I picked at the pasta, avoided the duff and wolfed the bread, which made me feel very full. I told myself that nerves and apprehension had dulled my appetite and the resultant benefit might be that I would be less likely to need that shit-pot. With only one chair in the cell, we started the rotation of taking turns to sit and eat. Mints went first, as I stood.

I followed Mints in dumping the tray outside the cell on the walkway for pick-up by the passman. Mints then explained to me that there would now be a 'count' and we would be locked up again whilst the screws had their tea. The count involved a screw sticking his head around the door, presumably to see that both of us were in, and then slamming the door closed and locking it. We were then locked up for what turned out to be about an hour and a half, during which Mints and I tried to relax on our beds, although I found it impossible to get thoughts of my family out of my head. I moaned on to Mints about my jeans being too wide at the waist and he said that he would try and get some laces so that I could make a belt of sorts. Fuck's sake, I'm in the jail. I need to get wise to what works in here, what the rules are, what the lingo is, how to do things, how to get things, how to suss who to trust – no one at the moment, I told myself. I needed to clue up and super-quick.

The cell door opened and the screw shouted, 'Bridges', without actually showing his face around the door. Mints shouted something about his detox but was ignored. I jumped up from the bunk and headed for the door with both hands fastened on to my jeans, pulling them up and holding them there. I then followed the screw along the landing to the left as far as the screws' office midway up the Hall. I was shown inside and another screw told me to sit down. He was wearing a black jumper over his white shirt. He asked me how I was. I nodded. Words were difficult for me because I thought that if anyone showed me even a modicum of sympathy or understanding, I might crack up. There was a very pregnant pause before he asked me if I'd like to call my family. I nodded again. He then explained to me that he would lend me a phonecard until I could get some cash into the jail and pay him back. I nodded again to signal my understanding of his proposal. He reached into his back pocket and handed me a 20-unit phonecard, total value £2. He then said that I could have first go at the phone, which was at the end of the Hall. Nobody else had been opened up yet, so I quickly stood up, took the card from him and stammered, 'Thanks.' He was the only residential screw in Bar-L who was in any way understanding of my situation.

I scooted along to the phone and tried to take a few seconds to compose myself before picking up the receiver, sliding the card into the slot and dialling my home number. By the time the connection was made, I thought that I was OK, but I was kidding myself. The sound of my wife's voice was enough to send me into chest-heaving silent sobs. I managed to blurt out, 'It's me.' She started to cry and through her tears asked me how I was. I then heard another cell door being unlocked, which brought me right back to where I was and what was required. I got myself back very quickly and set about trying to reassure my wife that I was OK, all the time watching the dial counting down the units used on the screw's card. I can't remember a lot more of that first call, other than saying that I loved her and would call again the next night.

I tucked the phonecard into my back pocket and just managed to get the handset into its cradle as another con arrived and slid by me to grab it. Phone access was strictly controlled by the landing screws – each day you told them whether you wanted to use the phone and when, afternoon or evening. You were then unlocked to use the phone and then locked up again. In Bar-L, we were locked up for 23 hours a day. No recreation or association time, and any excuse was made to stop us from going outdoors for a walk around the yard during the one-hour statutory outside exercise time. If there was a black cloud 20 miles away, that was enough to cancel it. We were then allowed to walk around the landing in single file, no less than one yard apart. The walkway was so narrow that two guys couldn't walk abreast, but that didn't stop some of the nuggets who were intent on chatting to their mates. Also, once you'd decided that you were walking, as opposed to lying stinking in your pit, you had to keep walking for the full hour. For some, that proved to be a bridge too far and there was always a shouting and bawling match between the screws and whoever had started to struggle.

Mints and I settled down for the night, complete with a small flask of hot water, our plastic bottle of cold water and a tea pack, which had been handed in by the landing passman. It contained some tea bags of indeterminate origin and brand, two coffee sachets going the same way, some whitener and eight sugar sachets – Silver Spoon, too!! Mints was deliriously happy when I told him that I didn't take sugar, 'cause he took loads. We played battleships, hang the man and noughts and crosses, and ended up with some daft music-trivia questions. Lights went out at 10 p.m. and we both got into our bunks. There was even a Waltons moment with 'Goodnights' passing between us.

It was fairly quiet for about 15 to 20 minutes and then it began. Some unintelligible shout started it all. Mints jumped up and hopped onto the top pipe to listen at the open window. More shouting, none of which I could make out.

'What's going on, Mints?' I asked.

He didn't turn around immediately, but then jumped down in the darkness and explained to me that the 'protections' were on the top floor of our Hall and threats were being issued to some guy called McPhee, who had been found guilty earlier in the day of raping a 79-year-old granny. He had apparently tied her up with the flex from a vacuum cleaner and then done the deed. The shouts grew in volume and seemed to be coming from inside our Hall, as well as from the Hall opposite. All of them were targeted towards McPhee. Then they stopped suddenly. Mints said that he'd answered back. I jumped up and tried to get myself alongside Mints on the top pipe so that I could hear better. I heard, 'Bring it on, ya fannies!' There was a second or two of a delay and then an absolute rammy, with the shouts getting louder and more frequent and seeming to come from all around us.

'He'll fuckin' get it now. What a wank!' Mints said.

'What do you mean?' I asked. He went on to explain that one of the guys who was shouting would get himself into protection by some means and do the deed on McPhee. He would be slashed as a minimum. He might get out with his balls intact, if he was lucky. Fuck's sake, I'd only been in Bar-L for about eight hours and this was how it was going to be. I'd better stop feeling sorry for myself and wise up – big-style.

The shouting went on for about another hour or so and then quietened down to what seemed like stage whispers. It didn't matter to me – I didn't sleep a fucking wink. It was the longest night of my life. It didn't matter that the nights are incredibly short at the end of July, it took ages for the sun to come up and even then my thoughts were drawn to what a full day held for me in that shithole. Mints was only up once during the night to use his piss-pot. I managed to get through. I'd been conscious of the amount of water I'd taken on the night before, but I was also aware that I would need to watch my hydration levels. I had no idea of the time.

Mints seemed to be sleeping well, breathing deeply and thankfully not snoring. The bed was a sheet of plywood covered with a thin slab of foam, which was useless in disguising the fact that I was lying on a board. The bedding was adequate, with a top and bottom sheet and a single blanket. The pillow had seen better days and probably too many cons' heads over the years. Maybe too many of them had cried their tears into this pillow.

My thoughts strayed to my wife and daughters and I wondered if they were managing to sleep. Get a grip – think about something else. Madness. It was impossible to get my thought processes working in the direction I wanted them to go. I forced myself to stop beating myself up. The culture shock I'd experienced was incredible. Sure, I'd been expecting a jail sentence, but not at that particular time and definitely not in this jail.

Eventually the peephole slid along and I could hear the screw moving down the landing, opening up the other peepholes. The screws' method of carrying out the counts was to check through the peepholes first and then go through the landings again, opening each door to check that everyone was alive by insisting on a response. During my three weeks in Bar-L, there were three suicides.

There was a lull after the screw had checked that Mints was alive. He grunted something about detox, but I missed the rest of it as I had started to get out of my bunk. The screw muttered something in response.

Half an hour must have passed before I heard the doors being unlocked on the landing. Ours was opened and the screw shouted, 'Slop out!' Mints jumped down from his bunk, grabbed his piss-pot and was gone. I followed on behind, making my way towards the Head. On getting there, the bank of sinks was well populated and the showers were in use, with a queue. I needed to go for a shit and managed to get into a trap that was free. The door was only about two feet deep, covering the bit between your knees and your midriff. Everybody could see you squeezing your guts out. I was determined to keep my personal hygiene high and wanted to shave. No razor. Mints was in the shower opposite, so I wiped up and went over to ask him where I could get hold of one. He shouted back, 'At the desk.' I went out to the desk to ask for a razor and was handed a pen. 'Sign!' the desk screw commanded. I scribbled my name next on the list and was handed a Bic disposable. Never thought about shaving soap. Just improvise. I picked up a small bar of off-white soap, which smelled ultra-cheap, and spent what seemed like ages trying to get a lather. No one was allowed out of their cells improperly dressed, so I had the stripy shirt on, jeans, no pants and the shoes without socks. The sinks were freeing up, so I jumped in and kept kneading my hands together to get the best possible lather going. The 'mirror' was a badly scratched strip of aluminium that ran along the wall about a foot above the level of the sinks. It was misted up with condensation and so I had to wipe it with my hand to clear it, only for it to mist up again almost immediately. The guy to my left, who was in the middle of washing under his arms, told me to squirt some washing-up liquid on the strip. I grabbed a brandless bottle of green liquid off the window shelf and spurted it onto the metal in front of me – Bingo! I said thanks to the guy and got on with trying to shave. The screws were patrolling continuously in the Head area and occasionally shouting instructions to various guys.

I'd been shaving for about two or three minutes when I felt a tugging at my right foot. I straightened up and saw a guy in a full squat at my right-hand side. I leant further over and saw that he was trying to take the lace out of my right shoe. I quickly moved the Bic to my left hand and banged the guy on the forehead with a swipe of my right fist. The butt of my hand caught him flush on the head and he fell over on the soaking floor. 'Fuck off!' I shouted at him, more in acknowledgement that this was precisely what I should be saying than anything else. He started to get to his feet and turned away. I watched as he left the Head but realised that I was at my most vulnerable here, so very, very quickly finished my shave and rinsed my face. I was about to jump into the shower when the screws started to shout, 'Time up.' Fuck! I'd need to get my arse in gear in future so that I could get a shit, shave and shower in the time available. I scooted back to my cell. Mints was already there, lying on his bunk.

My breakfast was lying on the shelf/table: a bag of brandless rice-krispies, a small bottle of milk, a bread roll and a portion of raspberry jam. I was hungry, so I got into it. You can't fuck about with breakfast cereal, can you? I fired the krispies into my plastic bowl, followed by almost all of the milk and started eating. Mints asked if he could have my sugar. 'Yeah, crack on,' I said. It would be the last time I gave anybody anything inside without there being something in exchange.

The screw checked we were inside the cell and then slammed the door and locked it. I was still savouring my cereal when the door was thrown open again.

'Bridges,' he shouted.

'Yeah,' I replied.

'You got a razor?'

'Yeah.'

'Do that again and it'll be the last shave you have in here.'

'What do you mean?'

He stepped past me to pick the razor off the shelf and held it up between his right thumb and forefinger. 'This,' he exclaimed, 'has to be handed in after each use.'

'I didn't know that!'

'You fuckin' do now. Don't let it happen again.' He stormed out and I tried to get back to my breakfast.

'Don't worry about it,' Mints said. 'Everybody's got to be a new guy sometime.'

I knew he was right, but I also knew that my 'new guy' status put me at risk. I needed to fit in. I needed to do that quickly.

Mints' detox was late. He apologised, before yelling at the top of his voice: 'DETOX!' After shouting like that for a couple of minutes, he lay down on his back on the filthy floor and started kicking the door with his feet. Just small kicks to begin with, but he progressed quite quickly to full-blooded thumps. The whole cell shook with the sound. Other cons were also at it and the noise in the Hall was incredible – just one big sound chamber.

He was at it for at least ten or fifteen minutes, and then the lock started to turn. He jumped to his feet and this bald screw whom I'd never seen before burst into the cell and asked what all the noise was about. Both of us kept schtum. He then quietly said, 'Minto, detox.' Mints was out of the cell in an instant, whilst the screw stopped to look around. 'Only got one chair, pal?' I felt like coming back with some sort of sarcastic response but thought better of it. 'These junkies,' he said. 'It's OK for you. You'll get yourself out of here and on to a drug-free wing soon. We've got to deal with them all the time.'

I grabbed my chance. 'Any possibility of getting me some reading material, a book or a newspaper?'

'I'll see what I can do,' he replied, and was off. He left the door open but pulled it to. Just the door being open made so much difference to the way I felt. Sounds crazy, I know, but I felt a whole lot freer. Passmen in Halls are afforded the privilege of being opened up when others are locked up: I could see the attraction at that moment.

My time in Barlinnie was fraught with the degrading experience of slopping out, but there was only one horrendous episode that soured my time with Mints in A Hall. One of the side effects of following a detox programme is that some guys develop constipation. Not a great condition to have in a slopping-out regime – just marginally better than having diarrhoea. Mints didn't have a shit for more than four days, during which time he was packing in the tatties and pasta and all types of high-carb, high-fat duffs that were on offer.

My appetite still had not recovered fully from the shock and although I'd managed to tie a few laces together to make a belt of sorts, my jeans were becoming more and more of a problem by the day. I'd come in a 38-inch waist, but after the first week must have been down to a 34.

Our problems with Mints' bowel movements began at around 11 p.m. on the Thursday night, four days after arriving in the place. Mints had been concerned that he hadn't been able to shit and was desperately hoping that when the moment came it would be during the day and he could get a screw to open us up and let him use the toilet. Shit's law! We had been lights out for what I thought might have been an hour. I still hadn't slept a bloody wink, other than snoozing through the day. The night-callers were hard at it, with shouts of a chatty nature rather than the threats of earlier in the week. The sky was still light when Mints uttered the fateful words.

'Sean, I think I need to shit.'

No panic, I thought. 'How do you want to do it, mate?' I tried to sound in control, when I was anything but. The size of the shit-pot precluded you from being able to stick your dick in as well, so Mints ended up sitting on the pot, which was balanced on the plastic chair, holding his piss-pot with his dick stuck in it. The first salvo was enough to convince Mints that there was no way that his shit-pot alone would be sufficient for the job. It was like a flock of sparrows flying out of his arse. The sound was bad enough, but the stench was absolutely incredible. He asked for the bottle of water so that he could pour some into the pot to try and reduce the effects of the smell. He was stuck there, poor guy, and had to ask me if he could pass me his pot and transfer to mine, as his was full. Shit-pots came with a plastic lid. I jumped up and got hold of mine, trying not to breathe through my nose, which was impossible. I was sure I was going to gag. 'When you're ready, Mints,' I announced. He stood up, his dick still in the piss-pot, shit still sticking to his arse, and left the shit-pot lying steaming on the plastic chair. What a fucking disgrace. It's the twenty-first century and we're still doing this.

I quickly stuck the lid from my pot onto the top of his one, although the amount of shit in the pot stopped it fitting properly. It resembled the shapes the characters in *Close Encounters of the Third Kind* felt compelled to mould . . . my sense of humour was coming back. He plonked his arse down on my pot and poured some water in again. His piss-pot was now almost full and I took that from him. Holding someone else's warm piss is strange. He sat and finished off over the next five minutes or so, and used loads of paper to wipe himself clean. The stench in the cell was rancid.

He was full of apologies. I told him that it wasn't his fault and that it wouldn't kill us. Would it? I also said that I was sure that after about an hour of suffering a disgusting smell, your sense of smell effectively shuts down, so not long to wait. The smell went, but I've no idea how long it took. It obviously never went anywhere, though, and our first inkling came when the screw opened the peephole prior to the count proper starting in the morning. His reaction as he walked away was enough for us to realise that the stench was still operating at full intensity. So it should have been, the shit was piled into both pots and must have been humming by then.

I felt sorry for the poor screw who opened us up and had to put his head around the door to check we were alive. His reaction was fucking priceless. He looked as if he was turning green in front of us. He almost gagged as he said, 'Morning.' He quickly engaged reverse and locked us up again. We waited another few minutes before we were opened up for slop-out. I said to Mints that I would take one of the shit-pots along, as his hands were full with both of his pots. He thanked me again and apologised.

I dived out first and signed for a razor. The screw looked at me as if to remind me about my recent fuck-up. I fired into the Head and made for the sluice, lifted the lid of the pot and stuck it into the running water. The force of the water shifted it from the pot but the smell hung around for a couple of seconds.

'Ye must have been needin' that, pal,' a voice said beside me.

'Yeah, I was.'

Dump the pot. Go for a dump, shave and then I'll maybe get a shower. It worked that morning, and even though the shower was filthy, just being under the water stream felt great.

CHAPTER SIX

After a couple of days, even without any meaningful sleep, I started to come out of myself a bit. I remember looking at the misted reflection in the aluminium strip in the Head and wondering if it was actually me. Who am I? Is this happening to me? Can I cope with whatever is coming up? The answers were provided over the next few weeks and over the more prolonged duration of my sentence.

The screw I had asked for some form of reading material slid into the cell on my fifth day and handed me a hardback copy of Wilbur Smith's novel *When the Lion Feeds*. It had been condemned by Glasgow City Council Libraries and found its way into the jail. It was a godsend. I devoured it. It was in tiny print and was meant to have 692 pages. I only read 686 pages. The sense of disappointment I felt was profound. The escapism the book afforded me was palpable and yet I was dragged kicking and screaming back to reality by the fact that some fucking idiot had ripped the last six pages out of the book. Mints confirmed that this was normal practice amongst cons and that you had to check first before you started to read any book. He'd forgotten to tell me.

My time in Barlinnie improved after I managed to fix a radio. Three doors along from our cell was one occupied by two guys who were on remand for murder. Their offence was shooting dead three members of the same family. Mints said that they were UVF hit men and that they'd wiped out the family because of a dispute over drugs territory. Unionist gangs apparently controlled wide areas of Glasgow's drugs business. Scobie and Brandon had been on remand for over six months. At that time there was a 110-day limit for remand prisoners, which meant that the Crown had to bring them to court before it expired. In exceptional cases, the Crown could apply for an extension and, subject to certain conditions being met, it was invariably granted. I heard later that the only eyewitness to their crime was a local postman who had narrowly missed being shot – a bullet hit the door he was delivering letters to at the time. There was no forensic evidence and although the postman picked out Scobie and Brandon in a line-up he later changed his original statement – no surprise there, then. No wonder the Crown were having difficulty getting them to court to face a meaningful case. Scobie and Brandon were about 15 years apart in terms of age but were exactly the same size and shape. Scobie was the elder, maybe about 39 or 40, and the more gregarious, whilst Brandon was quieter and more circumspect.

After the tea meal was served on my first Friday in the joint and whilst the doors were still open, Scobie came into our cell, which still stank from Mints' excretions the night before. He made a comment about the smell but then asked me straight out if I could look at their radio because 'It's fucked!' I said sure, I would give it a look over and see what I could do to help.

'Come on, then,' he said.

'What about lock-up?' I replied.

'Dinnae worry about that,' he came back.

I followed him along to their cell. I stood at the door open-mouthed as he turned round and said, 'Come in, for fuck's sake.' I slowly stepped in. Brandon was lying on the bottom bunk, reading a copy of the *Daily Record*. He tipped the paper forward and said, 'Hi, mate.' I nodded and grunted. Their cell was like the tardis. It looked a lot bigger than ours. But the impression of additional space was nothing compared to the level of fit-out. They had curtains on their window. They had carpet on the floor. The place smelled good. There was furniture in it, a small table and two substantial wooden chairs either side. There was a small chest of drawers. They both had thin duvets on their beds, with substantial pillows. They had two Thermos flasks and a cool box. What the fuck!

Scobie pointed towards their problem radio. 'Oh yeah,' I said, or something else that was meant to sound cool, calm and collected. Their radio was an old type of transistor that was powered by three PP3 cube batteries connected together and wired to the radio through an external input wire. It was a Heath Robinson arrangement, and so I asked Scobie if it worked OK and when it had packed in. He said they'd 'inherited' it from another con who had moved out, but it had packed in that morning. It looked like the problem involved the integrity of the connections between the various batteries. I asked them if they had an old sock. Brandon jumped up and opened the drawer under the table, which was stuffed full of socks and pairs of pants – any time I'd seen Scobie and Brandon, they had always looked very smart. Sounds crazy, but it was a fact. They always had clean, new-looking jail issue on.

Brandon threw me a sock and I spent the next couple of minutes stuffing the batteries into the sock and ensuring that the connections were in the right order and that the connection wire came through the open end of the sock. I then tied the leg of the sock tightly and reconnected the wire to the external power port of the radio. My heart was beating a bit faster than normal as I asked Scobie to try switching it back on. It burst into life and there were some heavy beats banging out of it. Scobie thanked me, as did Brandon. 'No problem,' I said.

As I turned round to leave, Scobie said, 'Hey, big man. What paper do you read?'

'*The Scotsman*,' I replied.

'There'll be one there for you in the morning and every other morning you're in this Hall.' Scobie went on: 'And, by the way, if it doesn't arrive, let me know and I'll fix it.'

'OK,' and I was gone, back to my cell. It seemed as if lock-up had been delayed, but maybe I was just imagining it.

When you are on remand, you have privileges that are not afforded to convicted prisoners. You're allowed a half-hour visit every day, if you can arrange one. (Once convicted and in Glenochil, I was entitled to three one-hour visits per calendar month.) My first visitor was my good mate Dave, whom I'd met during my time at the Royal Mail. He is a committed Christian and I felt that he would cope with me and my situation first up, rather than have my wife, daughters and other family members come in and see me losing it. Dave arrived on my fourth day and I almost lost it when I saw him – almost, but not quite.

My dad came in on my sixth day, a close family friend on my eighth. I had decided by then that I didn't want my wife or elder daughter coming in at all; however, they both came on my second Saturday after enduring a nightmare journey on public transport from Edinburgh but were turned away at the gate as they were two minutes late. They were on their way back out of the jail when a screw asked them why they were so upset. They explained and he had them shown into the visits room. We all cried when we saw each other, and my anger started to rise at the way they had been treated. It wasn't to be the only time I had problems with visits.

My copy of *The Scotsman* duly arrived the morning after the radio-fixing and I made sure to thank Scobie and Brandon when I saw them in the Head for the morning ablutions. One of the screws on the landing had the nickname Scooter. (He apparently had a twin brother who worked in B Hall who was also known as Scooter.) He was a sparky, wee, stocky bugger who was always raising his voice and making wisecracks. I was standing shaving as he walked along behind me and the other guys who were at the sinks. He had his truncheon out and was slapping it into his left hand as he walked – something he did all the time.

All of a sudden he comes out with: 'Mr Bridges, tell me, does this put you off crime for ever, or is that a rhetorical question?'

I was certain that a stunned silence descended on the place. I went back: 'You should never use words that you can't spell.'

He was pissed off with that and stopped right behind me, still slapping his truncheon. 'Ah, you mean rhetorical. Well, R–E . . .'

I spared him the rest by jumping in to say that there was an 'H' after the 'R'. The entire place exploded into raucous laughter – there must have been at least 20 guys in there – and Scobie, who was standing over at the showers waiting his turn, came out above the din with the classic, 'Scooter, ye had nae chance. He's fae Edinburgh, you're fae Motherwell.' Another laugh rose up into the acoustically excellent Head area.

'Get the fuck out of here. You're over time already,' screamed Scooter. I rinsed off and was careful not to make eye contact with him as I walked out. He whispered, 'Watch it!' as I passed him. I was glad it was Friday and Scooter was off at the weekend. He might have forgotten about it all by the time he came back on duty.

In jail, the regime changes at weekends. The lock-ups overnight are longer, starting at around 5 p.m. and extending through until around 8.15 a.m. the following morning. That's a long time when you're in a slopping-out environment. Fifteen hours in the same small room with someone you would not choose to be with is bad enough without the potential for either you or him having to fill piss- and shit-pots.

Breakfast on both weekend days was sliced sausage on bread rolls. You picked up two slices of sausage and a couple of rolls and made your way back to your cell. The sausage could have been used to pave your driveway; however, in some perverse sort of way, the change in menu signified that time was moving on; I was getting through. Actually, I'd got this far without any serious problems. Even the guy I'd dunted on the head at the sinks hadn't been seen again. Hopefully, Scooter would forgive my smart-ass comment and let me get through the next few weeks without too much hassle.

The weekend passed with only one significant incident. The rapist McPhee was sliced up whilst on protection. One of the guys who'd been shouting had managed to convince the screws that he needed to be in protective custody. He did the deed on the Sunday morning immediately after breakfast. There was loads of shouting and screaming as they led McPhee down the central stairway. I couldn't see anything, which was probably just as well – word got around that he had been very badly slashed on the face and neck and that his left cheek was 'hanging off'. Nice!

Whilst outside for the one hour of allocated exercise – it must have been a cloudless sky – I walked around the yard with a small Glaswegian guy called John. He regaled me with his stories of having been in the prison system all over the UK. He was, by his own admission, a career criminal, and not a very good one at that. He was 28 years old and had been in and out of various prisons and young offenders institutions since age 15. He was on remand for drugs-related violence and was due in court the next week. His chat was informative and revealing. He had spent time in Wormwood Scrubs, Dartmoor and Durham prisons and he explained that the English system afforded far easier time for cons and that the jails were run by gangs divided on a racial basis. He laughed when telling me that the black gangs who spent their time building muscle bulk and preening themselves were shit scared of being slashed, as their looks would be permanently changed for the worse. Consequently, John's time in English jails was trouble-free, as it was widely known that Scottish jails, and Barlinnie in particular, had a slashing culture with widespread use of blades and chibs. He chuckled when he said that huge black guys used to stand aside to allow him to pass along the landings in Dartmoor.

I was walking on his left-hand side and when we checked on one lap to overtake a group of guys in front of us I was then walking on his right side and turned to look at him as he was speaking. There was a huge scar that started just by his right ear and worked its way down to the space between his nose and his mouth. It didn't look as if the stitch job was the best one ever. The skin sank into the scar from both sides. He looked a scary guy, even though he was insignificant size-wise. Never underestimate anyone: you don't know what they are capable of.

Monday morning came and I was shouted at by a screw outside the cell. I pulled open the door, as it was just after breakfast and it had only been pulled to.

'You're going to B Hall. Get your gear together now,' the screw said.

Mints reacted first by saying that he would miss our games of battleships and hang the man. My first contribution was: 'What's that about?' Mints told me that it was a drugs-free Flat for remand prisoners, so there was no way he'd be getting there whilst on a detox programme. Better than that, he said there were in-cell toilets and the entire Hall had recently been refurbished.

Ya fuckin' beauty! My heart lifted for the first time in a week, but I quickly put a lid back on it when Mints said that he hoped I didn't get a rocket for a co-pilot. I was thinking 'better the devil you know' and all that as I was putting my stuff into my plastic hamper box.

The other doors were being locked and as our turn came the screw looked in and asked me if I was ready.

'Yip,' I said.

'Come on then,' he came back, and I stood up and bent over to shake hands with Mints. I wished him well and his response was to start asking who he was going to get in my place. 'Some junkie bastard probably! Come on,' said the screw, and I left the cell to follow him along the landing, down the stairs and out of A Hall and along to B Hall.

The place stank of fresh paint and looked new on the inside. I went through the admission procedure with a desk screw and was taken up to my cell on the top floor. I was first in and it felt like I'd arrived at the Paris Hilton. The cell had new bunks, a toilet with a door, a sink, a kettle and a small TV. Fuck me! This was *better* than the Paris Hilton. The door had been left open but pulled to. The entire Hall seemed to be quieter than A Hall.

After about ten minutes, during which I'd unpacked my stuff and spent the other nine minutes gazing at the easterly view over towards the M8 motorway, a screw came in and went through the Hall regime with me. Two things interested me particularly: I would be able to get into PT and I would get the chance to work if I wanted to. I'd do anything to get out of this or any other cell for an hour or two.

He explained that this was a drugs-free Flat for remand prisoners who were prepared to sign up to a compact not to take drugs and willingly be tested at any time. 'Where do I sign?' I said. I've never even had a cigarette between my lips, far less anything more serious or sinister.

The last thing he said was that the TV cost £1 per week. 'It'll come out of your PPC, so make sure you've got enough in it to cover the cost.'

I was on my own for about another hour or so. I never turned the TV on. Strange that. I was enjoying the calm, quiet atmosphere and didn't want it to end. The door opened and my co-pilot entered. His name was Ally Cameron. He was a brute of a guy. Smaller than me but well sculpted and complete with dyed blond short hair. He had his shirtsleeves rolled up and they stretched tight over bulging biceps. Other than that he came over as a decent bloke and I got on well with him during our time sharing. He was in for serious assault and was awaiting trial, having been fully committed. He had battered his wife after catching her and his best friend together in their bed. I only found out later that he had used boiling water to torture her after tying her up. He worked as a door steward at a Glasgow city centre club and could obviously look after himself. Other guys in the Hall probably knew about Ally's crime, as there were a few sideways looks when we were walking around the exercise yard. I was still wising up – it's a lengthy process.

That first afternoon in B Hall a screw came in and asked us about work. When on remand, prisoners are not obliged to work, but we both said that we would be up for it. He explained that it was in the kitchens each evening between the hours of 6 p.m. and 9 p.m. The wages were £6 per week and the bonus was that you would get a shower each night on return to the Hall. Oh, and each con got an extra half-pint of milk as well. Sounded like nirvana to me: every night out of the cell, and a shower and six quid to boot. He went on that it was hot, heavy work, which involved cleaning the kitchens and all the utensils, including all the food trays. I did the numbers in my head. There were around 1,700 prisoners in the jail, each of them eating off a tray. Fuck me, that was 1,700 trays to be cleaned in three hours! Almost 600 per hour, or ten every minute, or one every six seconds. How many of us are there?

I got a big kick from all of that, even though it was over in a second or two – my brain was still working and, what's more, it could still work at speed.

We found out that night exactly what was involved. I was allocated to the pots and baking trays – all new guys started there. The screw-chefs seemed decent blokes, who went through the drills with us before work started. I spent the whole three hours stooped at a crazy angle standing at a sink, wearing an off-white boiler suit, well-used wellies – which had no doubt housed several pairs of stinking feet – and heavy-duty black rubber gloves that came up over my elbow.

The pots just kept coming. When I finally finished the pots, the baking trays were next. I had missed the pink cake on the menu at lunchtime, but I never missed it at night. I spent ages running hot water over each tray and frequently skooshed some more washing-up liquid on each tray to try and soften the baked-on sponge. One thing for certain was that I would be losing weight – it was coming off anyway. I'd bulked up before coming inside on advice from the same family friend who'd kept me right with so many other things. My normal weight was around fifteen stone, however I'd managed to put on almost a stone and a half in the previous six months, though I reckoned that I'd lost almost a stone in my first week inside. The kitchen work would ensure that the rest came off super-quick: it was like working in a steam room.

The shift came to an end and my feelings of satisfaction were fantastic – sounds crazy, I know. The screw-chefs were pleased with the effort shown and the kitchen was spick and span when we left. On the way out, we were each handed a half-pint of milk and a lump of that bloody pink cake. I laughed when I took it from the screw-chef and he asked me why I was so cheerful. I told him that I'd just leaked some sweat trying to get the stuff off the trays – he laughed back. I liked him; he seemed a decent guy. As we all walked back to our various Halls, I felt satisfied that I'd done a decent job, even though it was just cleaning huge pots and trays. We got to the Hall at around 9 p.m. and were told by the landing screw that if we wanted a shower we should get on with it, as we only had ten minutes before lock-up. I fired my milk and cake into the cell, grabbed a towel and sprinted to the showers. There were only four of us from our Hall involved in the kitchen detail, so we each had a shower. It was fantastic to stand there in the warm water without any pressure to get out as quickly as possible because there were other people standing in a queue. Ally and I watched a bit of TV that night, but the lack of sleep from my first week was catching up with me. That, along with the heavy, sweaty work in the kitchen, meant I had the best sleep since going inside.

The following day was like every other weekday in the jail. Same old, same old. Routine upon layer of routine upon layer of routine. Only difference this day was that I'd managed to get my name down for PT. A game of five-a-side football beckoned at 2 p.m. It was a beautiful, warm day and I looked forward to it with relish. Only thing was that I didn't have any trainers; the landing screw reassured me that they had a selection available in the gym. The call for PT was made at around 1.50 p.m. and I hurried down from the top deck to meet up with the others at the front desk. I was bigger and heavier than all of them, and knew none of them. Nothing was said to me as we made our way to the gym area with the PTI. All these specialists in prison are screws first and specialists second. My overall impression of PTIs in the various jails I've been in is that they are different from the residential and operations screws. No idea why, but they were generally more amenable and less confrontational. The two PTIs I came across in Barlinnie presented as decent guys with a sense of humour. We walked a couple of minutes and reached the gym, where I was last into the kit box. A lot of the guys had their own trainers, but there was a scramble for the shorts and tops. I was standing there in nothing but my jail socks. I picked out the remnants of the kit, a bright orange top at least three chest sizes too small for me, and pulled it on with much grunting and tugging. The shorts were similarly on the ultra-small side. I must have looked a right sight – thoughts of the Michelin man came to mind. I picked out a stinking pair of old trainers and laced them up – I was here now and I was going to enjoy it.

The PTI clapped his hands and shouted for us to get outside. I was last out and made my way onto the AstroTurf, standing with the rest against one of the boundary walls of the pitch. The senior PTI chose a couple of likely lads to pick the teams. There were twelve of us, so six-a-side. Needless to say, I was picked last. The look of me was such that being last pick was a certainty. Quite a few of my team knew one another and all of them were keen to show their skills when in possession. I didn't get a pass for the first couple of minutes. I was putting myself into space, calling, shouting, waving my hands, but never got a sniff. We were two goals down in the first three minutes, mainly because our main man had been caught in possession twice and they had rapped a couple in past our goalie. Old rules applied – the goalie rotated at every goal, so our main man was next up – he volunteered, probably to ease his embarrassment.

Although I played rugby at representative level, my dad had played professional football with Southampton in the '50s and I'd been brought up playing football. My brother could have made it in the game if he'd wanted to. I was just gagging for a decent pass.

Bingo! One of my teammates slid the ball to me on the left-hand side. I came in off my left foot and hammered the ball into the bottom right-hand corner with the right. All my frustration, anger at myself, guilt, call it what you like, came out in that first shot. I'd hit it sweet as a nut and it rocketed into the net. 'Beauty, big man,' came the shout from our main man, adjusting his oversized goalie gloves and starting to clap encouragement to his team. All of a sudden I was getting ball.

The game lasted thirty minutes and I scored four in winning the match 7–4. Both PTIs made nice comments to me as I was getting changed. One of them asked where I'd learnt to play football – I replied that I was a rugby player! I waited three days for my next turn at PT, but I was first pick that time – respect!

My first weekend in B Hall was a nightmare. I must have contracted an ear infection and became aware of it on the Saturday evening after lock-up. Around 10 p.m., the pain was dreadful. Ally told me to press the alarm and see if I could get painkillers. I did so, and a female screw came to the door and asked me what I wanted. I explained to her through the peephole what I was suffering from and she said that she would see what she could do for me by way of getting some relief. An hour went by and nothing. The pain was getting worse. I pressed the alarm again. After about another 20 minutes, she came to the door. She opened the peephole and told me that she couldn't get any painkillers and that I'd just have to get on with it. What the fuck? I asked her to come back to the door by standing up against the hinged side, as there was a gap there. She did come back, but merely repeated what she had told me before. Ally was raging. I didn't sleep until about 5 a.m. By this time, I was almost completely deaf in my right ear. The infection moved to the left side over the next day or so, leaving me almost deaf. No painkillers, no antibiotics. Fuck all but deafness!

• • •

My departure from Barlinnie was abrupt, to say the least. During my second week there, my solicitor had arrived for a legal visit. She had come to say that she had applied to the Appeal Court for High Court bail, but wasn't hopeful at all and thought that I would be in Bar-L for the full five weeks, through to my reappearance before Lady Cosgrove for sentencing. I had taken all of that on board and was getting on with the job of trying to assimilate myself into prison life. The kitchen work was going OK. There was a continual turnover in our group of workers, which was understandable, as we were all on remand and either being sentenced or released on a daily basis. I made my way to the top job inside of a week. I was viewed as responsible by the screw-chefs, so my promotion was meteoric.

I moved to the tray-cleaning conveyor belt after one week on the pots and trays and two days on the floor cleaning – standing there, removing food from trays with a hand-held power hose, before handing them to another guy, who placed them on a conveyor belt for drying, was just the bizzo. Our team was invariably finished with half an hour to go and we were allowed to rest and relax in the changing room. PT was still going well and I'd made it to become one of the team-pickers. Unlike previous main men, I started off in goal and looked to get new guys on the ball as soon as possible. The PTIs liked that and noticed it was a deliberate ploy. I was still rapping in the goals as well.

The cell door opened early one morning. 'Court!' was shouted by the screw.

'Sean, what time is it?' Ally shouted down from the top bunk.

I looked at my cheap watch, which I'd managed to get out of my personal possessions. 'It's half-six,' I replied.

Ally jumped down from his bunk, pulled on his jeans and picked up his shirt. He slipped his trainers on and left the cell, still struggling to get into his shirt. I got to the door just as he was talking to the big screw at the desk. I heard the screw say, as he was pointing at me, 'It's fuckin' him!'

I watched as Ally made his way back to the cell. 'It's you,' he said.

'I'm not going to court,' I replied.

'Looks like you are, mate. I'd get going. He told me you've got 20 minutes to get ready and have your breakfast.'

'Fuck's sake!' I started to get my gear on and picked up my towel for a shower.

The screw caught up with me, as I was walking towards the Head. 'You'll get your breakfast in the dog boxes in Reception. Get a move on – I need to get you down there by 7 a.m.'

'Where am I going?' I asked.

'Edinburgh High Court,' he replied.

I shit, shaved and showered as quickly as I could and got my gear back on, even though I wasn't completely dry. The only things

I had in the cell were a couple of phonecards and some letters I'd received from my wife, my mum and other family. There was no question of me taking anything with me – I'd no idea why I was going to court. As far as I knew, I'd be back there that night.

At 7 a.m. on the dot, I was escorted down to Reception and left there at the desk. I was shown into one of the dog boxes and a passman came and handed me a hanger on which I found my suit, shirt and tie. In his other hand were my shoes. A screw behind him said that I should get changed into my own gear and hand the jail gear to the passman. I laughed as I pulled up the suit trousers to find that they were about four inches too big for me. I would need the belt tightened at least a couple of notches. I banged on the door for the passman to take my jail swag and the screw arrived to open the door and usher me out into the main Reception area.

At around 7.20 a.m., after my cereal, half-pint of milk and dry roll had been served in the dog box, I was ushered out into the main Reception area. There were two other cons already there. Both were younger than me, maybe in their late 20s or so. They were already cuffed and I quickly joined them. Tense your wrists and arms, I told myself. It made sure that the cuffs weren't too tight, as your wrists and arms relaxed. We were ushered out onto the loading bay and straight into the blue-painted minibus. The driver was already in position and there were another six screws standing outside it. I was waiting for more cons to join us, but there were only the three of us piled into the middle seat so that we could all be sitting together. The reason for this arrangement soon became clear: we were immediately double-cuffed. I was on the left-hand side of the threesome, and my right wrist was cuffed to the guy in the middle's left wrist. His right wrist was then cuffed to the guy on the right's left wrist. We were going nowhere other than as a three.

The guy in the middle asked the oldest screw whether anyone else was joining us.

'No,' he answered.

'A bit o' overkill here, eh, boss? Six screws plus a driver for three of us, fuck's sake!'

'Shut it. This trip'll be a whole lot easier if you keep quiet,' came back the senior screw.

We were then checked out of the jail through the sanitised area that surrounds the prison and all of a sudden we were on the road. Cars, vans, buses – I'd only been inside for three weeks, but they all looked strange. The fact that I could see ordinary people going about their daily business totally oblivious to me, us, sitting inside a jail bus, firing along the M8 in the direction of Edinburgh was confusing. I felt like shouting at them to look at us. As that thought flashed through my head, it was immediately replaced by another, which took over completely, and I was relieved that the bus had tinted windows – I wanted to remain as anonymous as possible.

It wasn't long before the man in the middle spoke to me and asked why I was going through to the Appeal Court. I said that I wasn't expecting it and explained my position to him. I had real difficulty hearing him because of the ear infection and also the noise inside the minibus. I heard him say that it had to be my request for High Court bail. Our conversation lasted a few minutes and he explained that I should never have been remanded in the first instance and that I had a great chance of getting out today. My heart lifted, but I forced it back down again. I just couldn't afford to think that way. I would be devastated to return to Bar-L if I allowed myself to get worked up about getting out. Instead I just asked him why he was going through. He explained that they were both going through to appeal their tariffs. That meant they were both lifers and were challenging their punishment periods, the minimum sentences that they each had to serve before they were considered for release. I asked him what he thought their chances were. He said it was a lottery and depended totally on the make-up of the Appeal Court bench, comprising three senior judges.

The journey lasted about an hour and a half and there was only one moment of note and that involved the two young screws who were stationed behind us in the rear bench seat. The senior screw was in the front with the driver, and there were two in front of us and one alongside me, albeit separated by a narrow aisle. The two in the back started talking together about half an hour into the journey. I could just make out what they were saying. I picked up that they were both new to the job and hadn't met before. They quickly moved on to discuss what they had each done before joining the ranks of screws. It turned out that they had both been stacking shelves in different Tesco stores and they rapidly got into serious chat about what fruits and veg they had stacked. The young lifer nudged me and then said in a loud voice, as he half-turned towards them, 'That just fuckin' sums it up. We've got a coupla shelf stackers in the back. What a fuckin' joke!'

'Shut it, you,' came the snarl from the old screw in the front.

The lippy lifer started laughing and so did his mate. We all laughed, and Lippy was still shaking a couple of miles on. The two young screws said precisely fuck all. They never spoke again during that journey.

We arrived at Edinburgh's High Court in Parliament Square on the Royal Mile at around 9 a.m. The two young screws from the back seat were first out, pushing past me and the screw sitting across the aisle from me. It was as if they couldn't wait to get out of that minibus. They stood outside the van for a few seconds, as the rest of us gathered ourselves to move. They both tried to stare out the lippy lifer but failed miserably. He knew what they were about and nudged me as we were being released from the double handcuffs. 'Look at that pair o' rockets,' he said. He proceeded to stare at them as he got off the bus and took his time about it.

The two young screws knew that they had bitten off more than they could chew and started looking uncomfortable as all nine of us gathered on the covered walkway surrounding the grand building. The driver took the minibus away for parking as we made our way around the building and into a side entrance. The old screw had a whispered word with one of the young screws from the back seat and the young guy nodded in acknowledgement of what had been said to him. The lippy lifer and his mate were full of beans and virtually skipped into the building, all the while talking about a day out in Edinburgh.

We were led through a magnolia-painted corridor with a high ceiling and eventually found our way to what turned out to be the waiting room. It was a scruffy room in what was the grandest of buildings. There were already a couple of other guys in the room, one of them accompanied by a screw. Our screws never came into the room with us, preferring to un-cuff us and remain outside in the corridor.

It wasn't long before the lippy lifer engaged one of the other guys in conversation. He asked him where he was from and he replied, 'Glenochil, I'm up for a tariff. That bastard over there is fae Peterhead,' pointing to the guy who was sitting with the screw. All of a sudden it made sense. The guy was a sex offender and effectively had to be 'under protection' during his court appearance.

Lippy tried to speak to the Peterhead guy, even talking over the screw sitting with him, when the old Bar-L screw popped his head around the doorframe – there was no door – and told him that his day trip to Edinburgh would be over quickly if he didn't shut his trap. He shut it – for now. We got tea served in Styrofoam cups.

Around half-nine, solicitors and QCs started to come in and talk to us cons. Mine was last in and she immediately explained that Neil Murray, my QC, was on holiday and unable to attend. Given his performance so far, I was relieved. She said that John Scott, a solicitor advocate, would represent me and that he would be along to see me soon. Just as she finished saying this, John came into the room. He immediately said that we should go out into the corridor to talk as the room was now almost full of people and overhearing everybody else was easy. Easy only if you could hear properly – and I couldn't. I joined John and the solicitor in the corridor and concentrated closely on his mouth, as he started to speak to me.

'Sean, you shouldn't be in remand. I'm going to bust a gut to get you out. You do not present as a flight risk and I'm certain that I can get you out today. The rules on being remanded in custody have changed recently and you do not fit any of them.' I think I started to shake at this point. Being given the hurry-up at 6.30 that morning in Barlinnie seemed a million miles away. I had to calm down and take that stupid grin off my face before I went back into the room. Lippy would spot it a mile away. I shook John by the hand and wished him luck. He looked at me as if to say: you're wishing *me* good luck?

I went back into the room, which was still full of people, and picked up my tea. There were just the dregs left and they were cold, but it gave me something to look at and concentrate on. I needed that then. I'd come from feeling nothing a few hours earlier, treading water and trying desperately to fit into a system and a culture that was totally alien to me, and now I seemed to be on the verge of freedom, even if it was only for a couple of weeks. My brain was swimming. Thoughts of my wife and daughters flooded my mind and I could feel my emotions starting to get the better of me. Fortunately, people were starting to leave the room, which made me feel able to re-focus. It wasn't long before it was the same crew as had started in the waiting room. The guy from Peterhead was up first, a few minutes later. I never saw him again and assume that he was whizzed straight back to his transport up to Peterhead. Lippy and his mate were next and they both sniggered and patted each other as they left to calls of 'good luck' from me and the guy from Glenochil.

They were back very quickly, I thought. They couldn't have been in there for more than 20 minutes. They weren't as chirpy when they returned. Before anyone could ask, Lippy said that they'd been knocked back, but that they had to look on the bright side, as their tariffs hadn't been increased.

'What do you mean?' I asked. Lippy's mate spoke to me for the first time and explained that the Appeal Court has the opportunity to increase the sentence on your appeal, even if that appeal is for the court to consider reducing the sentence. It wasn't long before they were happily chatting away together and pestering the screws in the corridor for more tea.

There was a gap before the guy from Glenochil was up. He looked a hard case and never spoke much. He also looked very tense and muttered something as the screw shouted his name.

More cups of tea arrived whilst Glenochil Guy was in court. I was needing a piss and asked the screw serving the tea if I could go to the toilet. After a huge sigh, he told me to wait a minute.

'I haven't been for more than three hours,' I said to him.

He just looked at me and shook his head. He went back out and then came straight back in and said, 'Come on, then.' I followed him out into the corridor and walked behind him until we reached a pitch-black cupboard with no windows that stank of piss. He leant inside and pulled a string, activating the light, and told me not to lock the door. I did the business and just hoped that my clothes didn't stink too much.

I followed him back to the waiting room just as Glenochil Guy was coming out of the court. He wasn't a happy chappy. He was shouting back into the court as he was being shoved and pulled out by two massive, fuck-off Glenochil screws. 'Give it up,' they told him as he calmed down a bit in the corridor.

I managed to get into the waiting room before he did and waited for him to come back in. His solicitor and QC came in before him and he was accompanied by one of the two massive screws. They tried to placate him, but he was having none of it. He'd obviously also suffered a knock-back. Jeez, don't tell me this three-man bench is in one of those moods where everybody gets whacked just because it's a Wednesday, I thought.

I had to be up next – there was no one else. It was after 11 a.m. and I was sipping my too hot, very weak tea when my name was called. I quickly laid the cup down on one of the two rickety tables in the room and stood and tried to compose myself. As I walked into the corridor, I saw that two of the screws who had accompanied us from Bar-L were straightening their hats ready for our entrance. Looks a bit formal to me, I thought. I was told to get in between them as we were going into the court in single file. We all but marched into that court in step.

I followed the first screw up into the dock, which is a long bench seat. The court itself was like something out of a Dickens novel. The ornate nature of the fittings and the paintings on the wall, accompanied by shelves and shelves containing various legal tomes, was intimidating, to put it mildly. It was also dim and badly lit. It was the middle of August and yet the ambient light made it look like the middle of January.

John Scott stood up and started speaking to the three judges, who were some six feet above him. Anyone looking up at them for any length of time would have suffered a serious neck complaint. I couldn't hear a thing. John was speaking away from me. All I know is that he must have spoken for at least a couple of minutes and raised his voice a few times, although even then I still couldn't hear him. The judge in the middle leant forward to ask the guy on the other side of the table at which John was standing – I assume the Crown agent – something, which again I couldn't hear, but in any case all the guy did was stand up and shake his head and I could hear him say, 'No, m'Lord.' I was looking at my solicitor, who was sitting at the table where John was still standing, and she showed nothing to me by way of facial expression. The three judges rolled their chairs together around the middle one and there was a confab that lasted ten seconds or so. When they broke up, I thought that I was a goner. Surely, if they were going to let me out they would have taken longer to consider it.

The middle judge said something and then banged his gavel. The screw on my right started to stand and pulled at my elbow to indicate that I should do the same. I got to my feet, not knowing what had happened. I looked towards John, but he was pulling papers together on the table in front of him. My solicitor was talking to John over his shoulder, so I couldn't catch her eye either. It was the screw behind me who muttered something as we were marching out of the dock and I turned half around to ask him to repeat it. 'Well done, big man,' he said, 'you got bail.'

I swear I took the biggest in-breath of my life. I actually started to relax long before I got back to the waiting room. I was conscious of the fact that I'd got a result as I walked back into that room. I knew I was the only one who had that particular day. The guy from Glenochil was on his own again and looking glummer than ever. Lippy immediately asked me how I'd done. 'I got bail,' I replied and all three of the guys in that room were delighted for me. It was one of those moments I'll never forget. Three convicted killers, guys who I'd cross the street to avoid in other circumstances, were all happy that I'd made bail and was getting out, even if it was only temporarily. Even Glenochil Guy was happy for me and made a point of shaking my hand as he left the room in cuffs, heading for his transport back to Glenochil.

The senior Bar-L screw showed his head around the doorframe and told the three of us that we would have our lunch here before going back to the jail. Sandwiches and crisps had been packed for us. John popped his head around the other side of the doorframe and beckoned for me to come out into the corridor. I joined him and my solicitor outside the room and shook John's hand vigorously. He told me that he had done nothing special and that I should never have been locked up on remand in the first instance. He wished me well and left. I thanked him again as he walked away from us.

My solicitor then spoke to the old screw, who was sitting with the others in a line of chairs, all of them hoovering up sandwiches and bags of crisps. She asked him when I would be formally released and he replied that I would need to be taken back to Barlinnie for processing. She went daft. 'You no longer have a warrant to hold Mr Bridges. Any further detention by you or the Scottish Prison Service could be deemed a contempt of court.' The old screw was having none of it and he was aided by one of the other Bar-L brigade, who interrupted to say that I had to be taken back to the jail to 'pick up his stuff'. The solicitor turned towards me and asked me quietly what I had to pick up. I told her that I had just over 20 quid in my PPC and fuck all else. She turned towards the line of screws, who were still tucking into their munchies, and said that I had nothing to go back for – my money could be sent on to me by cheque, if necessary. The old screw laid down his pack of sandwiches and stood up. He was quite an imposing-looking figure in his neatly pressed, super-white short-sleeved shirt, complete with HMP epaulettes. After a pause of a couple of seconds, he said in a quietly authoritative tone, 'Madam, Mr Bridges will be coming back with us to Barlinnie. That is the end of it. Further discussion is useless.'

My solicitor seemed momentarily stunned and once she had recovered some of her previous composure she told him that I at least shouldn't be taken back in cuffs. She turned to me and said that she would contact my wife with the news and that she would be in touch with me in the next couple of days. She then turned on her heels and started to walk down the corridor and out of the court building. As she walked away, the screws were sniggering and muttering away to themselves. One of them told me to get back into the waiting room and finish my lunch. 'It's getting cold,' he said.

I sat back down in the waiting room and started to eat my sandwiches, filled with the thinnest tuna filling you could imagine, stuffing a few cheap-brand crisps into my gob at the same time. I figured that the quicker we got back to the prison, the sooner I'd be out – I was wrong about that. I was also wrong in thinking that I'd be left uncuffed. It was the same double-cuffing routine, but this time it was all done before we left the waiting room, meaning an awkward walk for all three of us down the corridor and out of the court into the daylight.

The return journey passed without incident, with the two lifers getting some uncomfortable shut-eye on the motorway stretch. I couldn't sleep. Christ, I was wired to the moon. All that the passage of time had done since I left the court was allow me to think of seeing my wife and daughters again, as well as the rest of my family, but strangely the caper involving the solicitor and the old screw in the corridor had filled me with fear and trepidation that something might go wrong and I would be back in the cell with Ally that night. These two conflicting thoughts were sitting like devils on either shoulder, one saying that I would be out soon and the other shouting back that I was kidding myself, that all of this was a ridiculous dream and I should give myself a shake.

When we got back into Barlinnie, I could cast all the doubts aside, as we were uncuffed and the two lifers were escorted back to their

Hall. I was asked a few questions at the desk and then told to get back in one of the dog boxes to wait on paperwork coming through from the court in Edinburgh. I noted the time I went back into the box – it was a couple of minutes after one o'clock. I wasn't let out of that dog box until 5.30 p.m. The time on the faxed sheet that I had signed before being released was 13.10. The bastards had kept me there for over four hours for no reason whatsoever. As I was signing the release sheet, the civilian staff member behind the desk apologised for the fact that I'd been brought back through to the jail and said that I should have been released from the court. I looked at her and pointed to the time on the fax sheet and smiled. I said precisely fuck all. She knew what had been going on and looked suitably shaken that I'd sussed it. My contempt for screws and the system they operate in grew immeasurably in that single moment.

Two other guys appeared in the main Reception area accompanied by a screw manager – three pips – and were quickly dealt with at the desk. They had been granted bail at Glasgow Sheriff Court after spending a couple of months in Bar-L accused of theft. One asked me how long I'd been in, but before I could reply the screw manager, a guy in his 40s with a thin, grey moustache and a couple of tattoos on his forearms, which were framed by his perfectly pressed white shirt, spoke to give us details of what exactly the prison was giving us by way of transportation home. After all, we hadn't asked to be sent to Bar-L, so someone else was sure as hell going to pay to get us back where we wanted to be. I'd been handed my cash back, all £22.48 of it. The other two guys didn't have a shilling between them. They were each asked where they were going. One said Glasgow, the other, a smaller, weedier-looking guy, said Dumfries.

'That poses you a problem, my friend,' said the screw manager to the weed.

'Howzat?' came back Weedy.

'Well, we've only got one travel warrant for each of you, so you can get your warrant made out from here to Glasgow or from Glasgow to Dumfries.'

The Weed looked absolutely thunderstruck. 'How am I going to get to Glasgow?' he said.

'That's your problem,' came back the screw manager. 'Bridges, you'll need to walk to Baillieston to catch your bus back to Edinburgh.' I said nothing. I had no idea how far Baillieston was – all I wanted was to get out of that shithole soon as. I was prepared to walk back to Edinburgh, if necessary.

The Weed was still at it as we started to file out of the Reception and back into the very salubrious main foyer of the jail – if only people knew what went on behind the shiny main prison Reception area, all beautifully decorated and furnished. We all had one last thing to sign at the main Reception desk and I was last in line. It was only as we queued that I caught sight of my wife, looking absolutely fantastic. She was sitting in the Reception area and smiled a huge smile for me. I had to restrain myself from running over and lifting her up in a massive bear hug.

Weedy was still having a pop at the screw manager about his plight. He had opted to walk to Glasgow, maybe a distance of four miles or so, and had the travel warrant made out to get him from Glasgow to Dumfries. I was wondering how I would be feeling if I was the Weed. Totally skint, facing a long walk and then a train ride back to fuck knows where. As we left the front desk, I tapped the Weed on the shoulder and handed him a tenner. I said to him that it should be enough for him to get a bus back to Glasgow to catch his train. It might even have been enough for him to get a burger as well. I turned after saying it and caught the screw manager's eye. He looked uncomfortable. I was glad about that. I wanted that bastard to look at himself the following morning in the shaving mirror and ask himself if he was doing a good job. Or was he just being a bastard?

Weedy nearly burst into tears as he thanked me for the cash. I was too taken up by grabbing my wife and getting out of that fucking place. My brother-in-law had driven my wife through and was waiting to take us back home.

• • •

I was out for almost three weeks, which allowed me the opportunity to get my affairs sorted and reassure my wife properly that I could handle the jail time. My life was on hold for that period, but I was able to attend my mum and dad's golden wedding anniversary, which was fantastic. It would have almost broken me had I been in the nick and missed it. Also, our younger daughter arrived back from her trip to the States during my bail period and it was great to see her.

CHAPTER SEVEN

I had answered one bail call during my time back out before the case was called at the High Court in Edinburgh on 2 September 2002. The difference this time was that I knew I was going to prison that day. The only thing left to be decided was for how long.

I hadn't seen my QC since the appearance in Glasgow and his unfortunate suggestion that I go into protection. He impressed me less and less each time I met him. The temptation to get rid of him was real and relevant but was tempered by the fact that he had been with my case since the start and, although I was pleading guilty, a complete understanding of the facts was essential in putting forward my plea in mitigation. I needed that plea to be professional and comprehensive, indicating knowledge of all of the facts surrounding the fraud and showing an understanding of the reasons why I had committed it, as well as the roles played by fellow directors and their involvement in ensuring that the fake contract was fulfilled. It was clear to me, although admittedly I'm no legal expert, that I didn't get that plea. There can be no greater frustration than sitting there in the dock listening to someone talking what seems to be complete shit about you and what you're supposed to have done. He must have had his reasons for the arguments he put forward in court, but these were far from obvious to me.

The actual day started off strangely with me saying my goodbyes to my wife and daughters. We all knew it was our last chance to have kisses and cuddles in freedom, without being watched and assessed by screws in visiting rooms. I chose to leave early and arrived at the court around 8.30 a.m. I did this to avoid any media and also to protect my family from any connection to me in the media. The more I could do to reduce their exposure, the better. It worked, to an extent, although my sister-in-law, my wife's sister, received a knock on her door from a national newspaper. Fuck knows how that connection was made, but hey, people talk.

I met with the QC when he arrived at around 9 a.m. and my solicitor arrived shortly thereafter. We chatted about nothing I can remember now – it certainly wasn't about my case. He eventually broached the subject of my plea in mitigation and suggested that he should follow the line of making me look like a complete idiot who had fallen from the dizzy heights in business and been effectively ruined by my actions. He planned to detail the jobs I'd done since the fraud had been exposed and look for sympathy from a judge who had sent me to Barlinnie only five weeks previously. I remember sitting there with a frown and I actually started to shake my head. He was dressing up in his gown and other nonsense at the time he caught me shaking my head.

'Something wrong with that?' he asked.

'Yeah,' I replied. 'I think you should just tell it as it is. How it happened. Why it happened. How the actions of others allowed it to continue – all of that.' He seemed stunned by what he probably considered an outburst, but at this point I was really unhappy with my representation. I couldn't see where he was going with his questioning.

'Try and relax,' he said. 'It will be OK.'

But I didn't have confidence in him and what was to follow in court didn't help the situation.

I sat at the back of the court with my wife and the girls until my case was called. The rest of my family were all there except for my brother, who had gone on holiday the day before. There were a couple of reporters and a smattering of general public, the type who populate these places on a daily basis. One of the court attendants I had spoken with at an earlier bail appearance told me that it was the same people who came in most days, probably looking for some excitement, or in the winter for someone else to keep them warm. The old French women sitting knitting at the business end of the guillotine came to mind.

Lady Cosgrove was in her element in charge of 'her' court. I believed that it was totally useless to try and appeal to her better nature – she was the one who had remanded me in custody to that Glaswegian shithole. She knew what that involved, and if she didn't then she bloody well needed to visit the place pronto. One thing I thought I understood about the Criminal Justice System was that a sentence of four years or more was considered long term. Anything less than four years was short term. The differences were massive. A long-term sentence resulted in a conviction that would never be expunged, i.e. it would always have to be declared when applying for jobs, etc. A long-term sentence brought the con into the parole system, which meant that there was no automatic release at halfway, rather the Parole Board decided whether you were released or detained until the two-thirds stage of your sentence. Having said that I thought that I understood all that, well, the proportions involved meant nothing to me, and I never gave them much thought until the solicitor and QC visited me in the cells after being sentenced.

All I can say about the actual sentencing hearing is that it seemed like a farce. Neil Murray, the QC, was on his feet for what felt like an age, more than an hour, I thought. He was spouting off about stuff even I didn't recognise, and I was gradually getting more and more fretful about exactly how this was going. At one stage, he was challenging the Advocate Depute's assessment of damages, making an important point about the loss that had been suffered by the victims of the fraud. It was crucial that the judge understood the complexities of this issue, as it would affect my sentence, but I felt the point was not being made as clearly as it could be. I was confused and so assumed the judge must be, and I was really anxious to make sure that she understood all the circumstances. I was considering interrupting the proceedings to ensure that one particular point he was making was clarified. I knew that it would be difficult, but I needed to speak with him immediately.

Just at this moment, the Advocate Depute, Norman Ritchie, stood up and asked if he could address the issue at hand. Ritchie spoke for a minute or so, and his explanation made any further elaboration unnecessary. I was stunned – stunned and relieved. A prosecutor had helped me by clarifying a point to the judge. How often does that happen? I wrote to Norman Ritchie from my cell, thanking him for his intervention and received a gracious response.

The whole thing was over by 11.45 a.m. and the judge told everyone that she would break for a quarter of an hour and deliver her decision at midday. I was not allowed to go back to my family and instead had to sit in a secure room in the cells area under the court. It was a long 15 minutes. I thought about my family, sitting waiting in the court. I hoped fervently that the sentence would be less than four years. I had never been given any indication by the solicitor or the QC as to length of sentence, despite asking them both on several occasions.

Eventually, midday came around. I was led back up into the court and sat in the dock flanked by two policemen. The judge asked me to stand and so I stood up, as did the two cops. I can't remember how she started off – sometimes these things stick and sometimes the buzzing in your head dictates that they don't. I do remember her calling me the 'architect of a grandiose scheme'. No way! She also said that my actions had harmed several people. She had to be joking! Nobody lost a penny through my actions. It was the archetypal victimless crime. How could she not see that? Fuck's sake, she'd sat through all of the Crown's crap in Glasgow and Neil Murray's performance here in Edinburgh, and still she hadn't got it.

Then it came. 'Mr Bridges, I'm sentencing you to four years' imprisonment. You will further be disqualified as a director for a period of ten years. The sentence will take account of your period in custody on remand which was . . .' She started to shuffle papers at this point, whilst Neil Murray stood up and offered her a period of two weeks. What? I'd been inside Barlinnie for longer than two fuckin' weeks! That hairy bastard of a QC had been on holiday whilst I was inside that shithole and here he is offering up a chunk of time to a High Court judge who doesn't know the answer. I was never closer to exploding in that dock than I was then. Between this pair of nitwits I'd lost a few days of my life. Instead of my sentence being backdated by 17 days, it was only backdated by 14 days. Mightn't sound like a lot, but given the fact I thought four years for what I'd done was totally fucking ridiculous, another few days merely added insult to injury. Lady Cosgrove finally worked out when the sentence was deemed to have started – she seemed to have difficulty in counting back 14 days over the turn of a month.

'Take him down,' she announced. That was the second time this woman had said that about me. I had then, and still have now, total contempt for her.

I was focused on ensuring that whatever sentence she came up with I wouldn't be stunned or shaking, crying, breaking down or generally making a tit of myself. I got to know plenty of guys during my time inside who had buckled or even collapsed when sentenced. No fucking way was I going down that road. I didn't have a lot of time to stare her out, and she never looked up after she said those three fateful words, and in any case I was being shoved by the cop on my left to get out of the dock and down the stairs to the cells. I managed to turn and look at my wife and the girls, who were huddled together and visibly upset – they all knew the significance of the length of the sentence. Two seconds later I was under the court, shoved all the while by the cop behind me. I understood their keenness to get me down to the cells. It was a potential flashpoint for violence and other protests.

I was stuck in a holding cell with three other guys who were eating packs of sandwiches. 'Wha' did ye get, big man?' said one.

'Four years,' I replied.

There was no further chat for the next few minutes and then I was called out to see my 'legal team' – the screw's term, not mine. I was shown into a goldfish bowl-type room; the QC and solicitor were already there, waiting for me. Maybe it was my imagination, but to me they both looked a little smug. The QC started off by asking me what I thought of the sentence. I responded by saying I thought that it stank, given all the circumstances. I went on to say that the judge in her pre-sentencing summing-up had used terms that made me think she had not fully understood all the facts of the case and that my sentence was inordinate because of that – at least I think that's what I said, as my brain was spinning like a fucking top. The QC then said that he thought it was a fair result – well, he would say that, wouldn't he? – and that had the judge sentenced me at the end of the Glasgow hearing, then I might have got between six and eight years.

It doesn't take long for your brain to clear and all of a sudden this new clarity kicked in. I went for it. 'Don't give me all of that shit,' I said. 'She couldn't have sentenced me in Glasgow without hearing pleas in mitigation, and, while we're at it, why was it that the Advocate Depute stepped in to clarify a point you were making?'

He looked shaken, and had started to stand upright during my rant. I stayed seated and tried to keep the level of my voice in check. He quickly moved on to tell me that with full parole I would be out after serving one-third of my sentence, 16 months, and that I would more than likely be housed in open conditions for the bulk of my time inside.

This guy, a senior legal professional, got both of these predictions completely wrong. I would have expected him to get the first one dealing with parole completely correct, given the sphere he was operating in on a daily basis. His comment on easy time in open conditions was well wide of the mark for me – not his fault, just reality.

He concluded by telling me that he had met and discussed the parole situation with my wife and family and also that he considered the lodging of an appeal against sentence to be a waste of time, as his opinion was that it was fair. I really wanted to grab him by that straggly beard and swing him around a bit. Maybe slap him a few times as well. I got up and without saying anything to either of them – the solicitor had stayed silent throughout – moved towards the door. I got the eye of the screw behind the desk and called to him that I was finished. I kept my back to them until the screw came over and unlocked the door, and then I went back to the holding cell. I was becoming more and more incensed with my legal team and my feelings would be heightened later in my sentence.

I was tossed back into the holding cell and handed a pack of sandwiches and a bottle of water. There was a strange atmosphere in the cell. I was aware of it from earlier, but it was even more obvious now. I thought that it might have had something to do with the fact that there were two new guys sitting there along with the three originals. No chat, not a word. Strange that, given all of the other cells I'd been in. Thinking like a hardened con even now. Get a fucking grip of yourself, I thought. I ate the sandwiches without tasting anything, thinking about my wife, the girls and the rest of my family and how they were doing. Tried to get positive by telling myself that at least I knew now exactly how long I was going to do. Nothing could be worse than A Hall in Barlinnie, surely. Didn't they get home visits from open conditions? Wasn't Archer only in maximum security for three weeks? Your brain works treble overtime when the old adrenalin is pumping so violently through your system.

Still no chat. There's something up here, I thought. I could feel it. I glanced round and took in as much as I could without looking directly at anyone in particular. Various body positions, from totally laid-back to bent at the waist to pacing around, making everyone else feel uncomfortable. One common theme: all five of them were smoking. I could die from passive smoking if they don't move us soon. I smiled inside.

There were six of us, so when the screws came to cuff us for transport to HMP Saughton, which is Edinburgh's prison, we were cuffed to another guy but not cuffed to ourselves. This made walking a bit easier. The first real sign that something was up came as the cuffing went on. The second pair were about to be cuffed, I was in the third and last pair, when one of the guys stepped back and asked to speak to one of the screws away from the rest of us. They stepped back a few paces and there was muffled chat. When they returned, the guy was pushed back to stand with me, and my partner was promoted to be cuffed to the other guy in the second pair, who turned his head slowly and looked at my new partner in an openly threatening fashion. The guy in front was a small, insignificant-looking type, whilst I was now cuffed to the complainer, who was my height and build. The way I was feeling I just wanted to get to the jail, get through the Reception process and start settling in as best I could. I didn't want any hassle. I didn't want to get involved in anything dodgy. I just wanted to do my time and get the fuck out as soon as I could. I'd thought about all of that so often over the past two and a half years or so and here it was now as my total reality and the only thing that I should be focused on. Even the spell in Barlinnie seemed to be years away instead of just a couple of weeks.

We walked out to the minibus and were seated by the screws so that my partner and I were at the back and the small guy and his partner were at the front. Interestingly, no screw came in the back of the minibus with the six of us. There were two of them in the front seat, along with the driver. Made the trip from Barlinnie look like total overkill – six screws and a driver for three of us!

My cuff partner started to chat not long after the bus started to move. How long had I got? What for? Where was I from? All of this before we had reached the bottom of the Mound.

'Look, mate,' I said, 'I'm not in a particularly talkative mood just now. Can we leave it there?'

'Yeah, sure,' was his reply.

I was relieved and just started to focus in on what was waiting for me as a convicted man. I knew that the privileges, number of visits, etc. would be far fewer than for someone held on remand and I tried to prepare myself for what was waiting for me. The rest of the journey was over too quickly. It was the last I was to see of the world outside prison walls for a number of months; I had tried to take notice of cars, people, buses, vans and all the other sorts of normal everyday life that I wouldn't be involved in for a while – the memories would just have to do me.

Soon enough we were going through the main door of Saughton. The driver and one of the other screws went through the check-in procedures with the guard on the gate and we were inside. Very quickly, all six of us were ditched off the minibus and into the main Reception area. We were shown into a room opposite the main desk, featuring a full-width window about four feet deep. There were already six guys in there, so I sat down and prepared myself for a wait. There was a wall-mounted bench running around three of the walls, with the window wall being the only one without seating of any kind. My cuff partner sat close to me opposite the window wall, whilst two or three other guys milled around in the middle of the room, the rest being scattered around on the bench seats. One of the guys milling about was the guy who had looked threateningly at my cuff partner before we were stuck in the van. He was on tiptoes some of the time, whispering into the ears of the two other guys who were standing up. Something was up, but, to be honest, I was feeling too sorry for myself to bother too much. It didn't involve me, so I'd just let the fuckers get on with it.

Over the next couple of minutes, more guys were brought into the loop, including a tall, thin, shaven-headed guy dressed in a T-shirt and jeans with a tattoo of barbed wire encircling his neck. He patently had no chance of impressing the judge. He had a spider's web tattooed on the left side of his neck and the words 'No Fear' underneath the wire right across the front of his throat. I was once told by someone who knows about these things never to be intimidated by anyone with tattoos, piercings, a shaven head or body art. He said all they want to do is make a statement – and it only hides a deep-seated insecurity if that statement is 'I am hard. Don't mess with me!' All of that flashed through my mind as Tattoo got up and became one of the 'millers'. There were now six of them walking about aimlessly, including the Whisperer. I was looking down at the floor and didn't really notice anyone other than the Whisperer, but the other five had by now positioned themselves in front of the window, effectively blocking the view in from the Reception desk.

Suddenly, the Whisperer took two or three giant running strides and launched himself feet first at my cuff partner, much like a kung fu-type jump-kick but just a bit more agricultural. I was sitting hunched forward with my hands on my knees and Whisperer shot past me before I could move away properly. Fortunately, my cuff partner, who was sitting only a couple of feet away from me to the right, had spotted the move and took evasive action. Whisperer missed totally and the frantic efforts he made during the last few feet of his journey to try and make some form of meaningful contact looked absolutely hilarious. It was as if he was having a seizure whilst flying through the air unaided. It didn't take him long to get back on his feet and continue with the attack. I just moved a bit away from it, sliding along the bench to my left. My cuff partner was at least three stone heavier than Whisperer and slapped him a couple of times to fend him off.

Tattoo couldn't resist the temptation to get involved and, as the dancing continued, he head-butted my cuff partner on the back of the head. The sound of head-butting is like no other. It's like a dull thud that carries a certain resonance, as if a tuning fork has just been struck – there's a musical note to it. It hurt the guy, no doubt about that, and gave Whisperer renewed encouragement to carry on his futile attack. My cuff partner didn't even get time to turn around and see who had butted him, as he was fending off Whisperer. The butt had obviously hurt Tattoo as well, but he was putting on a brave one, the reddening lump in the centre of his forehead notwithstanding – nothing else he could do with 'No Fear' splattered all over his throat in giant capitals.

It must have been all of ten seconds since the first desperate lunge by Whisperer and the pain in Tattoo's forehead was kicking in three or four seconds after his head-butt. The slapping match continued and was leading to a stalemate, which was just fine by me. Surely the screws would see what was going on and stop this farce soon. I could see that Tattoo was considering taking a more 'hands-on' involvement in the proceedings. I stood up and looked straight at him – he looked straight back. I barely shook my head, more out of nerves than trying to look cool and hard at the same time, but it worked. 'Dinnae worry, big man. Nae point in ruinin' that good suit o' yours.'

Just at that point, two screws came charging into the room and broke up the cuddling match. The two guys were taken out of the room and the rest of us were told to sit down and were called 'fuckin' animals' by one of the screws as they left – I didn't get that last bit. I got to know Tattoo well during my time in Saughton and he was a decent, if totally misunderstood, type of guy: a typical tattooed, shaven-headed warrior.

The two pugilists – a loose term, you understand – were split up and it turned out that Whisperer had grassed up my cuff partner to reduce his sentence and initiated the attack to try and deflect any potential attack on himself. This was my introduction to the very strange world of how jails work. Whisperer spent the rest of his time on protection, whilst my sentence ran parallel to my cuff partner's. He had been sentenced to four and a half years for the armed robbery of a petrol station.

CHAPTER EIGHT

Imagine your first day at a new school. Think of the fear and the apprehension – and then multiply it by a thousand, a million or whatever number your brain can quantify. All of those feelings are more acute now that you're an adult and should be able to cope with most things. Shit, every feeling of insecurity you've ever experienced washes over you in huge fucking waves. The new boy's arrived! Wonder what he's like? Some of the undesirables will be considering you a new opportunity. The screws will be wary until they get to know you – such wariness initially leads to you being treated as the biggest threat to security in the Hall.

Fear is the biggest feeling you experience by a street length. It dictates how you deal with every situation. It drives your ability to form relationships. It deprives you of sleep. It's never, ever, gone, even at visits. I have been asked numerous times since my release whether or not I was frightened inside. My answer is always the same: I was scared all the time. I felt as though if I wasn't scared, then that was precisely when I would be at my most vulnerable. Anyone who says they're not scared, at least on admission to prison, is lying.

I made a few pledges to myself before I was sentenced. All the usual stuff: get more education, read more books – hopefully, ones that were complete – try and help others where I can and don't get drawn into making comparisons on lengths of sentences. I also promised my dad I would come out the same guy as I went in. I succeeded in a few of them but totally failed on the last two.

The ludicrous disparity of sentences is incredible. I knew a guy inside who had been sentenced to five years for a VAT fraud. That was my benchmark for comparisons and still is. There were others who had committed unspeakable sexual acts on children doing three years or less; a guy who had threatened his neighbour for over ten years, eventually killing him in the street with a cricket bat, was doing a five-stretch for culpable homicide. A variety of others who were in for acts of horrendous violence were doing ridiculously short sentences – all far shorter than mine. The only cons who are whacked when it comes to sentencing – apart from fraudsters, that is – are those convicted of supplying class-A drugs. Their sentences are diabolically long and out of kilter with the gravity of the crime. I know what I am saying is controversial; it's not intended to be for its own sake, but it's exactly what I feel from having experienced it close-up. Their lives are chaotic and are effectively halted by huge sentences, meaning that they revert to type on release – they have nothing else to fall back on. They then get caught again, get a longer sentence, then an even longer one, and so on.

I knew absolutely nothing about drugs or the issues surrounding them before I was sentenced, other than what I'd read or watched on TV, but everyone needs to know that the entire jail system revolves around drugs and the system's futile attempts to reduce consumption by cons. My views now are well researched and moulded by first-hand experience, and I'll detail them later in this book.

． ． ．

Being processed through Reception at Saughton was a bit less painful than at Barlinnie. The screws in Saughton seemed altogether more human than the squad at Bar-L. They spoke to me in a quiet and far less intimidating fashion than the Bar-L screws had. Maybe it was me and I was just imagining it all because the prison was about a mile and a half from my home. Maybe it was because I now knew exactly how long I'd been sentenced to and I was wallowing in self-pity, guilt and thoughts for my wife, daughters and other family and friends. I never, ever, thought that I would be grateful for having served time in Barlinnie, but I was at that particular time. In spite of the caper in the waiting room, Saughton seemed to be an entirely different ball game – less threatening and less intimidating. I got this feeling during the Reception process and it was to continue throughout my time there.

I was interviewed by a nurse, who went over my health and fitness, and was also seen by another screw, who mapped out exactly what would be happening to me from the following day. Oh, and by the way, did I smoke? 'We'll try and get you in with another non-smoker but can't promise it' was his answer to my negative response. I would be going into A Hall, which was for new arrivals and was also used as a downgrade facility. 'Progression' is a massive word inside – so, therefore, is downgrade. For all cons who are serving sentences of more than 18 months, progression is the driver. It brings greater privileges, maybe home visits as well, yet it also puts hurdles in your path – hurdles that numerous guys fail to get over. It also allows the informant, or 'grass', network to flourish. The more guys have to lose, the greater the lengths they'll go to to hang on to what they've got, even if it means sticking others into the screws. The fact that these 'others' might be entirely innocent of doing anything against the rules makes no difference – desperate men do desperate things. I was to suffer on two occasions from exactly such a situation. The screws effectively propagate this growth in grassing because of sheer laziness, a feature of screw life in jails. It's easier to react to information given to you by some fuckwit than have to go around ferreting it out for yourself. The result is an atmosphere of mistrust, generating unease and sometimes culminating in violence within the general population.

I wasn't thinking about progression or any of that at the moment I was asked to strip off and handed out jail jeans, underpants, socks, shoes and a vivid-red polo shirt with a snazzy logo – 'HMP Edinburgh – A Hall' – on the left breast. The screw hadn't mentioned that A Hall was still slopping out. I didn't pick that up until I was in the Hall and being handed my shit-pot and piss-pot. I was completely wrong in my notion that it was only in Barlinnie that inmates still slopped out. In Saughton at that time, September 2002, there were two Halls that slopped out and I was going into one of them. The other was Forth Hall, which was the ultimate downgrade facility, housing guys who were either not prepared to sign up to the Voluntary Drug Testing compact (VDT) or those who'd failed Mandatory Drug Tests (MDT).

As I'd been held on remand in Barlinnie I hadn't been exposed to any of the real systems in operation within the Prison Service in relation to drugs. Now that I was convicted, the entire machinery concerning drugs and their impact on prison life was made very clear right from the start. I signed the VDT compact during the Reception process and was asked about my drugs use – there had never been any. I was told on arrival at the Hall that I would be tested as soon as possible. I was also told that until and unless I produced a negative sample I would be staying in A Hall – slopping out and all. Let me take it now, I thought. I'll piss in whatever you want me to. The test didn't take place until the following day.

I was two'd up with a guy called Davie, who was serving 90 days for assault, involving some sort of a domestic dispute. He seemed decent enough and never bothered me at any time, although he chain-smoked, which did bother me. He'd been in Saughton before and knew the ropes. The cell we shared was bigger than the one in Bar-L and its two beds were just that – beds, instead of bunks.

There were two problems for me on arrival in the cell, one minor and the other most definitely in the major category, both of them caused unnecessarily by the laziness of screws. I was meant to have been issued with a plastic beaker to accompany my plastic plate and cutlery. I was told at the desk that they would have to get down to the storeroom and get one for me, so meantime I'd just have to use a Styrofoam cup. I used that fucking cup for four days. The major problem I had on arrival in the cell was that there wasn't a pillow for my bed. 'I'll try and get you one,' said the screw as he locked the door. I was moved on to D Hall a full week later and still hadn't been issued with a pillow. There will be some of you reading this who might be thinking, 'Aw, he never had a pillow. So fuckin' what?'

My point is that there were pillows available and that, according to rules not drafted by me, I was entitled to one, but because of the sheer laziness and indifference of the Hall screws I didn't get one. My old friend the chipboard screen was in place, behind which one did one's business, and there was fuck all else in the cell aside from a small cupboard, the door of which was hanging off on one hinge, that sat in between the two beds. It had also been a cream colour at some point in its history.

I'd come in with over 40 quid in my pocket, so my personal cash was well stocked. The screw on Reception sold me a couple of two-quid phonecards off my cash, so I could make calls to my wife that night without going into hock with anyone, screw or con. I thought at the time that some form of information sheet would be handed out to me as a newly convicted prisoner, giving details on how the regime worked, complete with timings, info on visits – how to apply for them, allocation, etc. – and other important stuff, like canteen details. But as was my experience throughout my time inside, the less information given out by screws, the more they feel in control. As the entire system depends on the screws at least feeling that they're in control, you would think it all made sense. But it is a total fallacy. There are a lot more cons in a jail than there are screws and the only reason that riots, flare-ups and smash-ups do not occur more frequently is down to the goodwill and good sense of the cons. No information was given out on an individual basis at either Bar-L or Saughton and all that did was to cause further uncertainty and confusion, which resulted in an extended period of settling in. It also proved to be a demarcation method of establishing hierarchy within each Hall and within each prison – the more you knew about how things worked, the higher up the ladder you were. Make no mistake, there is a hierarchy in every prison and every Hall, even within those Halls where prisoners are on protection.

I never slept on my first night in Saughton. Too much battering around in my head, along with trying to get comfortable on the rolled-up scabby towel I was using as a makeshift pillow. My feelings of guilt and responsibility to my family were at their most acute since the shit had hit the fan for me two and a half years earlier. How would my wife and daughters cope for the time I was inside? How would I cope with that amount of time? Would I survive it? I'd been told by the screw during the interview at Reception that because I was a long-term prisoner (LTP) my long-term jail of allocation was HMP Glenochil, near Stirling, and that the likelihood was that I would be transferred there at some point in the near future. I didn't even know where Glenochil was. I did know that Saughton was close to my home and, as my wife didn't drive, it was ideal for visits. Just sharing the same bit of sky was comforting to me, and also to her, as we discussed after my release.

I was piss-tested the following day. The procedure is that the drugs screws arrive at the cell – unannounced, obviously. They take great care in ensuring that they get you out of the cell as quickly as possible, so that you're unable to dump anything or pick anything up, and march you to the testing place, one in front, the other behind. The testing area in Saughton was across the courtyard at the centre of the prison compound. I was stuck in a dog box for about 15 minutes and then summoned to the desk, where the procedure was explained to me by one of the screws who was by now wearing surgical gloves. I had to piss into a plastic beaker, which had a temperature strip on the side. A what? I sure as hell wasn't going to show my naivety by asking what the fuck a temperature strip was needed for (it wasn't too long after that I found out). I would just piss into the beaker for these screws and get back to the Hall. His explanation continued, saying that my sample would be split into two new samples, both held in new plastic phials, and they would then be sealed in front of me and bagged, along with my signed declaration that I hadn't taken any drugs. Oh, and by the way, the results would be back in a few days.

I just got through all of it in a stupor. What was all this about? They must know I'm not on drugs, I kept telling myself. By the end of my sentence, I was a fucking expert at the whole caper. I had been tested 15 times.

One of the trade-offs for having an early piss-test was that I missed the half-day induction session where cons were informed of what went on inside Saughton. It also featured a one-on-one interview with a screw from Throughcare – a jail term for the process of assisting cons to get through their sentence and trying to ensure that they don't come back inside. I got info on visits and mealtimes and other important bits of shit from Davie, my co-pilot, who was patient with me and answered every question I had in between long drags of his ultra-thin roll-up of Golden Virginia.

I had managed to get through that first phone call with my wife without either of us breaking down. The fact that I was close by was far more important to her than it was for me and she sounded strong and focused on the positive side of things – that we now knew exactly how long I would be serving. The QC had explained to her and my daughters, my mum and dad, and my sister and brother-in-law that I would be out after one-third of my sentence, i.e. in 16 months, if I got full parole. We both said that this meant I would only have one Christmas inside and that I would be back home for Christmas 2003. I could do 16 months inside – I knew that.

I was sentenced on a Tuesday, tested for drugs the following day and sent to induction on the Friday of the same week. Sleeping had been crap: no pillow, strange place – no, make that a *very* strange place – and a bed that was a one-inch-thick slab of foam on a piece of hardboard. The food was crap, and I mean total fucking crap. Hey, get over it, you're in the fuckin' nick! The grub at Barlinnie was light years better than this shit. (I later found out that Saughton had a deserved reputation for serving the worst food in Scottish prisons.) There was absolutely no chance of me using the shit-pot 'cause there was fuck all to get rid of. I wasn't at my best, you could say.

There were more 'open' times anyway, including a two-hour period of 'recreation' in the evening, except at weekends. Recreation involved sitting in a large school-hall-type room with one small TV that was invariably running wall-to-wall soaps throughout the period of rec. No, thanks – I got hold of a book.

Induction was an informative exercise for me – very, very informative. I was interviewed by a thoroughly decent screw called

Stuart, who went over all my details, including the sentence handed down to me. He told me that with full parole I would be released after two years, i.e. halfway through my sentence. If I didn't get parole, I would serve two-thirds of my sentence, some two years and eight months. I immediately challenged him on the terms he had explained to me. I told him that my QC had not only explained the one-third of sentence to me but also to my family. As diplomatically as he could, he told me that the system had been changed some years earlier and that long-term prisoners had to serve at least half of their sentence now before consideration for parole. I was totally devastated. I was going to have to do eight months longer than my QC had told me and my family. I started to dread the upcoming phone call to my wife that Friday night. As it turned out, the phone call went much worse than I'd anticipated and we had to stop the call short because my wife was too upset to speak. She said that she would contact the solicitor, who was in attendance when the QC had told them about the one-third rule, and try to get an explanation.

Weekends drag in jail. Sounds obvious, I know, but the lock-ups are lengthy at weekends. The one from Saturdays at 5.15 p.m. through until 8.30 a.m. on Sundays is particularly difficult, especially if you're slopping out. That first weekend in Saughton was diabolical for me. I couldn't get thoughts of how my wife and the girls were feeling with the news on my minimum terms. My feelings were tinged with anger and frustration at the QC and my solicitor. How could someone who is a senior figure within his chosen profession get something so basic so fucking wrong? That question hammered around my brain for the whole of that weekend and still resides in its deeper recesses.

Monday brought allocation to a workshed. There were a number of sheds in Saughton, including painting and decorating, joinery, hairdressing (violent guys with scissors, oh fucking no), industrial cleaning, textiles and laundry. The screw manager in charge of labour allocation came into our cell at around half-eight on the Monday morning and asked me what shed I fancied. I told him that I didn't care and that he should put me wherever he wanted. 'OK, then,' he said. 'I'll put you in textiles. Nessie'll sort you out.' I couldn't give a fuck who Nessie was, and the way I was feeling there was no way she'd be sorting me out.

My frustration and anger was moulding a changing attitude that continued throughout much of my time inside. It has turned me into the person I am today.

My first day in textiles was actually that same Monday afternoon. One of my other pledges to myself was that I would always go to work – I never missed a day's work inside. The guys in the shed were friendly and the fact that I didn't smoke meant that I was instantly seen as posing no immediate threat to their precious snout. There seemed to be plenty of tea breaks, taken around a large table at the front of the shed, which was just that, a huge barn of a room full of industrial-sized sewing machines and massive tables used for measuring lengths of material. My wife is a talented seamstress and I smiled as I thought about her reaction to me sitting behind this monster sewing machine.

Training by the said Nessie, a scary, fat female screw, was rudimentary, to say the least. I was handed a small pair of scissors, which were numbered, from a locked cabinet on the back wall. The workshed produced sheets, duvet covers and pillowcases for that jail and others. All of the products were made up in the same soft-peach-coloured material. I say soft peach – it might have been light shitty brown. My first task was to put a hem along both ends of a length of material which would eventually become a sheet. Nessie explained the use of the pedal and how I slotted the material under the needle carriage. It all sounded really easy and looked even easier. I say it *looked* that way because I didn't realise that the motor pedal was on a hair trigger and one press with my size-nine right foot was enough to fire half of the sheet through the machine and leave the line of stitches careering through the centre of the piece of material. Nessie recognised my difficulty, came over right away and gave me a playful clip around the back of my head. She extricated the material from the machine and asked if I would be good enough to unpick the stitches so that the material could be re-used. I grunted in response.

'You'll get used to it,' she said as she walked away.

She was right. Two weeks later, I was firing out sheets and duvet covers like nobody's business. It would be wrong, totally wrong, to say that I was enjoying it; I wasn't. However, it did pass the time and I was being rehabilitated. What's more, I got paid for it. A grand total of £6.50 per week meant that I could buy three two-quid phonecards and, along with what I could draw down from my PPC, I could get what I wanted from the canteen to supplement the bloody awful food in the place.

My piss-test had come back negative – surprise, surprise. I had spent a week slopping out and was moved to D Hall, which was sent up by the screws and prison management as a 'Drug-Free Hall' – it had a huge sign outside the main door to that effect. It went something like: 'Please be aware! You are now entering a drug-free environment'. Some fucking hope! I was moved into a double cell with another non-smoker. Hallelujah!

My co-pilot was Jim Henderson, who was almost a year into a three-year sentence for a violent attack on the man who was messing about with his wife. Three years seemed lenient to me, and others, including the Lord Advocate, who appealed the sentence, with the result that Jim's term was doubled to six years. It very nearly drove him out of his mind. He was in his early 40s but probably looked older than I did. He suffered from sleep apnoea, the symptoms of which are very loud snoring and a tendency to suffocate yourself before regaining your breath with an unbelievable snort that could wake the dead. I kid you not.

My first night with Jim was my worst nightmare. We'd chatted through the evening. The cell had a TV and a kettle and, most importantly, its own toilet and sink. Things were looking up. We went to bed around midnight. The light was put out and I tried to get to sleep. It was bunk beds and I was on the bottom.

The guy on the top moves and shakes the frame more than the guy on the bottom – simple laws of physics – and the further away from the fulcrum, the less effort needed and all that. I was prepared for that, having been bunked on the bottom with two different co-pilots whilst in Barlinnie. After about 20 minutes of silence, other than the usual shouts and cries of a typical jail night, I heard Jim whisper my name. 'Sean, Sean,' I heard. I thought about responding, and later wished I had, but felt that whatever it was he was after could wait until the morning – we were both going nowhere, after all. A couple of minutes after my lack of response, I could feel the frame of the bunks start to move rhythmically. Oh fuckin' no! He was having a wank. And if only I'd said something, it wouldn't be happening. I was just going to have to lie there and think about anything other than what was going on a couple of feet above my head. It was all over in no time and I was relieved when he gave out a big sigh and the deed was done. My problems, however, were just starting, as he fell asleep in no time and was soon snoring like Desperate Dan. I got up at some point to go for a piss and tried to make myself a couple of earplugs out of toilet paper. They helped a little but were inadequate in stifling the noise coming from the top bunk. I found out the following day from other cons in the Hall that nobody would share with Jim because of his condition. Other than that he was a cracking guy and we had loads of good chat over the time we spent together both in Saughton and latterly in open conditions.

Fortunately, Jim was moved to the low-category E Hall the following Monday, so I only suffered three nights of his snoring. My new co-pilot was a young guy from Edinburgh, who was serving two and a half years on a drugs-possession charge. He was in and about all the shit that was going on in D Hall in relation to drugs. Fuck all to do with me, and as long as it didn't affect me in any way these guys could get on with it.

That particular Monday evening turned out to be a seminal moment in my sentence. It was during the rec period and must have been around half-seven. I was waiting on my turn for the phone – two phones, sixty-four guys, means a queue. I was sitting in the cell on my own, watching something on the telly, when a screw came in and slapped a form on the top bunk. He told me that it was my category allocation and that he would be grateful if I would sign it. I got up from the plastic bucket chair and stood beside him.

He was standing with his pen in his hand and offering it to me. I asked him if I could read it before I signed it, and he huffed a bit and continued, 'You're a high-cat 'cause you're doing a four-stretch, LTP – makes sense, eh?'

The form was called a PSS1 and was A3 size, folded to make a four-page A4 document. The front page was information only. The back page was a series of signature blocks, whilst the middle two pages comprised a Yes/No flowchart, described by the screw as an 'algorithm'. For me, it was a simple flowchart. I'm certain some screws loved to use the term algorithm, as it made them sound superior to the cons, something that was prevalent throughout my sentence.

This particular algorithm had as its first question, and the words are branded into my memory: 1) Is the prisoner within twelve months of the commencement of a four-year sentence or longer for violence, including murder, a sexual offence or any offence involving drugs?

I felt sick. They'd answered 'Yes' to question one. This had taken me immediately following the flow of the diagram to a category assessment of 'High'. I did a double-take and asked the screw if I could look more closely at the form. He wouldn't let the thing go and there were a couple of mad seconds where we were pulling it back and forwards between us. He finally let it go and, becoming ever more sure of myself, I recited question one to him.

'How did you come up with a "Yes" answer to question one?' I asked.

He then took the form back off me and started to re-read the question. 'You're a high-cat 'cause you're just starting a four-stretch.'

'That's right,' I said, 'but I'm not starting a four-stretch for any of those crimes detailed in question one.'

He was getting pissed off. He'd probably never been challenged on one of these assessments before. 'Are you going to sign it? It'll be right, y'know. The Hall manager and Hall Governor have both signed it already, see.'

'No fuckin' way am I signing that thing. If the answer to question one is "No", I go straight to being a low-cat. I should be a low-cat anyway. First offender, crime involved no violence, no drugs, no threat to anyone or anything – a fuckin' high-cat, are you kidding?'

He quickly picked up the form and walked out of the cell, saying precisely fuck all, although the look on his face displayed his feelings towards me. He'd have to do some work, for fuck's sake.

I heard no more about the category cock-up that night. I came back from firing out sheets at lunchtime the following day and was asked to go and see the Hall manager before taking my meal. No problem, I wanted to delay eating all of my meals in the place.

Mr Grant was an ex-soldier, as are a load of screws. His office was on the same level as my cell, on the first floor of the Hall. It was immaculate, as was Mr Grant, with his sparkling, well-pressed white short-sleeved shirt and black tie.

'Mr Bridges,' he said, as he stood up and asked me to take a seat at his desk. 'I believe that you have concerns over the category allocation we have given you.'

'That's right,' I replied.

'As per our operating guidelines, we are required to categorise you within 72 hours of you arriving in this jail. You will realise that we are well beyond that stage now and we need to categorise you as soon as possible.'

He'd just fucking blown it. Why tell me that he was under pressure?

'I would be grateful if you would sign the PSS1 and just let the system pick up on your perceived anomaly,' he continued.

I'd never felt calmer since the start of my sentence. I told him in a flat, considered tone, carefully choosing every single word, that there was absolutely no way that I was going to be signing any form of any kind that didn't make sense to me, regardless of the pressures he was under to have me sign it. He couldn't look me in the eye, merely continuing to look down at the form and starting to shake his head. I was thinking to myself: don't fill the silence, keep schtum. It's his bag, he needs to respond.

'I'll ask you again,' he said. 'Will you not just sign it for now? The system will pick up any mistake.'

I sighed loudly and gave him my retort. 'Mr Grant, your faith in the system is far, far greater than mine. I will not be signing anything that doesn't make sense to me.' He eventually looked up, thanked me for my attendance and said that the meeting was over.

There was a screw in the Hall whom I'd played rugby against and also gone through a couple of coaching courses with. He was a decent bloke, but I was ultra-conscious not to be seen talking to him a lot. The more drugs there are in any Hall or prison, the greater the level of sophistication displayed by the grass network, leading to increased levels of suspicion. There's no way back into the general population for grasses. They go on protection, never to be seen again. Anyway, he came into my cell later that same night and asked me to sign the PSS1. I stood up and started to bristle, as I thought I was going to have to go through all of it again with him. All he said was, 'Hey, you were right. You should have been a low cat. You just need to sign for it.'

'You'll forgive me if I read it over,' I came back, starting to calm down.

He handed me the form and I gave it a full scan. I was indeed categorised as a low-cat prisoner. I duly signed the form. That single action sparked a problem situation for the Scottish Prison Service that was to run throughout my sentence. The 'PSS' on the form stood for Prisoner Supervision System; this system was new, having only been introduced in April 2002, less than six months earlier. Worse still for me, as it turned out, was that it had apparently been devised by an operations director at SPS headquarters who was now the No. 1 Governor at Saughton. I'd just driven a coach and horses through his new baby. My battle with Governor David Croft was just starting, although neither of us knew it at that moment.

CHAPTER NINE

It wasn't long before I was moved into a single cell. I was an LTP, after all, and that brought certain privileges. The guy in the single next to me wasn't an LTP. He was called Dom and he was the Hall kit passman. He was an important guy in the overall scheme of things, hence his single-cell status. I traded my tea packs for decent swag from Dom. He traded the sugar and tea for other stuff, including smack, but at least I was well dressed. He also came in handy when I came back inside from exercise after it had been raining.

The screws – especially a female one we nicknamed Vinegar Tits – hated it when I stayed outside to walk around the yard in the rain. One of the other cons had recently won a complaint about outside exercise. According to prison rules, everyone is ordinarily entitled to one hour's worth of outside exercise each day, regardless of the weather. Vinegar Tits particularly hated being outside in the rain when there was only me walking round and round. I did it to breathe fresh air. I did it to look through a small gap in the fence and see the Pentland Hills. I did it because I was entitled to do it and, yeah, sometimes I did it to piss off the screws. 'Bridges,' she used to shout at me, 'don't think you're getting a change of kit when you get back inside 'cause you're not.' I never, ever, responded, just kept walking round. She never sussed that Dom had some dry swag already waiting for me.

My wife had contacted the solicitor with the news on how long I would be serving and she had promised to contact the QC for his views. The solicitor came in to see me about ten days into my sentence to explain that the QC was certain he was correct in what he had told all of us and that he was investigating the situation. He was, of course, completely fucking wrong! His letter to me, received via the solicitor, states that 'the minimum terms served have been changed due to a recent administrative change by the Scottish Prison Service'. The 'recent administrative change' had taken place in the 1990s, around ten years previously, and it was a change initiated by statute and had absolutely nothing to do with the SPS.

The solicitor visited me to hand over the letter and said, 'Neil would be glad to come in and apologise personally to you.'

'I don't think that's a good idea,' I replied. 'I think I might just pull him over the table by that straggly beard and batter the fuck out of him.'

She looked shocked, but I didn't give a toss. I kept asking myself how someone in that position could make such a basic mistake. Surely at least one previous client had been sentenced to four years or more.

Get your head around it and move on, I kept telling myself. There was precisely nothing I could do about it anyway, so why use up brain cells worrying over it.

Cons had started to come to me with their problems and complaints. Word spreads fast inside such a confined community and news of my triumph on the categorisation issue swept like wildfire through the jail. There were loads of other guys who had been wrongly categorised, and so I was also being approached by cons in the Hall and had others at work asking me to look at their problems or complaints. All the time, I was assessing everything. I have an analytical mind. I like to understand how things work or, in this case, how things don't work.

Very quickly I came to the conclusion that the prison was nothing other than a human warehouse. The laziness shown by the majority of the residential staff (the screws who manage the Halls) when married up to the currency of indifference that pervaded the place created an inertia that couldn't have been destroyed by the use of a nuclear device. The SPS, government ministers and whoever else wants to pitch up and spew out all of the crap that some other wee civil servant writes for them can go and take a running fuck to themselves. The only statistic that matters is the one detailing how many ex-prisoners re-offend within a prescribed timeframe – the usual measure is two years. This statistic has remained almost static at around two-thirds for years. In other words, 66 per cent of ex-prisoners re-offend within two years of release. Fuck, if this was a hospital it would be shut down tout de suite. Just imagine it. Patients arrive at this imaginary hospital with a health complaint and are supposedly treated and discharged and then, within two years, two in every three patients return with the self-same problem or, even worse, a far more serious problem squarely based on the initial problem having not been properly treated. How long would the government allow this hospital to continue to exist?

What are our prisons good at? They are very good at keeping people locked up. Hardly any prisoners escape from closed conditions and therefore society feels safer for that. I've no idea precisely how difficult it is to keep a load of people locked up, but using my fertile imagination I can't see it being too taxing to come up with a secure system for keeping cons behind their cell doors. Prisons are undoubtedly very successful at generating repeat business. They ensure that they will always have repeat customers and when these repeats are added to new customers, they are all of a sudden bursting at the seams.

Let me be incredibly cynical just for a moment or two. If I, or anyone else for that matter, could come up with a bulletproof plan to reduce the current prison population by 50 per cent in the next ten years, whilst at the same time reducing re-offending rates from 66 per cent to, say, 50 per cent by the normal measure, this plan would never see the light of day. No matter how well researched, no matter how well budgeted, no matter if I or you managed to get it in front of the principal decision-makers, it would never be given serious consideration. Why not, you should be asking. Well, the answer's simple. Half as many prisoners require half as many screws, on a simple rule of thumb. A reduction in re-offending rates inevitably means a further reduction in screws. Fewer screws means fewer opportunities for promotion, lower pensions, loads less administrative staff and far fewer empires worth building. Believe me, the empires built up in the Prison Service are fucking massive. All of that fails society and will continue to fail society unless and until someone has the balls to attempt to change the culture inside prisons, and I'm not talking about the culture amongst cons.

I have been asked by loads of people both during my sentence and since release what I would do were I in charge of the Prison Service. Asking for a blank sheet of paper, I respond by saying that I would get rid of at least 60 per cent of the screws as a starting point. I know that's ridiculous, but I did ask for a blank sheet of paper after all. I know this is a generalisation, but the culture amongst screws is invariably one of sheer laziness. This either leads to indifference or has its roots there. What is the incentive for any Prison Service to rehabilitate cons? You will no doubt answer 'job satisfaction' or simply say 'that's what they are there for', but when you think it through, you realise that it would be like turkeys voting for Christmas. As I said before, fewer cons means fewer screws, means fewer governors and administrators, and ultimately fewer politicians, supposedly in charge of all those little empires. It's all about self-preservation.

■ ■ ■

Due to my now being a low-cat prisoner, all of a sudden better jobs were open to me within the jail. All of the external passman jobs were for low-cat prisoners. These jobs are outside the residential Halls and, as always, involve cleaning, more cleaning and then, just for a change, some more cleaning. You might just have to make the screws a cup of coffee at some point, or several points, during the day as well. The labour allocation manager came to see me one day when I was running off a few dozen sheets in light shitty brown. He said that the chapel pass was available and asked would I like to have the job? He explained that the wages were marginally better than the textiles job, £8 instead of £6.50 per week. He said that it was a 'cushy number', which in jail parlance means there is very little to do. He also said that the chaplains and the priest always 'looked after' their passmen. Christ, I could do with some spiritual help. I told him that I'd think about it and tell him the following day. He seemed a little put out by that answer, but I was doing just fine in that shed and time was rolling along for me. The last thing I wanted to do was change to something I didn't like.

I went back to the Hall that night and spoke to two guys I'd become friendly with. Both were in for drugs offences and, like me, both were LTPs. Neither of them was in and about the drugs scene at that stage, although both of them were destined to fall off that particular wagon later in their respective sentences. One was to become a supergrass at the open prison I ended up at. Remember, desperate men do desperate things.

I decided, after advice, that I would take the chapel pass job and told the screw manager, as agreed. He told me to start the following Monday, leaving me a final couple of days in textiles. Even Nessie was sad when I left. She muttered something under her breath. The last thing she wanted to show was any compassion.

I was in my third week in Saughton. Things had changed for me fairly dramatically since I'd arrived. I was in a single cell – the difference was incredible. I was on my second job. I thought that I'd sussed out who the headers were and who were the cowboys. I'd experienced no violence towards me up to that point and, although the Hall was awash with drugs, the fact that everyone knew I was clean kept all that shit well away from me.

My fourth week in Saughton changed all that. It was the Sunday afternoon and I was lying on my bed reading a newspaper from the previous Wednesday during an open period just before the early tea meal when a guy I didn't recognise came into my cell. He was mid-20s, medium build, with short, sandy-coloured hair and he looked decidedly agitated. He stood in the doorway with the door pulled onto him so that he was blocking sight and sound from getting in or out.

'Geez yir tea pack, big man!'

I didn't have a tea pack. I gave all my tea packs to Dom for clean swag. I'd looked over to him when he came in and then looked back at the paper, my brain working overtime.

'Geez yir fuckin' tea pack, I'm carryin'!' he said, raising his voice.

In the next few seconds, I swear there were a thousand thoughts flashing through my mind. I was thinking about my wife and daughters, my mum and dad, brother, sister, their families, why I was here, guilt, responsibility and then all the way to: will I survive this? Is this guy willing to kill me for a tea pack? Something switched me over and a strangely calm feeling came over me. Firmly, and in a deep tone that came from somewhere near my boots, I said, 'No!'

My response shook him and, as he thought about his next call, I eased myself up onto my elbows. In a loud, exaggerated stage whisper, he said, 'Dinnae gie me that shit. I told ye, I'm carryin'. I'll dae ye damage!' He was still wedged between the door and its frame, although he was now more in than out.

'I can't see it,' I came back.

'Cannae see what?'

'The weapon you're carrying.'

'Whit are ye talkin' aboot?'

'Well, I thought I'd be able to see whatever you're carrying, because you'll be needing a fuckin' bazooka to get a tea pack out of me today, now fuck off and bother some wee laddie!'

At that point, I swung my legs off the bed and stood up.

'Hey, big man, nae need to git a' steamed up aboot a tea pack.'

I moved one step nearer to him, leant forward and said, very quietly, 'Fuck off!'

He did fuck off. I sat down again and my legs were shaky. That didn't last long, but just long enough for me to realise that this might just be the first of these capers. I also remembered what that old family friend had told me before I was sentenced: 'If you have to go rolling about with some cunt, then that's what you'll have to do. You might take a tanking, but you'll not go on protection and the last thing these cunts want is to roll about with anybody. They'll leave you alone after that.'

I had to get out of that cell as soon as I could after the altercation with the halfwit. It was like falling off a bike – get back on as soon as you can. What if that little shit had some back-up and they were waiting for me somewhere? What if they were all tooled up? Well, I'd just need to find out, and pronto. I opened the door with a powerful swing and stepped out on to the landing and looked around. There was no one anywhere else on the landing. There were cons playing table tennis and snooker on the ground floor, a few screws standing around the desk area and most other guys were in their cells, relaxing on a Sunday afternoon. There was certainly no sign of the guy who'd come into my cell.

I walked along to Davie's cell. He was sitting watching his telly and smoking a giant roll-up. Should I say anything about the incident? Say fuck all, I said to myself. I'd try and act as if nothing had happened and see what comes up, if anything.

The rest of the day went without incident, although I'll admit to some relief when the screw locked my cell door at 5.15 p.m. – having almost 15 hours on my own was somehow reassuring and comforting in a crazy sort of way.

I started on the chapel pass the following day and it was indeed a 'cushy job'. Move the chairs, sweep the floor, strip it down and polish it once a month – loads of coffee, loads of biscuits and an acoustic quality inside the chapel that was fantastic for singing. I love to sing and music means all that is good for me in life.

Cons were able to get their own portable music centre and ten CDs into the jail by means of a property form and a week's delay for inspection. The equipment was virtually taken apart to determine whether any drugs were secreted anywhere within the unit. I didn't feel able to get my music in just yet. Too many memories attached to so many songs meant that I would have to wait until I'd settled in a bit more. Part of that process involved me singing in the chapel.

Initially, I waited until I was on my own and picked a couple of songs that I knew well and which wouldn't stretch my voice too much – I hadn't sung for a while. I graduated to singing for the young female chaplain, who enjoyed being serenaded whilst she went through her paperwork. Eventually, I was taking requests from all the chaplains and the priest. Colin, the senior chaplain, was a character and a half. He wasn't meant to smoke in the chapel but secretly kept his fag burning in a drawer, which he would quickly close if one of the management team came in. It was hilarious to watch. We had some great chats and he became a close friend.

Not long after I started in the job, Colin asked me if I would consider becoming a 'Listener'. Listeners are cons who act as internal Samaritans. They are trained by the Samaritans over the course of two full-time weekends and provide a listening service to all cons requiring their services. Screws are duty-bound to call a Listener if any con asks for one. Colin gave me some literature about them and I agreed to read it. My initial feeling was that it was too early in my sentence and that I was still needing time to adjust to life behind bars. I didn't feel that I could offer any kind of meaningful service to anyone who was struggling, far less someone who was feeling suicidal, given that I was feeling low myself and still at the start of my sentence. That fact didn't stop the Hall manager, a hugely fat guy called Mattie Sim, from asking me if I would like to meet the Chief Inspector of Prisons, who at that time was Clive Fairweather. I told Mr Sim that I'd just started my sentence and wondered what good it would do if I went along; there were others who were more experienced in the workings and failings of the system. 'Aye, that's right,' was his response, 'but at least you'll be able to put a sentence together.'

I stayed back after lunch one day and along with two other cons, neither of whom I knew, was introduced to Mr Fairweather, spending about thirty minutes in his company. He asked questions of us, and the other two guys were quick to respond, especially when it came to the topics of food, underwear and why Milky Bars had been withdrawn from the canteen list. I completely missed out on that last one, but it didn't take me long to understand the importance of Milky Bars in any jail.

It was a useful exercise apart from enjoying Clive Fairweather's company for a short time. It showed me that there was someone on the outside, someone independent, someone who was there to listen and hopefully respond, and I loved the fact that I was conversing with someone other than a screw or a con; someone who didn't have a chain full of keys attached to his belt and who wasn't wearing jail swag. I took a whole lot from that very short half-hour.

It was later that same afternoon, as I was sitting in my cell watching *Richard and Judy* – the things you do – when a brown, A4-size envelope came sliding under my door and hit the leg of the chair I was sitting in. (I tried like crazy not to lie down on my bed during lock-up periods during the day, as I was convinced that it would help me to get to sleep at night if I didn't.) My feet were up on the bunker, which was the large slab of worktop that ran down the complete length of one side of the cell. The envelope was face-up and showed my name, prison number, cell number and Hall. It didn't have a stamp on it and so before I even moved to pick it up I'd decided that it had to be internal mail. The daily distribution of mail always took place before the lunch meal was served. I took my feet off the bunker and bent down to pick it up.

Opening it and sliding out the contents, I could feel myself getting slightly more attentive. This was no ordinary piece of internal mail: this was the trial judge's report. The facing page had all the usual guff on it – name, date, judge's name, name of the court and a variety of reference numbers. I flicked through and there were nine pages, neatly stapled together in the top left corner.

I settled back to read the document, not knowing how I would feel, having all of what went on committed to black and white. Yeah, there were feelings of anticipation, but they were tainted by others of embarrassment, guilt and responsibility. All the feelings I'd experienced before starting to read the report were washed away by a form of mental tidal wave after I'd got only halfway down the first page proper.

I knew precisely what I'd pled guilty to. I could recite the precise terms of the various parts of the indictment. I'd signed the plea book in the High Court in Glasgow, pleading guilty to heads of indictment (a), (d) and (e). Yet in her report, the judge had stated on page one that I had pled guilty to four heads of indictment. I sat bolt upright. I looked at my watch and calculated that there was at least another hour before we were opened up for evening recreation, allowing me access to a telephone. It was the longest hour of my sentence. I read the whole report over and over – nothing else contentious. What am I saying, nothing else contentious? It seems I had been sentenced on the wrong basis. Head of indictment (b) related to a charge of defrauding a business partner of £150,000. You would agree a not insubstantial charge. It was total crap and was the first one dropped by the Crown months before the court appearance.

I shot out of the cell when the screw opened us up for evening rec. I'd got my solicitor's phone number from legal papers I had in my cell and decided I would leave her a message, asking her to come in and see me urgently but not telling her why. You'll be wondering why I called this particular solicitor, given my feelings towards my QC. A distinct lack of any reasonable alternative would be my answer to you.

I phoned my wife afterwards and decided that I wouldn't tell her over the phone but would wait until our next visit and explain what had happened face to face. The last thing I wanted was for any of us to get our hopes up of anything positive happening on the back of this discovery – that would have been a total bam-up for everyone.

Cons who are appealing either their convictions or the lengths of their sentences are entitled to certain privileges, the most useful one at that time being the chance to purchase an extra two phonecards per week on the basis that you were likely to be making more phone calls to legal advisers. Phonecards were a big currency item inside: debts were settled using phonecards; guys were taxed for phonecards. Taxing inside jails involves basically bullying other cons out of their goods. Those goods could be drugs, food, phonecards, bedding or anything else that one of the bastards wanted. The bullying sometimes extended to a full-on assault; there was one guy who was tortured with a disposable lighter, his forearm being burned until he told the taxers where his stash of smack was hidden. The entire Hall was buzzing after that one and the poor guy spent the rest of his sentence on protection, with one very badly injured right arm. Those bastards would need to kill me to get anything I had – my anger at a system that allowed these things to happen was growing exponentially and I had to find a way of channelling this in a positive way.

CHAPTER TEN

The solicitor came to see me a couple of days later. It was mid-morning, so I knew that we had plenty of time: it was at least an hour before I was due back in the Hall for lunch. The young operations screw had come to the chapel for me, and I'd said that we needed to go via the Hall to get the relevant papers. I fired up to my cell and picked up the judge's report, still in the same brown envelope.

Meetings with legal advisers are held in private, for obvious reasons. In Saughton, a relatively new suite had been opened up for legal visits and it provided comfortable rooms. Fiona was there, waiting for me, as I was shown into the main area. The screw behind the desk called a number to her and we both headed towards the allocated room.

'I got your message. Sorry for not coming out earlier, I've been really busy,' she said.

'No problem,' I replied.

'Are you OK?' she asked. 'Anybody causing you any problems?'

I didn't answer any of her questions – time was too precious to me. 'The trial judge's report,' I announced. She looked at me quizzically. 'Tell me about it.' She went on to explain that the trial judge produces a report on the proceedings and that this report is sent to the convicted person's solicitor between two and four weeks after the court appearance.

There was a stall in my delivery – I wanted to get this right and make maximum impact. 'What would you say if I told you that I have the trial judge's report in my hand now?'

'I'd say that's impossible.'

'What would you say if I told you that this report details that she has sentenced me on an incorrect basis, on me pleading guilty to four heads instead of three?'

'Let me see it,' she demanded.

'I want to know what you'd say to that.'

'Let me see it,' she repeated.

'Listen, I want to know, hypothetically, if you like, what your thoughts are on what I've told you – that this report contains a major discrepancy involving the basis for sentencing.'

'Well, if what you say is correct, that the judge has sentenced you on the wrong heads of indictment, you have the right to appeal the length of your sentence. Will you let me see it now?'

I passed her the envelope.

'How did you get this?'

I told her exactly what had happened, missing out none of the details, but I got the feeling that she had some doubts about my story. While I was a convicted fraudster, there were things worth lying about and others where there was zero profit in telling anything other than the truth.

'Did it come in this envelope? Have you shown it to anybody else?' she asked.

'Yes and no,' I replied.

'Who else knows about this?'

'No one, not even my wife and daughters,' I replied, wondering where the fuck she was going with this. What was all the Secret Squirrel shit about? I didn't give a monkey's how the report had got to me; the only thing that I had to question was whether this report was genuine and not some sort of wind-up. Given all the work involved in putting it together, I felt that there was no way it was a wind-up. The only way you get anything out of winding someone else up is when you're able to see it happening in front of you – and that hadn't happened in this case.

'There's no doubt this is genuine,' she said, without any prompt from me. I was thinking 'you fuckin' beauty' when she went on to say that she would need to take it away and discuss it with the QC and put together grounds for appeal. My brain went into overdrive. I didn't have a copy of the report. I hadn't told anyone about it, never mind showing it to anyone else. Did I really want that particular QC involved again on my behalf?

'I'm unsure about having Neil Murray involved in this,' I told her. The problem was that he'd been involved in the case from the start and it would have been a bit daft to have to start from the beginning again with someone new. Fiona told me not to worry, that the mistake with the term was just a bad day at the office for him. I wasn't convinced. However, the only way to proceed other than handing the report over to her was to walk out and try and get in touch with another solicitor. Hindsight is a 20–20 science which never allows for the emotional influences that colour most decisions. I was left with the dilemma of wanting desperately to progress this 'new' situation as quickly as possible but having to decide whether my existing legal team was the one to handle it. Appointing a new solicitor would inevitably result in delays and, foolishly, I felt that time was of the essence. If I'd just taken a step back and thought about it for a bit longer, another day or so, I might have appointed another solicitor.

I handed over the report, but kept the envelope. Fiona gave me another quizzical look, but I explained that the envelope was some form of receipt for me. Crazy, I know, but it was all I had.

The tone and content of her questions had me feeling that I was doing the wrong thing by handing the report over to her. I told her more than once that I needed the original sent back to me as soon as she'd photocopied it – I emphasised not the copy, the *original*. It took almost a month and numerous phone calls made by both my wife and me to get that report back, and even then it was the copy that came back.

Since an appeal hadn't been lodged on my behalf during the statutory period of 21 days after date of conviction, my appeal would have to go before a judge, who would decide whether or not there were sufficient grounds to allow an appeal that technically was out of time. I explained this to my wife and daughters at our next visit. Our elder daughter was a trainee solicitor at the time and so she did some research and confirmed that the normal route for the judge's report was from the Crown Office directly to the convicted person's solicitor. All three of them thought that the way I'd received it was mighty strange, to say the least, but we were all buoyed by the fact that there appeared to have been a fuck-up. Surely my term in prison had to be reviewed, given the fact that the judge had sentenced me on four charges instead of three.

'We'll just have to try and not get too excited about any prospects of a reduction,' I remember saying. Even at that early stage in my sentence my confidence in the system was cracking; soon, it would be ripped asunder.

■ ■ ■

I decided to apply to be a Listener. This sounds crazy, but the main reason for my application was that the training took up two whole weekends and that sounded just fine to me. Weekends in any jail are shit: no work, too much time locked up, too many rockets running about trying to get hold of whatever they're after.

In local jails like Saughton and Barlinnie, there's a massive problem in maintaining Listener services. It's principally because of the transient nature of the prison population and partly due to the nature of the work, which attracts the wrong type of people. Once trained and certified as a Listener, a con is provided with a 'yellow pass', which effectively allows him free passage to all parts of the jail at any time when a Listener call has been made. This provided an opportunity for less scrupulous types to get into the Listener Group and basically transport drugs around the jail with free passage.

By the time of my application, the screws knew I was clean and that there would be no problem with the drugs issue. The only thing they had to be convinced of was my ability to handle intimidation by the dealers. Mattie Sim asked me outright what I would do if someone asked me to take a package to another Hall during one of the Listener calls. I told him that I would tell that person that he was asking the wrong guy.

'What? You wouldn't come and tell a member of staff?' he said.

'That's the last thing I'd do!' I replied. 'If it means a roll about, so be it, but fuck all is getting moved about this jail by me.'

He only shrugged and got back to what he was doing – precisely nothing.

Training for the Listener service was conducted by Samaritans from the local branch. They brought great M&S food for our lunch each day and treated all four of us with respect and dignity, and displayed a genuine interest in each of us. They were fantastic people. The course involved lectures and a lot of role playing. The emphasis was on 'listening' skills. Sounds barmy, but that's what it was. Getting people to open up and talk about problems without offering solutions, even if you knew what the solutions were, was difficult to implement.

I've always been a good listener. I've been complimented on my debating style and my ability to argue effectively on numerous occasions. I base that squarely on my listening skills; I love to ask supplementary questions based on previous responses from the person I'm talking to. It shows one thing – I'm listening to what they're saying. It also signals to them that they need to take care in what they say, precisely because I'm listening and hearing everything. I knew I would find it difficult not to solve someone's problems if I knew what the solution was – but that wasn't the only difficulty I experienced being a member of the Listener Group.

• • •

Four weeks into my sentence, I was still desperately trying to settle. The potential for an appeal had stirred up everything for me – my brain was whirling.

At that time, Saughton had five convicted Halls and one remand Hall called Glenesk, which was the most modern, having been built only a few years previously. A Hall was for inductions and also housed those cons who did not want to progress to other Halls. There were quite a few of them, including a comical-looking, baldy guy with a Groucho Marx-type walk who insisted on moving about the Hall naked from the waist up. When he had to go out of the Hall to see the doctor, the screws had to persuade him to put a shirt on. He was mentally ill and was a regular customer at the surgery. There are so many like him, it's heartbreaking to see.

Forth Hall was the ultimate downgrade Hall and, like A Hall, slopped out at that time. Everyone in Forth Hall was guilty of some form of infringement of the prison rules. D Hall was supposedly the first progression into a 'Drug-Free Environment', so the sign said. Fuck off! If the Trade Descriptions Act were applicable to prisons, there would be a potential prosecution for the comedian who put it up. E Hall was for low-cat prisoners, who enjoyed a more relaxed regime and additional visits. At that time, it wasn't for me, because I was an LTP and it was only for short-termers. I'd no idea why that was and, to be honest, I didn't really care at the time.

Pentland Hall was what's known as a National Top End and housed mainly life-sentence prisoners who were reaching the end of their term inside. It provided a sort of halfway house between closed and fully open conditions. Cons there undertook work and study placements in the community, though during my time at Saughton there were some absconders. Pentland was also a route into the jail for drugs.

Everyone in Saughton, apart from those in Glenesk, had to wear jail-issue gear. You could get your own socks and pants sent in, and some gym gear, but no outer clothing. I never sent anything to the jail laundry, as it had a deserved reputation for 'losing' your decent stuff. Fuck, there was even a black market for CKs in the place, regardless of their age or condition. I washed all my pants and socks by hand in a sink and made up for the lack of heat in the water by steam ironing them to get rid of any germs. I was the only guy to iron his pants and socks and took some inevitable flack for it.

The jail-issue gear also had a colour scheme that was *interesting*, to say the least. A Hall was red, Forth Hall was green, D Hall was navy blue and E Hall was light grey. The only Hall housing protection prisoners, B Hall, was the brightest fucking yellow you've ever seen. Things had to be bad enough for all the poor bastards in that Hall, including the beasts, without putting them into bright-yellow gear. Pentland Hall, with its lifer population, had the boys strutting about as if they owned the joint in black storm trooper gear.

As my time inside continued, I came to realise that lifers were probably the least threatening of all cons. The number of first-time offenders amongst lifers was amazing – wrong place, wrong time, too young and all that. I know that's a generalisation, and there were a few total bams among the lifers I met. Some of them shouldn't be released – and I mean never. Mind you, there were more determinate sentence prisoners I met during my time that I wouldn't ever let out either. These guys could do some poor bastard serious damage; some already have.

I'd been building a reputation for getting success for guys who complained about one thing or another. There was a guy in D Hall called Stu Anderson who was on the methadone programme. He was generally considered to be a junkie, ironically even by the convicted drugs dealers in the Hall – there was even a hierarchy amongst the guys in for drugs offences. Stu was a prison rules expert. He kept a copy of the rules in his cell, which was number 12 on the first Flat. It had been used as the holding area for condemned men waiting to be dangled at the end of a rope. It had a door halfway along its outside wall which supposedly opened up on to a shaft where the poor guy would walk, and then the trapdoor would be sprung and that would be that. I think Stu secretly enjoyed telling and re-telling that tale and talking about all the spooky visitations he'd experienced since he took up occupancy. He would always go into great detail with any prospective new co-pilot – as a consequence he was invariably on his own and not two'd up.

Stu provided a valuable service to cons in the Hall who wanted advice on potential complaints, the only problem being that he was considered a junkie and so was viewed as unpredictable and unreliable, therefore his client base wasn't as wide as it could, and should, have been. Stu was no mug – he just looked it, with his permanently dilated pupils and ranting style. I took to him immediately. I was determined not to pre-judge anyone, including screws. I spent hours in Stu's company and enjoyed all of them. One day he explained to me how the title 'screw' came about. It goes back to the nineteenth century, when prison officers used to tighten the screw regulating the grinding wheel which cons pushed round and round, grinding grain. Cells were also called 'Peters' for some reason that Stu couldn't remember – but it was nothing to do with Peter Sellers.

Our association started quietly enough, with Stu coming to me and introducing himself and immediately asking me what I thought about a particular rule in relation to what cons could get into the jail as personal property.

Your 'rep' gets to be known very quickly. I was a white-collar criminal, it was well known throughout the jail. Everyone knew I wasn't a dope, including all the screws. Everyone also knew that I was clean. The only thing they didn't appreciate at the time was that I wasn't the kind of 'white collar' who fitted into a well-worn slot. Most of the other white collars I met inside, and there weren't many, had decided to keep their heads down and ride out their sentences with as little hassle as possible. A few went directly on to protection and were never seen in the general population. But I had plans for my time inside. I wanted to get something out of it. It was the only way that I could turn the situation around and regain some of my dignity and self-respect. Turning this negative situation into some sort of a positive experience proved to be the biggest challenge I'd faced in my life to that point.

Stu and I soon became the first port of call for anybody with a complaint in D Hall. Our reputation spread rapidly throughout the jail and soon Stu was bringing complaints back for consideration from his shed at the industrial cleaners (he was brought in to clean cells covered in shit after 'dirty protests' and following a suicide). I'd managed to get myself on to a Level 3 course in computing for two mornings a week and an art class one morning a week, so my fellow classmates were providing Stu and me with plenty of work. I was astounded at the number of cons who had genuine complaints and whose previous representations under the prison rules had been either ignored or batted away.

There were a couple of fundamental problems with the prison complaints procedures. Did I say a couple? Well, I've always enjoyed a good laugh. Here goes . . . Firstly, 70 per cent of the general population in prisons have a reading and writing age of 11 years or less – not a made-up statistic, a government one. All the information given to prisoners is by way of written handout or is posted on a noticeboard. A massive proportion of those cons who are illiterate or who struggle with reading and writing will not admit to their problem on admission to prison. I knew a lifer in open conditions who insisted on getting the Section newspaper first every day; it wasn't until he asked me to fill in a form for him that I realised he couldn't read or write, it was all just a front.

Sure, education assessments of basic English and numbers tests are given during the induction process, but these tests are administered in a group situation where the strugglers ask others for answers and always get them. Imagine you've just arrived in a prison and you're sitting one of these tests and a guy behind or beside you asks what answer you've got for question three. You're a brave fucker to ignore him and all his mates who are just waiting on the same answer. I sat these tests on my own, as I'd missed the induction group because of my piss-test. A simple method of ensuring that no one slips through the net would be to administer these tests individually. At least then there would be something on which to base an education plan. One of the single biggest tragedies of the current system is that the vast majority of prisoners leave prison with no greater level of formal education than when they were initially convicted. Instead of prisons being called 'Universities of Crime', perhaps society should demand that otherwise 'dead' time is resuscitated and education requirements are properly assessed and addressed during sentences of any length over three months.

Back to the complaints procedure, which is based squarely on an individual's ability to understand how it works and requires the ability to read.

Complaints are written on a form called a CP1. These should be readily available to all cons, but inevitably there's a rigmarole that has to be gone through in getting hold of one, including explaining to a screw or screws exactly why you want one in the first place – a not too subtle method of intimidation used by loads of screws to try to cut down on their complaints workload. This CP1 form effectively acts as a bouncing ball, going back and forward from con to screw, back to con then to management, and so on. The system is effectively based on attrition and it tests all cons' determination to see it through to a conclusion. Imagine your complaint is about a decision made by the screw on your landing – a frequent occurrence. You fill in the first part of the CP1, and guess who answers your complaint initially? Yeah, you got it, the very screw whose decision you're complaining about. Total fucking madness!

You then fill in part two and that goes to the Hall manager, who invariably backs his member of staff, regardless of whether he's acting within the prison rules or not. So you decide to go to the next stage, and that involves the ICC, the Internal Complaints Committee, normally chaired by one of the Governor's management team and made up of two others, at least one screw and sometimes a civilian member of prison staff. The pressure builds on this committee, as they are effectively the third stage and there have already been two stages in the process, both of which have rejected the prisoner's complaint. They also want to be seen to support prison staff.

So, you disagree with the ICC's decision to reject your complaint, all the time detailing on a new section of the form the reasons why you want to progress to the next stage. It moves to the Governor's desk, and you're probably at least two weeks into the process. The Governor gets a week to respond and, of course, he or she invariably responds in the same way as the three previous respondents. It's easier that way. You would think that that would be the end of it, but no, there's another stage to come.

The final piece of the jigsaw comes by way of the Scottish

Prisons Complaints Commissioner, who is an independent arbiter of complaints made by prisoners who have exhausted the internal procedure. Just say that you've managed to maintain your drive and determination through to the stage of getting your complaint in front of the Complaints Commissioner – it might have taken you at least a month by that stage – and your submission convinces him that your complaint is valid and that the prison is in breach of the prison rules in not rectifying said complaint. Well, there's a further twist waiting in the tail. Regardless of whether the Complaints Commissioner decides in your favour, he has zero – that's right, zero – statutory powers and the prison Governor can effectively ignore his recommendation, even if it's turned into a formal one, where SPS headquarters are informed. Anyone feel capable of explaining to me exactly why there is a Scottish Prisons Complaints Commissioner if his decisions and recommendations can be set aside as and when it suits the Prison Service? And is this system inclusive for all cons or just for those who can read and write? Does the way the system operates engender confidence and trust? Is it robust enough to withstand close scrutiny? The silence is deafening.

The one thing that Stu and I decided on early doors was that we weren't going to get involved in chasing lost causes. As such we were actually doing the jail a favour in not promoting frivolous or vexatious complaints. Our success rate was fantastic. Carefully considering each grievance, interviewing the complainant, studying the prison rules and writing a well-composed, effectively argued case brought virtually guaranteed success. It also brought my existence and skills to the notice of the management team, which I assumed could only be a good thing.

● ● ●

Singing in the chapel was brought to a sudden halt when the guy I'd taken over from was released from the 'digger' and demanded his old job back. (The digger is slang for the Segregation Unit, solitary confinement for the really, really bad guys.) I was shunted onto the pass job at Estates. Another boring cleaning job, of which there were plenty in the jail. I spent a couple of weeks there and then got asked if I fancied moving to the pass job at Throughcare. I jumped at the chance. It was widely recognised as the top job in the jail and, although it was cleaning, cleaning and more cleaning, there were civilian staff based there, along with two of the best screws I came across in my time inside. Steve and Willie were guys I'd be happy to meet and have a chinwag with now. In fact, I've met Steve a couple of times since my release; he's a diamond of a bloke. They were both in the right job: reassuring cons who'd just arrived in the old tin pail and were struggling. They also offered a type of pastoral care for those guys who were having problems on the outside: failed relationships, loss of accommodation, etc. I loved working there and received fantastic support from Steve and Willie throughout, never mind the rest of the staff, all of whom I got to know well.

It was good news as far as my appeal went as well. A letter arrived from the solicitor informing me that a judge had allowed my appeal to proceed to the first sift, even though it was out of time. Well, let's just see how far this goes, I thought. The next stage was to prepare a 'formal grounds of appeal' and that had to be done by the QC.

As far as legal proceedings go, all cons need to show incredible patience when trying to progress things from the inside. You just feel that you're cut off from everything – in effect, you are. Solicitors can't just phone you up and tell you what the hell's happening; they have to write or arrange a visit. All of that takes loads of time and, given that the system is unwieldy at best, cons are way down the priority list. After all, they're not going anywhere fast.

CHAPTER ELEVEN

I got information during my fifth week in Saughton that an LTP had, in fact, made it to E Hall, which was the low- and medium-cat hall that offered additional privileges. It stood me up. I had other cons coming up to me, especially those whom Stu and I had helped with their complaints, encouraging me to get on the case and get myself over to E Hall pronto. That's how it was for me during the whole of my sentence: my mates wanted me to progress through the system even though losing them to that same progression left a huge hole at times.

I knew the LTP in question. He was in doing a four-stretch for drugs. He'd only done eight months of it, so I wondered how he could possibly be a medium-cat, given the first question on that stupid fucking algorithm. How had he managed to get into E Hall, which was supposedly only for short-termers? He spent all of his time in education, supposedly studying some computer course or other. He fancied himself as a Yogi Bear character: smarter than your average con.

It was easy to make his acquaintance and get into his head. He was in the same classroom as me for computing, though he was working on something fancy on the other side of the classroom. He knew who I was and what rep I carried. There was no way he was going to make the first move to talk to me – the last thing he wanted to do was expose himself to someone who was probably smarter than he was. That's why it was dead easy for me to get close to this guy

– he loved the fact that I'd made the first move, it massaged his all too considerable ego. I heard later that he'd even bragged about the types of conversations that were available to him now that he'd got to know me! All I wanted from our 'chats' was info on how he'd managed to get himself a low-cat so early in his sentence and into E Hall as an LTP.

It transpired that he'd complained to the Governor that he'd been categorised 'high', as he was a first offender and, in his own opinion, did not present as a threat of any kind. The Governor had backed down and also agreed to his request to move to E Hall. Suspicions existed at that time about his 'grass potential' and they later proved to be well founded.

When I thought that I had all the ammo I needed, I went to see big Mattie Sim and told him of my intention to formally complain about the fact that I had been refused a move to a Hall in the jail that was designated for my particular security category.

'Mr Bridges,' he said in a strangulated tone that mirrored exactly how his trouser belt must have been feeling, 'you are not going to be one of those prisoners who is going to cause us problems with firing in all sorts of complaints, are you?'

'Mr Sim,' I responded, 'I can guarantee right now that you will only receive complaints directly from me when I consider that I have a case for complaining, either under the prison rules or the rules which are set locally.'

He shifted in his swivel chair, which squeaked and groaned with the movement. He was struggling to respond. Don't fill the silence, I repeated to myself. Keep fuckin' schtum!

In shifting forward and turning around a bit, he ended up not very far from me, and there was nothing in between us, no desk or anything else for that matter. It flashed through my mind that he might whack me but that thought flashed out quicker than it arrived.

'I'll support your application for a move to E Hall,' he whispered, 'just don't tell anyone that I said that. Is that a deal?'

I thought for a couple of seconds and went back with, 'I'll keep all of it to myself only if you make it happen. You're one of the senior managers in this jail and you have a load of clout. You know that the local rule has been blown apart and so I need you to make it work for me. Now, is that a deal?'

He said precisely fuck all for a good ten seconds or so – it felt a whole lot longer than that. 'OK,' he whispered. 'That's a deal.'

I got my move to E Hall ten days later.

One of the last things I did whilst in D Hall was to sell my piss. All the smack users in the Hall knew I was clean and one of them came and asked me if he could get some of my piss, as he felt that he was going to be tested sometime soon.

The growth in heroin as the principal drug of choice in jails stems from the early '90s, when Ann Widdecombe was the Home Office minister in charge of prisons. It was she who introduced drug testing for cons. Most who wish to take drugs in prison would opt to use cannabis, but the problem is that it stays in your system for up to 30 days. The drug actually clings to the fat in your body. Heroin, on the other hand, can be flushed out of your system by taking in copious amounts of water, almost enough to drown you. Smack users would get up around 5 a.m., or 5.30 at the latest, and start to flush. They took on litres of water at an incredible rate and basically spewed, pissed, shat and coughed the water out over the next two or three hours. If they were tested, the result would be what was termed a 'dilution'. In some jails, although not in Saughton, a dilution was counted as a failed test, or positive result.

One of the other methods used to try to circumvent the system was the use of clean piss. The con planned to fill a finger of a surgical glove with my piss and then tuck it up and under his foreskin. During the actual test he would nick the 'nipple', as it was called, with a fingernail and let my clean piss mix with his own. His test would be at worst inconclusive. The only thing remaining was the price – a jar of 'Gucci' coffee sealed the deal. Well, it was Nescafé. Anything with a decent brand name in prison is called Gucci, so Nescafé was called Gucci coffee. Tetley tea bags were also called Gucci, and so on.

I was also told why there was a temperature strip on the sample bottle: it stopped guys from pouring in piss or water directly from a container into the sample bottle, as it would be detected as being cooler than body temperature – which explained the foreskin-tucking thing and the need for a 'nipple'. Goodness knows what the circumcised guys did!

· · ·

My first rota duty for the Listeners came around not long after the final weekend of training. There were grand plans for a formal presentation of certificates by the Governor at a ceremony to which our families would be invited; I wasn't sure about that and, in any case, as it turned out I didn't receive my certificate until I'd been shipped out of Saughton.

I'd been in E Hall a week or so and realised that there were more problems with drugs in there than there were in D Hall, if that was possible. There was also a palpable feeling of mistrust and suspicion. This was the first time in my sentence that I'd experienced these feelings and they were caused by the fact that it was a progression facility. Cons had plenty to lose by being downgraded and stuck back into D Hall or, worse, Forth Hall. This led to the grass network working overtime, more incidents of violence, frequent movements in and out of the Hall and absolutely no reduction in the level of drugs available in the place.

It was a Tuesday evening and a screw came up to me whilst I was playing table tennis in E Hall's separate rec area. He said that there was a call for a Listener in B Hall. Fuck, I thought. B Hall was only for protection prisoners. Well, here goes. I couldn't knock it back anyway, so I got changed and the screw let me into the main corridor of the jail, complete with my bright-yellow pass. It would match the outfits where I was going.

The manager to B Hall opened the door for me. He knew who I was as I'd seen him along at Throughcare a few times, although we'd never spoken. 'Sean, we've got a problem with one of the guys,' he said. 'I've tried to calm him down, but he wants to see a Listener.'

'Can you tell me his background?' I asked. That was allowed and was preferable to going in totally blind. The Hall manager gave me some details, informing me that the guy had been convicted of grooming young girls over the web.

'OK, let's go and see him,' the Hall manager said and walked in front of me to the guy's cell. The hall was absolutely dead. Everybody was locked up. It was only 7.30 p.m. on a Tuesday night; lock-up in E Hall on weekdays was 9 p.m. and I remember thinking how desperate I'd need to be to even consider going on protection.

As the cell door was opened, I found the guy sitting there with his head in his hands. His cell was clean and in order and he looked OK physically. The screw left us, telling me that he was leaving the door pulled to and that if I needed anything just to shout. I wasn't going to be in any physical peril with this guy. He was much smaller than me and weighed far less. He was a bit weedy, in fact, and looked to be in his mid-40s. Don't tell me, he's your typical caricature of a child molester. You should try getting up close with these guys, it's fucking creepy.

Anyway, the training kicked in and I started to get this guy to open up and tell me what his problems were. Nice'n'easy does it, don't rush it, take your time, let the guy think about each answer to each question and don't provide solutions to any of his problems I told myself as he started to tell me his story. It all came out in a seemingly well-rehearsed monologue over the next half-hour or so. His problem wasn't that he'd committed the crime – he'd pled guilty at first opportunity. It wasn't that he'd been sentenced to two years in prison. It wasn't that he would be serving ultra-slow time on protection. It was that he'd abused two other children and was shitting himself that one or other of them would go to the police and he would end up in court again with an even longer sentence – all of it to be spent behind his cell door.

As all of this spewed out of his mouth, I desperately tried to maintain eye contact with him. My feelings for him were neither here nor there, it was my role to try and help him. After he'd finished, he slumped forwards in the chair and again held his head in his hands. I felt physically sick. I wondered if he was getting himself off just by telling me his story – it was something the Samaritans had warned us about on our course. Nah, he wasn't – I don't think.

I spent a while trying to reassure him that if these other children had kept their own counsel up to now the chances were that they'd continue to do so. Fuck! I was offering my opinions on possible solutions to his problem rather than allowing him to develop solutions himself. 'Do you think so? Do you really think so?' he kept asking me. I had to get out of that cell – and now!

'Look,' I said, 'I think you've got plenty to think about by way of trying to get settled in here without doing your brain in, thinking about what might happen if the kids speak up, so just try and put it to one side and get your head around the fact that you're going to be here for a year.' At that point, I stood up, opened the door and stepped out to see the landing screw looking at me over his glasses.

'Finished?' he called.

'Yup,' I replied. I looked back into the cell. The guy was walking over to me with his hand outstretched. Oh fucking no, I thought. I slowly raised my right hand, took his, exerted no pressure whatsoever and said, 'Good luck.'

I've no idea what he was saying to me. There was a loud buzzing in my ears. I felt a massive shiver go right through my body; it seemed to linger, and fire up and down my spine for ages afterwards. I stepped out of his cell, the screw locked it and then escorted me back to the main door to the Hall and let me out into the corridor.

I was shaking a bit. I looked down at my right palm and wondered what I'd done and why I'd done it. I needed to wash that hand, and double-quick, too. I also wondered exactly where the hand I'd shaken had been over the years. I needed to get back into E Hall and chat to some of the good guys to get my mind moving away from all of that shit.

■ ■ ■

E Hall had its own rec area, which included a pool table, a table-tennis table, a couple of treadmills and an exercise bike. I used the facilities every night and during the day at weekends. The weight was falling off me, due to the combination of diabolical food and the exercise regime. Within about four weeks of being sentenced, I'd got back down to the weight I was when I was playing senior rugby some 20-odd years earlier. I tried to eat sensibly, but the shit just kept coming.

Every meal was jammed full of high-value carbohydrates: chips with everything and enough bread to start your own baker's shop. Fruit and fresh vegetables were a distant memory. Chicken was an option in one form or another every single day, and sometimes more than once a day. I invariably chose 'chicken', as I once went for beef stroganoff and spewed half of it back up. The other half of the 'stroganoff' was inedible fat and gristle and had been left on my plate. Never again.

By this time, it was early December 2002 and I'd been in E Hall for a couple of months. Each prison has what's known as a 'visiting committee', which is made up of lay people who are interested in ensuring that the prison is properly run and that cons are treated properly. Notice I use 'properly' and not 'well'. The visiting committee at Saughton was made up of the usual local worthies: retired councillors and the like. When the VC, as it was affectionately known, visited the jail, it was a fairly big event. Not as big as for the Justice Minister, but big enough to create a stir and have the screws bowing and scraping for a few hours – a sight worth seeing on its own.

This particular day, as the VC went round the jail doing what they do, I went to work in Throughcare as normal. I completely forgot that they were in the jail until I got back to the Hall for the lunch meal. E Hall's rec area doubled as a dining hall. Tables of six were spread around the Hall and the screw in charge of 'feeding' called up each table in turn for service – but only if you were all present and correct and sitting with your arms folded. God help you if you'd forgotten your menu. Shooting would have been far too kind an end, though possibly preferable to being shunted to the back of the queue.

Whilst we were waiting our turn to be called up for service, the Hall manager came up to the table with an elderly, very distinguished-looking gent dressed in a rough tweed jacket that would have killed lesser mortals, dark-green trousers and a pair of brogues, which he'd probably had for decades and had shone to a discernible twinkle. The Hall manager was an insignificant, spineless bastard who could no more manage than fly in the fucking air. He took a deep breath and introduced Sir Montague McPherson-Jones or something like that. I can't remember his name, but it was long and posh and double-barrelled, and he was definitely a Sir. Fuckwit Manager continued by telling us that this guy was the chairman of the VC and he wanted to have lunch with us. We started to snort and snigger in concert.

Tattoo, the guy from the fight at Reception, was one of the guys at my table. He was a big, gruff, loud guy and came out with: 'Does he ken whit he's fuckin' lettin' hissel in fur? He'll no eat this shit.'

The whole Hall heard that one and there was raucous laughter until one of our guys realised that we'd missed our turn for service and so we all got up and made our way to the service hatch. The VC chairman would have to wait. Poor Sir What's-his-name was left standing alongside the manager, watching us being served and walking back to our table. When we all made it back, he was sitting two places to my left – everybody always, but always, kept the same seat at his allocated table: violence was frequently the result of the shameful act of disrespecting someone else's seating position. Fuckwit Manager started to recite the day's menu to our lordship and after careful consideration he went for the 'chicken fricassee'. This'll be interesting, I thought, that's what I'm having.

One of the main problems with the food in Saughton was that it was cooked in a central kitchen and then transported by heated trolleys to the various Halls. It might have been stuck in a trolley for over an hour before we were served the meal, by which time it was congealed and just plain disgusting.

The manager scuttled off as Sir What's-his-name tried in vain to make conversation with guys who were trying to stuff their faces with the shit on their plates. Meals were rushed if your table was among the last to be served, as the pantry passmen wanted you out soon as, so they could get the place cleaned up and get back to lying in their scratchers. Responses to all of Sir What's-his-name's questions were monosyllabic or restricted to double grunts. His fricassee arrived quickly – he got a plate and a half, plus loads of fresh-looking chips and some garden peas.

'Where the fuck did the peas come fae?' shouted wee George to my immediate left. Another burst of laughter accompanied by a sideways look for George from Fuckwit Manager. George desperately tried to retrieve the situation with the classic, 'Disnae matter tae me, I dinnae even like peas.'

George was one of loads of guys in the Hall for driving convictions. I couldn't believe how many were inside for relatively trivial offences when there must have been community sentences that were surely more appropriate. Or there certainly should have been.

Anyway, I was chewing my way through the meal and leaving huge bits of it – same old, same old. After a couple of forkfuls, Sir What's-his-name called over to Fuckwit Manager, who was standing close by, presumably to protect his charge from the dangerous and uncouth criminals. Fuckwit Manager bent down to listen to what was being said to him by his esteemed guest. He needn't have bothered bending down 'cause Sir What's-his-name said in his big, booming, well-cultured voice, 'I thought you said that this was chicken!' Fuckwit desperately tried to sound in control. He started to step away from the table with the words, 'Yes, that's what I was told, sir.' He walked quickly to the service hatch to check the information he'd been given. There was a noticeable delay at the hatch, as the pantry passmen and the screw in attendance at the hatch looked at one another, wondering exactly what to say. The entire dining hall held its breath.

I was sitting with my back to the hatch, which was a good ten yards away, looking at my meal. So, Sir What's-his-name thinks this isn't chicken, I thought. Well, it can only be turkey if it's not chicken. Whilst I was moving the fricassee around my plate – no chips or garden peas for me – Fuckwit returned and tried desperately to get Sir What's-his-name up from the table by beckoning to him. The old guy wasn't for moving and so Fuckwit was forced to come to the table and say that yes, it was chicken.

'No, this is turkey!' was Sir What's-his-name's instant retort. 'Furthermore, it's a very cheap cut of turkey, which I think is normally used in the composition of dog food.'

I dropped my fork. Tattoo went mental. Standing up, he shouted at the top of his voice, 'They're feedin' us fuckin' dog food!' A variety of barks and howls started up from other tables as they reacted to Tattoo's outburst. Then slowly the realisation of exactly what had been said by the chairman of the VC spread around the dining hall. A few more screws filtered in, in anticipation of problems. One of them had got on the blower, no doubt, warning that there could be a smash-up after an innocent mix-up over chicken or turkey. I kept moving my fricassee around. I had to see this meal through to the bitter end.

Sir What's-his-name resumed his meal and asked me if this was the usual type of 'chicken' served at mealtime. I responded by saying that I only took the 'chicken', as the beef, or meat, was dire. As far as I was concerned, I said, this 'chicken' was the chicken they'd served in all meals I'd eaten in the gaff. 'Well, it's definitely turkey,' he replied. 'And I should know – I used to farm these birds.'

It looked like he knew exactly what he was talking about. Fuckwit's face was a picture. He was standing surrounded by about six screws. He couldn't look me in the face. It was as if he wanted the ground to open up and swallow him; I just wondered if the ground would think he was turkey or just plain 'chicken'. I thought I knew the answer to that one.

The repercussions of that lunch meal reverberated for a couple of weeks. Some guys decided that they would make formal complaints on the basis that they were being served dog food. I didn't help to process any complaint on that basis – there was absolutely no point.

The VC chairman made a formal complaint to the Governor, and the Governor's written response was pinned up on noticeboards throughout the jail. The Governor had no option but to admit that the prison kitchen had been using turkey instead of chicken, but he denied that it was in any way a cheap cut of turkey. Yeah, that'll be shining bright! And all the menus were changed to read 'turkey' instead of 'chicken'.

At the time I was in Saughton, the jail budget for food was £1.57 per prisoner per day. I watched a news programme whilst I was there, which was making a huge thing over the fact that school meals were restricted to a cost of £1.40 per pupil per day, while convicted prisoners were allocated £1.57. They didn't mention that the £1.40 covered the cost of one meal for a child and not for a whole day's food for an adult, as was the prison budget. No point in letting the facts get in the way of a good story, eh?

Incidentally, since leaving Saughton in February 2003, I've never eaten turkey. Just the smell of it turns my stomach. At Christmas, I eat beef. My wife and girls are OK with that and if it's OK with them, it's OK with me.

CHAPTER TWELVE

Visits for convicted prisoners in Saughton were limited to five half-hour sessions per calendar month. Once I got over to E Hall, my entitlement increased to six per month. The visits room was always packed at the times I took my visits because my wife and daughters were all committed during the day; getting visits at weekends was almost impossible. Other guys who could take visits during the quieter afternoon periods were rewarded with better quality time with their friends and families. There were always loads of screws in attendance in the visits room. They were principally on the lookout for drugs being transferred by visitors to cons; there were more than a few times when half a dozen screws jumped on some con and his visitor who were slipping packages to one another, either quite straightforwardly by handing them over or more surreptitiously via lengthy kissing sessions.

Visits were tense occasions for all concerned. Visitors had to go through the entire gamut of search procedures before being allowed into the waiting room, including occasional dog searches. My mate Dave and his wife Fiona visited me in November 2002 and brought along their eight-week-old daughter, Sarah. I was thrilled to see them but angry and sad when I was told that Fiona had been forced to strip Sarah down and even remove her nappy for inspection.

The drugs issue dictated how the jail was operated, regardless of whether you were clean or not. The laugh is that from what I have heard some screws are complicit in both getting drugs into prisons and not picking up on who was holding stashes once they are in. The bulk of the residential screws must have loved it when the Hall was awash with smack. Heroin dumbs down life for the user – remember *Trainspotting*? Some guys gowch after taking the stuff, meaning that they turn into virtual zombies who are incapable of doing much, and if that includes not bothering the screws at all, then that's just fine by the screws. Heroin addicts are easy to spot, with their dilated pupils and carefree attitude as they emerge from the initial effects of the drug.

The value of Milky Bars was explained to me by Stu Anderson. Heroin is smoked in jail most of the time; some is injected, but far and away most of it is smoked. The powder is poured on to a piece of foil and the powder is heated from underneath using a disposable lighter. The resultant fumes are inhaled through a 'tooter', a small pipe, which could be a biro pen without the ink refill, always remembering that the small hole that allows an equalising pressure for the pen has to be closed off. During my time inside, there were plenty of downgrades after drug paraphernalia was found in cells.

You would think that one way of scuppering the practice of smoking the drug would be to stop selling anything containing foil in the canteen. The foil has to be clean, unprinted stuff, making prison Milky Bar consumption per head of population the highest anywhere in the country.

Most coverage of drugs in prisons refers to feats of derring-do, detailing how ingenious cons get packages inside. Yeah, cons do stuff drugs up their arses. They also fish for drugs packages that have been thrown over perimeter fences and walls. And drugs are transferred at visits.

But, and this is huge and needs to be said, drugs are also being brought into British prisons by the screws – a fact that is well known within the prison population and one which was acknowledged by a Home Office report in 2005. Lord Ramsbotham, the former Chief Inspector of Prisons, acknowledged recently that: 'Without the staff, these things couldn't get in.'

There are good screws in the system – just nowhere near enough of them. The problem for the good screws is that they are inundated with work because every con knows which ones are worth going to and which are the ones to steer clear of. That makes the good guys' workload unbearable at times and slows things down.

'There are more criminals in white shirts than there are in jail swag,' I was told by another con not long after I'd started my time. I didn't know what he was talking about but soon heard the stories about bent screws who team up with gangsters on the inside to make themselves a tidy profit. Square-up is made in cash by accomplices on the outside.

Poor bastards are getting themselves and their families and friends into all sorts of debt by using the stuff. Guys who don't pay get battered or slashed and inevitably land up on protection.

The money involved in the drug trade in prisons is utterly phenomenal. A report I read just the other day quoted the former head of drug treatment policy at the National Offender Service estimating that the trade in heroin is worth £140 million across the 140 jails in England alone. Drugs in prison cost roughly five to ten times what they cost outside, which reflects simple supply and demand, meaning that profits are incredible and easily adjusted to the fact that there are additional cuts to be made in the margin.

It's not just the potential financial benefits that bring prison officers into the loop. Some will have been threatened by the cons with damage to their families; they have people on the outside who identify where they live and do their homework. Unless and until screws are searched as they enter each prison for duty every single day, with such searches including the use of trained dogs, the amount of drugs in prisons will continue at current levels, if not increase.

CHAPTER THIRTEEN

My appeal started to falter as Christmas approached. The solicitor got in touch to say that the QC wasn't certain that there were sufficient grounds for a formal appeal.

The Joint Note by Counsel stated that, while they recognised that Lady Cosgrove had made an error regarding the counts of indictment, they did not believe this had affected the sentence I had been given. Although they felt that an Appeal Court might be dismayed by the error as a matter of form, any appeal would allow the Court to review the whole circumstances of the case and impose a fresh sentence as of new. They felt that the deficiencies in the judge's note would not be sufficient to found any argument that the sentence should be reduced.

You could have knocked me over with a feather. Wait a minute, a judge had decided that the appeal should be allowed to proceed to the sift, even though it was out of time, and so he was willing to give me a chance to present my grounds for appeal. I disagreed with my QC and felt, in the circumstances, that it was worth making an application for leave of appeal to see what the sifting judges' opinion would be. So time to get rid of both the QC and the solicitor, but I wasn't going to do it in writing or over the phone; this had to be done face to face.

I telephoned Fiona Cooper and left a message, asking her to come in and see me. She appeared a couple of days later. She asked me how I was, what I thought of Neil Murray's comments on my appeal, how I was getting on and how my family were, all before I was able to get in even one word. I put it down to nerves. I took a deep breath and slowed the proceedings down before saying, 'You're no longer part of this. Neither is Neil Murray. My only regret is that I didn't do this long before my court appearances.' I then turned around, opened the door, made my way back to the desk and told the screw that I was finished.

'That didn't take long,' he said.

Fiona was still sitting in the consulting room as I was escorted out of the legal visits area. I never even glanced at her.

I had to get a new solicitor, and quickly. By this time, I'd met a guy called Davie Wayne. He was a massive character in the jail. This was his third sentence in a life of crime that had spanned 25 years. He was a thief, plain and simple. His problem was that he lived in a small place midway between Edinburgh and Glasgow and any theft that showed similarities to his methods would result in Davie being put immediately under suspicion. He had been transferred back to Saughton from open conditions, as he had outstanding charges to face. One of the rules about progressing to open was that cons were not allowed to have outstanding charges waiting to be heard. Davie had, as usual, managed to get around this problem by a combination of flannel and good humour. I got to know him well during our time together in E Hall at Saughton and also shared with him briefly after being moved to Noranside later in my sentence. His stories were legend and included the one of him and his oppo ram-raiding a cash and carry one night with inside info on exactly where the cigarettes and rolling tobacco were located. Only problem was that the info was wrong and instead of coming away with a load of valuable stuff that could be easily turned over, they ended up with thousands of pairs of ladies tights, all in American tan. They still had loads of pairs left, stashed in a garage somewhere, even though they'd been giving them away to women and their husbands for years in order to try and get rid of them.

Davie caused mayhem in Throughcare one day by eating one of the civilian staff's sandwiches. He was stuck with us in Throughcare to keep him out of trouble until his case came up. He just couldn't resist that M&S sandwich in the fridge and hoovered it one afternoon. It took all my persuasive powers to convince the Throughcare manager not to put him on report for it. We laughed like crazy when he recounted the story at Noranside after I met up with him again.

Davie put me in touch with a diamond of a solicitor in Dick Whyte, of Adams Whyte Solicitors. Dick came in to see me very soon after I made contact with his offices and was just what I needed at that time. He really seemed to know what he was talking about. I spent over an hour with him and recounted all my woes. He sat through most of it with his mouth wide open as he looked at the various letters I was passing over to him and listened to what I was saying.

He asked me why the QC thought there weren't any grounds for an appeal. I just shrugged, incapable of offering anything by way of a coherent answer.

'OK,' Dick said. 'Let me get on with appointing a QC and I'll get back to you when I have one. Meantime, if there's anything else I can help you with, or there are any questions you have in relation to this appeal, just get in touch with me.'

He handed me his business card as he got up. I felt as if a massive weight had just been lifted from my shoulders, and shook his hand firmly, thanking him for coming to see me. As he left, he commiserated with me about my situation, and I appreciated that.

▪ ▪ ▪

My dietary regime had by now started to settle down. In Saughton, as in other Scottish prisons, the menus are filled out weekly in advance and there are three of them, meaning that every few weeks you're on the same stuff. It wouldn't be a problem if the food was decent, but . . . What it did do for me was throw emphasis on trying to ensure that I ate the right things and didn't take on too much carbohydrate, including chips with everything.

The prisoner's diet has long been a bone of contention with the Chief Inspector of Prisons, who has highlighted the paucity of fresh fruit and vegetables in prison menus. Food is a huge thing in jail – some say it's the only thing. This means that small treats assume massive importance. Toast is a big thing. I know it sounds mental, but toast is a vital part of jail food. Whilst I was in D Hall, each Flat had a toaster that was wheeled out during evening rec for use by all. The numbers using said toaster were exceptional for an average household two-slice toaster. The queue to use it was lengthy, but as long as everybody maintained discipline, then everybody got their toast before lock-up.

My second week in D Hall saw the toaster exploding and catching fire. Some halfwit had managed to get hold of a couple of sausages from the kitchens, probably stuck down his Ys for transfer, and thought that he would cook them in the toaster. The thing was taking considerable abuse anyway, being used almost continuously for well over two hours each weekday night, without having uncooked sausages thrust into its slots. When it gave up the ghost, the residential screws made a right song and dance about how stupid the guy had been. A notice was put up on the Flat noticeboard the following day, stating that there would not be a replacement until the 'Arsonist Sausage Toaster' came forward. No chance of that happening then; no more toast for me in D Hall.

My fitness levels were getting higher and higher. I was loving it. My table tennis was improving as well. I had played to league standard when I was in the civil service 25 years earlier. Hey, you never lose it! It's just that the speed goes a wee bit. I was taking on all-comers in E Hall and doing them up like turkeys. Oh no, that fucking bird again! The guy who gave me most problems at the old T/T was a huge black diamond thief from London. He was doing two years for passing a fake credit card in an Edinburgh store but was expecting a gate arrest when he was due to be released. He was certain that police forces from down south had been informed that he was in prison and would be looking to arrest him in connection with diamond thefts from jewellers in and around London.

Gate arrests must be the worst form of jail torture. You are actually out of the jail but then arrested as you set foot on the other side of the main gate. What makes it worse is that the only person who doesn't know about it is the prisoner – all the screws know. What a bam-up!

Alex was due to be released just before Christmas and was gradually becoming more animated as he convinced himself that he would be the subject of a gate arrest and driven down to London. I took advantage of his state of mind to thoroughly turn him over at the T/T in the run-up to his release. He always gave me a good game and as the annual championships were coming up over the Christmas period, I was delighted to be honing my skills. I went on to win the T/T title with ease and was awarded five £2 phonecards and an orange as my prize.

Other than my younger daughter's 21st birthday in October 2002, Christmas that year was my worst time behind bars. Her birthday was dire for me and I found the visit the day before heartbreaking. I'd got one of the cons in E Hall to draw a huge teddy bear on a sheet of A1 and had him colour it in using bright colours. I managed to write a birthday message to her using a wide-nibbed felt pen without my tears dropping onto the picture. I was allowed to take it to the visit but couldn't speak the words I'd rehearsed so often while handing it over to her. All four of us couldn't speak for a minute or so, desperately trying to regain our composure in a suitably packed visits room. That was the hardest visit I ever had.

The second hardest was the one I took immediately before Christmas. I'd booked a double visit, giving us the opportunity to spend an hour together. Everything had gone as normal up until the end of the first visit session, when those guys who had only booked single visits were due to leave the room. The screws started to trawl the room, identifying those who were only on single visits. They came to our table and asked me to finish off. I explained that I'd booked a double visit but was brusquely told that I would have to sort that out with the Hall staff when I got back there. My wife and daughters all got visibly upset, but I tried like hell to reassure them that I would be back soon and not to worry.

I kept my temper well in check on the way back to the Hall. I realised that John, a guy from my Hall whose family had travelled up from the Borders to see him, was in exactly the same position as me. He was well steamed up about it, but I managed to get him calmed down, explaining that going into the Hall and reading the riot act could work against both of us. He agreed and kept a lid on it.

On getting back to the Hall, Fuckwit Manager was waiting in the desk area. I spoke for both John and me in explaining the situation. Fuckwit said that unfortunately our visit request slips had been lost and therefore they could not verify whether we had booked double or single sessions. I asked him why, then, given all that he'd said, they hadn't mentioned anything about it before we attended the first session – at least then we could have prepared our respective families.

'We thought that it would sort itself out,' came the limp response.

'What does all of this mean for John and me?' was my retort.

'Well, let me check whether there's room for you to be accommodated at the second session,' he said as he picked up the phone.

Both John and I stood there, hoping like hell that Fuckwit got a positive response, but you could tell after two or three seconds that things weren't looking good. As the call was winding down, I could tell John wasn't taking all of this too well. Neither was I, by the way, but there was a way of handling this and there were loads of other options which were definitely not solutions to this particular problem.

Fuckwit came off the phone to break the bad news to us: there was insufficient space available to accommodate either of us at the second session. I pleaded with him to allow John to go back, as his family had travelled so far, but he was having none of it.

It transpired, of course, that both of our families had sat in their originally allocated seats and tables in the visits room throughout the entire second session waiting for us to come back in; there was loads of space. It was just that these bastard screws were completely indifferent to our plight and, more specifically, John's situation, with his elderly parents and wife having made the long journey by road for a stinking half-hour visit session.

John's mood was dark, very dark. Fuckwit was muttering on about what would happen if and when our original visit request slips were found. I could just feel something happening on my right side and was in the process of turning my head to look when John lunged over the desk, grabbing Fuckwit by the V in his V-neck sweater and dragging him over the desk. John was a relatively big guy, and strong with it. Fuckwit was no match for him and soon his feet were dangling in mid-air on the business side of the desk. It wasn't long before the other screw behind the desk pressed his rape alarm and I knew I only had a few seconds to get John off and to try to defuse the situation. I'll admit I didn't try too hard. Two reasons really: one, that I wanted to give Fuckwit a hiding as much as John did; and two, the thought of being drawn into a melee and facing some good old solitary in Saughton's digger and a loss of privileges at this time of year was way, way too much to risk. Stand back and let John get a few good digs in and hope like hell he stops before the cavalry arrives. Too late, the cavalry arrived quicker than I thought they would and John was slapped down and restrained before his short trip to the digger, head held down with his arms stretched back and pointing to the sky. Poor bastard! His case was heard in the Orderly Room the following day, by which time our missing visit request slips had turned up – they'd fallen down the back of a desk. John was given a slap on the wrist and was back in the Hall by lunchtime that day. He was still hurting from the incident and so was I.

I decided that I would complain about our treatment and completed a CP2 form, which can be used to complain directly to the Governor about issues to which only he can respond. I had the Deputy Governor and the Governor in charge of visits independently visit me to apologise for the fuck-up. They offered both John and me an extra double visit, without it affecting our monthly entitlement for January. It wouldn't matter what they'd offered us, the sourness of that whole caper – the lack of care, kindness, call it what you like – is something I can still taste now.

My wife and girls were badly affected by the experience; they just couldn't get how anybody could be so unnecessarily cruel for no good reason. I'd kept all the stuff I'd seen and witnessed well away from them since the start of my sentence and tried in vain to move the visit fiasco aside as quickly as I could.

Ask any con about Christmas in prison and you'll get the same answer: diabolical! Christmas Day is like any weekend, with a long lock-up to look forward to, no work of any kind and ultra-glum looks on the faces of the screws who are unfortunate enough to have drawn the shortest of short straws. The quality of the food isn't any different, although breakfast on Christmas morning that year was a bacon roll. Ya' fuckin' beauty! The only bacon I'd come close to since being sentenced was the stuff the screws fried in their desk area every Sunday. I'm certain they did it for a bam-up.

Thoughts of what my family were doing at various times during Christmas Day dominated the way I was feeling. I insisted that they stick to our traditional Christmas Day routine, as far as they could, and also phoned them a few times during the day and spoke to everybody who was at our house. My feelings of loneliness were most acute at that time, although they were never far away anyway.

One thing brightened up my Christmas Day. Steve and Willie, the two good screws who I worked with in Throughcare, had bought me a 'meal for one' from Asda. More specifically, it was a chicken tikka masala, with rice and a nan bread. I stuck it into the microwave on our Section at about 8 p.m. and savoured every mouthful. It made me feel human again.

It was during the second week in January that my attempts to get myself moved on from Saughton and into more relaxed conditions started. E Hall, being a low-cat facility, exported guys to open conditions on a regular basis. The self-same Prisoner Supervision System that specifically excluded me from its operating parameters was the thing standing in the way of a move to open conditions. I was a first offender. My crime involved neither violence nor drugs. I had been a low-cat since day one of my sentence and yet, on enquiring about the possibility of moving on, I was told that it was impossible, as I'd not served enough of my time in closed conditions. I was referred back to the terms and conditions of the

Prisoner Supervision System, which had apparently been dreamt up by Saughton's esteemed Governor, David Croft.

Prisoners at that time had to be serving a sentence of 18 months or more to qualify for a possible move to open conditions; beyond that basic qualifying criteria, prisoners obviously had to be low-cats and have served a proportion on a sliding scale of their sentence in closed conditions. The only problem with this system was that, as with the categorisation issue, it didn't cater for someone in my circumstances: an LTP, who was low-cat on admission.

I decided to ask for a meeting with Croft. I thought – wrongly, as it turned out – that if I kept it friendly and well away from the official complaints system, then I would have a better chance of achieving my aims and objectives. I put in a request for an audience with the Governor and waited for a response. I knew exactly what I was going to say to him and how I was going to put my arguments across – logically and in a well-considered fashion and, above all else, calmly, regardless of how the meeting was going.

Croft came to see me one lunchtime without giving me any prior notice. No worries, I was well prepared. He insisted on meeting with me in the desk area of E Hall, which at the best of times is like Piccadilly Circus but over the lunch break is at its most busy. Cons attend the desk to make various requests and the place goes like a fair. He spent most of our meeting, which lasted about 15 minutes, looking beyond me at what was happening at the desk; he even got involved in an argument that started between Fuckwit Manager and a con who was moaning about where his porno magazine had gone. It'd been sent in by his girlfriend and had vanished after arrival at the jail. It wasn't the first and it wouldn't be the last.

I tried to get my argument across, going over all of the points I'd listed in my head, but eventually I decided I would stop until he gave me his full attention. He noticed I'd stopped speaking about five seconds after I'd actually shut up. He threw me a quizzical look, then went on to tell me he'd been in the Prison Service for over 30 years. I didn't acknowledge the long-service comment and just continued to emphasise my point about why I was a perfect candidate for open conditions and why I should be moved – now. He was a big, old guy, receding hair and a Halloween cake-like face. I could feel myself tensing up as what sounded like a well-rehearsed response started flowing from his big gob. No, no, no, no! Did the guy have anything reasonable to come back with, or was it just the standard shit that prison officers would trot out to any poor dumb bastard? I listened to him blow himself out and then asked, 'Why?'

'Have you not been listening, Mr Bridges?' he said.

'Mr Croft, I've been hanging on your every word, although I feel now that most of them were worth letting go of. You just haven't answered my question in any reasonable fashion!'

He seemed shell-shocked but quickly recovered his composure. 'You're coming up to having served five months of your sentence. What would the public think if they found out that you were transferred to open conditions after serving only five months in closed?' he said.

Now we're getting down to it, I thought. 'I don't care what the public think about me, my sentence or anything else, for that matter. All I want is to be accommodated in conditions that fit my security category.'

'Unfortunately, Mr Bridges, *I* have to be concerned about what the public think,' he replied.

I could feel myself getting steamed up, but desperately tried to hold on to it – nothing would be gained by losing it with this man, here and now. I waited a second or so, and then went back with, 'So, Mr Croft, your system of progression is dependent on public opinion.' Before he could answer, I looked down, so that we couldn't make eye contact, and continued, 'I just wonder what the public would think of your system firing multi-convicted drug dealers on to open conditions after serving only a few weeks of their sentences. There was a guy moved to open last week who had been convicted for a third drugs offence and had been sentenced to three and a half years. He was moved on to open after serving just three weeks in closed. Three weeks!' I was holding three fingers up as I emphasised the point.

All he did was sigh. 'Mr Bridges, you are an LTP and that makes a huge difference to how your sentence is managed.'

Again, I asked, 'Why?'

He stood up, told me that I'd taken up enough of his time and finished off by explaining that I should make a formal complaint using a CP2 form if I still felt unhappy about things.

Unhappy about things – I was fucking raging about things. This guy was in charge of running this jail, one of the biggest in Scotland. He was a major player in the Prison Service in Scotland and yet I thought he was a fucking doughnut. He left with a swish past the desk area, muttering his goodbyes to Fuckwit and another screw who was at the desk. Neither of them looked at me as I got to my feet; they must have heard all of it, and I thought they looked suitably sheepish.

I asked Fuckwit for a CP2 form as I passed by the desk. He handed it to me without making eye contact. Just as I was leaving the desk area, Croft arrived back and called to me from behind. 'Mr Bridges, I was thinking on my way back to my office that, as an LTP, you should be accommodated at HMP Glenochil and not in this prison.'

Here it is, I thought. The threat of transfer to Glenochil is his way of dealing with this problem. Maybe I've become too hot to handle.

I said nothing.

'You did hear me, didn't you?' he said.

'Yes, I heard you. What response did you expect, Mr Croft?'

'I just thought that it was worthwhile reminding you of that fact,' he said as he turned on his heel and repeated his goodbyes to his staff.

What a prick, I thought to myself as I analysed this short meeting and its aftermath over and over again: his apparent lack of proper attention during the first half of the conversation, which effectively contained all my points supporting my position; his blanket refusal to consider that I'd made any viable arguments in favour of a move; his dismissal of me when he'd had enough and then his implied threat to ship me out to Glenochil. All of it made me feel angrier and angrier but ever more determined to get it sorted.

I filled in the CP2 in my usual style and hoped for a speedy response – no chance of that happening, but hey, stay positive.

. . .

It was my week on the Listener rota again and up until the Thursday night it had been a quiet week with only one callout to deal with: a mentally disturbed guy who was in one of the suicide cells in D Hall. He'd been sentenced to 30 days, of which he'd have to serve 15, and the poor bastard was struggling. Stevie Wonder would have noticed that the guy was mentally ill, but this is 2002. We're in the system and this is where mentally ill people go when they've done something wrong, even though that something is very minor. I couldn't do anything for the guy – he would need to see a psychiatrist, but probably wouldn't. It was a strange type of jealousy I felt towards him, all to do with the fact that in two weeks' time he was out – I had another nineteen months to go.

The Thursday evening of my rota saw me get another call from the suicide cells in D Hall. I arrived at the Hall, where big Mattie Sim was on duty. 'You've got a celebrity to see tonight, Sean,' he said, with a sardonic smile.

'Is that right?' I replied.

He just smiled again and led me over to the sui' block. He opened the cell door and introduced me – staff weren't allowed to introduce Listeners by name and we were trained not to give out our real names to cons, but that went by the way most of the time. I recognised the guy immediately: it was Nat Fraser.

He had been convicted of murdering his wife some years earlier and disposing of her body. He had been sentenced the previous day to 25 years of a life sentence. He would be in his 70s on release – that is, if he ever got out. He stood up from the thin mattress that lay on the concrete plinth running down the far side of the sui' cell. He was dressed in a short dressing-gown thing that other guys in textiles specialised in running off. It looked dire in the light, shitty-brown colour. The sui' cell had a desk and chair, both nailed to the floor, and a stainless-steel toilet bowl with no seat. The only other thing it had in it, other than the mattress, was a digital LCD clock, which ticked over the seconds. It was sunk deep into the wall, just to the left of the cell door. Christ, if you weren't suicidal when you went into that cell, you sure as hell would be in double-quick time.

Nat looked cool, though. Did I say cool? Given the fact that he'd just had 25 years of a life sentence rammed up his jacksie, he looked unbelievably cool. He explained that the reason he'd requested my attendance was so that I could have a word with Sim to try and stop other cons in D Hall from banging on his door and shouting threats through its hinges. The suicide cells in D Hall were on the ground floor opposite the desk, you see. All the recreation took place on that floor, including table tennis, pool and snooker. All the cons in the Hall gathered there twice a day, mornings and afternoon, to join the 'route' to work or education. Each prison has a route, a main corridor that normally feeds into every area of the jail. Imagine being in one of those cells and having total bams banging on your door, winding you up, shouting abuse at you and threatening you several times a day, only because it suited the screws for the cells to be located there, plus the fact that they preferred not to have to walk further than the length of their noses.

I said that I would speak to Sim about it and that if it continued he should make a formal complaint. I explained that it was standard practice to put newly sentenced prisoners who'd been given substantial time into suicide cells. 'So that they can settle in,' I explained. He nodded his understanding but went on to say that he had too much to live for. His kids were standing by him, he said, and he was the victim of a police fit-up. I'd brought a plastic chair into the cell with me and sat down to listen to his story; it was fascinating. I have to say that he is either innocent or he is the most cold-blooded killer in history. At the time of writing this, Nat is awaiting the result of his appeal heard in November 2007.

There was one other event of note during January 2003. It was when a young guy in E Hall called Alan suffered an epileptic fit about 10 p.m. one evening after lock-up. He was in the single cell next to me and a load of guys, including me, heard the thump of him falling off his bed and hitting the deck. I didn't move immediately; there were always strange noises at strange times and I'd programmed myself not to react unless I thought it would affect me in some way. A few seconds later, another con banged on my door and told me that Alan was in trouble.

One of the privileges of being in E Hall was that your individual cell doors were open during lock-up periods – it was only the Section doors that were locked. There were about 14 guys in my Section. I jumped down from my bed and went next door to find young Alan on the floor and fitting violently.

'Get a spoon,' I shouted to Stu, who had come in behind me. I knelt down at Alan's head. He was reddening up, but I could see he wasn't breathing and that soon he'd start turning blue. 'Stu, where's that fuckin' spoon?' I shouted. Stu came around the door standard just as I had finished yelling at him.

I tried to open Alan's mouth to insert the spoon and retrieve his tongue, however it was proving impossible to get his mouth open far enough to get the spoon in. Nothing else for it but to try and prise his jaws apart as he relaxed out of the fit and hope that all this happened in time. I shouted to Stu to press the alarm at the main Section door to alert the screws. Alan was going to need some medical attention when he came out of it.

Eventually, I got his jaws apart enough for me to slip the spoon in and push his tongue back into place in his lower jaw. As I was doing so, he started to bite down again and caught the index finger on my right hand in between his front teeth – I couldn't get it out. It was fucking painful and it was made worse by overhearing an argument between Stu and the night screw about why the screw should open the Section door and why Alan needed medical attention.

I'd managed to get Alan into the recovery position and it seemed as if the fit was subsiding – I couldn't wait to get my finger out of his gob. It had a bite mark on it for the next three days, although thankfully the skin wasn't broken.

Finally, three screws came into the Section and literally dragged Alan out. My abiding memory of that night was the sight of him being lifted out, his feet dragging along the Section corridor. He made a full recovery and was back in his cell two days later.

■ ■ ■

It wasn't just complaints that I helped write for cons; simple stuff like writing letters to family and reading their replies was also part of my function. I was someone cons could trust; sounds crazy, given that I was a convicted fraudster, but maybe they saw the real me as I settled into my existence inside the prison.

A really small guy who was in for drugs possession and answered to the nickname 'Moose' – not because he looked like the North American deer-like beast but because he was so small, and the Scots vernacular for mouse is 'moose' – asked me if I would write a letter for him. He was a bubbly wee guy who was always bouncing about; he looked as if he was on happy tablets, but wasn't. I said I would and asked if he could come up to my room the following lunchtime so that I could get the details and compose the letter for him. It all sounded so familiar. I'd been amazed at what other cons were prepared to have me write on their behalf, including lurid details of their sexual intentions to girlfriends or wives. I'd also written some tear-jerkers, mainly in response to a Dear John letter received from a former girlfriend or wife. I steadfastly refused to write abusive letters for anyone. But Moose's requirements were the most upsetting for me, and his letter is one I'll never forget.

He had been brought up by his granny who, now aged 72, was terminally ill and had only a short time left to live. He became upset as he was telling his story and started to cry as he said the words he wanted me to write for him. I desperately tried to detach myself from what I was writing down and managed to keep myself together until he had finished his dictation. I wrote the letter for him that evening and called at his cell during evening rec to read it over to him as matter-of-factly as I could, mainly to get *me* through it as opposed to *him*. He thanked me for helping him out and promised me some Gucci coffee for my time.

What I hadn't anticipated in helping Moose write his last letter to his gran was the possibility of a reply being received. One lunchtime a week or so later, he appeared with the reply and asked me to read it to him. Writing this account now is upsetting enough. I won't go into detail, but suffice to say, both of us ended up with tears streaming down our faces. I had real difficulty in finishing the letter, but eventually managed.

There is the saddest postscript imaginable to this particular story. Moose's gran died about a week after he received her final letter to him. He applied to the Governor for special escorted leave to attend her funeral but was knocked back due to 'lack of escort staff'. I wrote the appeal for him against that decision but all to no avail. He didn't get to his gran's funeral. The way the system treated him after her death was simply cruel and totally unnecessary and he was a different guy afterwards from the one I had known before his gran's death.

CHAPTER FOURTEEN

Life inside had been fairly straightforward for me since the Christmas period. New Year was a non-event, and I tried to get my head around being there for a few more months whilst I fought with Croft over a move to open conditions. His formal response to my CP2 complaint was an absolute classic.

The CP2 is a simple two-sided A4 form. The prisoner details his complaint on the front and the Governor replies to said complaint on the reverse. I detailed my complaint by hand as succinctly as I could and used a list to emphasise the various points in support of my argument. Croft, on the other hand, who also hand wrote his comments, seemed to ramble on and on; in fact, his response actually ended up continuing around the form over the identity details and printed instructions at the foot of the second page. Regardless of how it was written, the answer was a big fucking NO! It seemed I wasn't getting a move any time soon. As it turned out, that was a load of shit – I got a move in double-quick time, only it wasn't to open conditions.

I'll never forget that day for as long as I live. It was 20 February 2003 and, as usual, I was at work in Throughcare, cleaning the place and serving teas and coffees to order. At 9.55 a.m., I was called into the office by Willie and asked to sit down. He was ashen-faced. He started off by saying that he had bad news for me. Initially, I thought something had happened to someone in my family. Both my parents were in their 70s and it had been a recurring nightmare of mine that something would happen to either one of them whilst I was inside; Moose's experience only heightened those fears. Willie put me out of my misery quickly.

'You're being shipped out to Glenochil. Sorry, mate.'

'When?' I asked.

'They're coming to get you now. The bus leaves at half-ten.'

'You're fuckin' joking!' I said.

'I wish I was,' he said in muted tones.

Just at that moment, two ops screws came around the door of the office and asked if I was Bridges. I just nodded. 'Come on, then. Let's get you on this bus!' said the first one. That's the last thing I needed at that point: a cheery bastard who's not got a clue what's going on.

Willie did the right thing and asked me to stand outside the office whilst he spoke to the other screws. He obviously told them what the score was and to go easy on me during the move. They paid attention to what he'd said, but only until we'd left Throughcare, where they re-assumed the swaggering, self-confident arrogance that comes with a white shirt and HMP epaulettes.

It's worth saying here that screws in Scotland are employed by the Scottish Prison Service, not Her Majesty's Prisons, as they are in England and Wales. There was a suggestion made some years ago that the letters 'HMP' were not appropriate for uniformed staff epaulettes and other outerwear worn by screws in Scotland. The screws were having none of it; they threatened strike action in support of their position, which was to keep the HMP tags on the shirt epaulettes whilst wearing the SPS logo on other gear. Tells you loads about the demographics of the screw population; I was to witness more of it, at much closer hand, on arrival at Glenochil.

I was escorted back to E Hall and was hurried along to get my stuff together; both of these eedjit screws were loving it. I asked if I could phone my wife to tell her of my move, but that request was refused.

I got into the Reception area just after 10.20 a.m. and saw that there were another five guys waiting for the same wagon to Glenochil.

The looks on their faces were just how I felt: confused, upset and totally petrified but desperately trying to handle things. Two of them were passmen from D Hall and I knew them. The other three guys I also knew to look at but had never met.

The two D Hall passmen were both from Dundee. One was doing a five-stretch for drugs, whilst the other was doing six years for a violent assault on a guy who had purportedly attacked his girlfriend. The big problem for both of them at that particular moment, as we were all standing in Reception, dressing up in our own clothes, awaiting transfer, was that they had visits booked for that afternoon and their relatives were coming down from the Dundee area to see them. When I walked into Reception, they must have been on their fourth or fifth plea to make a phone call to cancel their visit. The Reception manager just kept saying that they would be able to phone when they got to Glenochil – we all knew that was a load of shit and so it turned out to be. Their visitors duly arrived at Saughton only to be told that they'd been shipped out – and, of course, their requests to make a phone call on arrival at Glenochil were laughed at.

Getting back into my own gear was a laugh; I must have lost at least a couple of stone in weight. My belt was tightened another three notches until it bit in a new hole and the trousers felt really baggy on me. I smiled to myself, but that smile didn't last long. I couldn't get thoughts of Croft out of my brain. Though there had always been the possibility that I would be sent to Glenochil, it seemed to me that he just couldn't handle the fact that I'd challenged his wonderful new system and argued that it was fatally flawed. He's another one I'd run over, if I got half a chance. The only difference being that I might also reverse over him, just to make sure!

I was trying not to think about what was in front of me, while my anger was growing at how I and the other guys were being treated, just like lumps of fucking meat, being transported to another processing plant.

We were all filled with fear and trepidation at being transferred to a long-term prison that was full of LTPs and lifers. Scotland's most dangerous criminals were held there. Glenochil had the justified reputation of being Scotland's toughest jail – run by the screws in a fashion that was akin to a boot camp. It had suffered damaging riots in the early '90s and a stand was taken to sort out the problems using an iron fist. It worked and that hard-line approach had ensured that the place had been riot-free for almost a decade. HMP Shotts, midway between Edinburgh and Glasgow, was the other LTP prison in Scotland. It had a reputation for unrest and was commonly viewed as a cons' jail, whereas Glenochil was rightly viewed as a screws' jail.

The trip up there was interesting. Moving jail at any time during your sentence is an intimidating prospect; moving Halls within the same jail is bad enough at times. I spent twenty-four months in five different prisons, was in eleven different Halls and eighteen different cells. In that minibus on that particular day, we had to endure a screw from A Hall, who had been press-ganged into escorting us up to Glenochil, moaning on about missing his pub lunch and his game of darts. It took about 75 minutes to complete the journey.

When we arrived, we were quickly thrown out of the minibus and the screw driver led us into the Reception. We were, of course, all double-cuffed. The Reception area in Glenochil is a bleak place, but don't take my word for it, read it in the latest full report on the prison from the Chief Inspector of Prisons – he actually uses the word 'bleak'. It was ultra-bleak that particular Thursday lunchtime as the six of us sat on a bench waiting to be uncuffed by the screw from Saughton. The driver was agreeing the paperwork with the senior Reception screw at the desk whilst Eric Bristow was uncuffing us. After the Saughton screws left the building, we were all called up, one by one. In full hearing of the rest, our personal details were trawled over – this practice has been stopped after a formal recommendation by the Chief Inspector. I felt certain that it was the first of the methods used to de-humanise new inmates and get them well under control from the outset. I wasn't called up until the very end. I used the time productively to look around the place. One thing I noticed was the amount of Rangers FC paraphernalia splattered all over the wall immediately behind the Reception desk. There were prints, pennants, scarves and other pieces of tat all over it. Thank fuck I wasn't a Celtic fan, I thought.

Moggy, one of the guys on the minibus, was a Celtic fan and as I was gazing at all that shit on the wall, he was being processed at the desk. Moggy was a rebel who sported a Mohican hairdo and loads of tattoos, mostly of a crappy quality, all over his body. Celtic FC tattoos dominated both his forearms. His chat at the desk was fairly muted to start with until the screw started to mouth off about Moggy's Celtic tattoos. The screw had a short-sleeved white shirt on and proudly showed Moggy a close-up of his Rangers FC and Red Hand of Ulster tattoos. The screw was well into his posturing when Moggy turned to the rest of us and said, 'Hey, guys, we've got a raving fuckin' Hun here!' The screw went mental in about one second and issued a warning to Moggy, suggesting that he be very, very careful during his stay in Glenochil. Moggy responded by telling him to fuck off and promptly turned and sat down beside us. The screw told him that he wasn't finished with him yet, but Moggy, a thin, wiry guy, just told him to continue with his questions and he would answer them from where he was sitting. The screw had no option but to continue and Moggy's stand set the tone for the way we were all going to handle what was an unnerving ordeal.

Once everyone was processed, we were all told to strip, but instead of it turning into an embarrassing caper for all of us, I cracked a joke, so did Ken, and before we knew it, we were all laughing – standing there in the scud, but laughing all the same! Both the screws looked totally disorientated, as if they'd never seen anything like it before. We were issued with jail swag and all of our own gear was folded and stored by the Reception passmen.

One of the gripes I had with the Reception screws revolved around a can of shaving foam I'd bought from the canteen list at Saughton. The screw going through my stuff told me that no pressurised cans were allowed into the prison. I'd bought it from the Saughton canteen list, I explained.

'Disnae matter, mate. Some nutter stuck one o' these in a microwave and blew the fuckin' thing up!'

'When was that?' I enquired politely.

'Oh, maybe three years ago or so,' came the limp reply.

'Three years ago! Everyone who's come through here in the past three years has suffered due to the actions of some nutter three years ago. Are you serious?'

Yeah. He was, in fact, deadly serious and failed to respond to my question about his sincerity. This small altercation told me so much of what Glenochil is all about – total subjugation and control of prisoners.

'Dinnae worry. It'll be in yir property when you leave the place,' he said.

It wasn't! Just like loads of other stuff that was routinely snaffled by the screws on delivery to the prison, or was stolen from prisoners' property after their arrival at the jail.

We were all herded across to the surgery to go through the routine of medical assessments with one of the jail nurses, and then we picked up what gear we were allowed in and made our way over to D Hall, which was the induction facility at Glenochil.

In comparison with both Barlinnie and Saughton, Glenochil is a modern prison, having been built in the 1980s. There was no slopping out at Glenochil and it was all single cells at that time. It nestles in the valley south of the Ochil Hills in Clackmannanshire – memories of the views over these hills still send a shiver down my spine.

We arrived in D Hall and were shown onto the first Flat, which housed all prisoners new to the jail. The only way you could be admitted to Glenochil was by transfer from a local jail like Saughton or by way of a downgrade from open conditions, probably for having been found guilty of some infringement involving drugs. This prison was made up of four residential halls, A, B, C and D, and a segregation unit, or digger, which had accommodation for up to twelve really bad boys at any one time. Each Hall had a rec hall, pantry and offices on the ground floor and three Flats above. Each Flat had three Sections, each Section housing 14 cons, hence 42 cons per Flat, 126 cons per

Hall. Four Halls makes a total capacity of 504. The actual capacity was just less than 500, as there were always cells that were out of commission for some reason or other at any one time.

The six of us were allocated cells on the middle Section of the first Flat on D. We were handed bedding, which included a stinking duvet and a thin pillow. I was told which number cell was mine and I made my way along the Section towards it. On opening the door, the stench hit me. I had wrongly assumed that as this place was a modern build it would be clean and tidy inside; generally the jail was, however the arrivals hall wasn't included in the cleaning regime. The mattress on my bed was covered in stains, some of which I could identify, others which I didn't even try to place. Just like the duvet, the mattress stank. I'd been left a large plastic bottle of Imperial Leather talc by a guy who had been recently libbed from Saughton and my first job in cleaning my new house was to get this mattress smelling a bit better. I must have used loads of that talc on the mattress and the duvet, as the whole place smelled sweetly. The only problem was that the stench from both mattress and duvet gradually managed to fight its way through the talc, resulting in a strange smell in my nostrils that didn't quite make sense to me.

We'd all been given packs of sandwiches in Reception and a small pack of orange juice. We were told by the Flat screws that we should eat our 'lunch' now and would be spoken to individually during the remainder of the afternoon. All the cell doors in the Section were still open and I got to thinking that maybe that's the way things were here, with the Section being locked up but the individual doors left unlocked. Just as I was thinking that, one of the screws popped his head around the door, said nothing and then locked me in.

There was only one piece of paper in the cell and that was the instruction sheet for the 'Night Sanitation System', or NightSan, as it was called – the substitute for not having a toilet in the cell. There was a sink in each cell, along with a TV and a kettle. A charge of £1 per week was charged to your PPC for your use of the television. Some guys had so little that they had to have their TV taken out. The profits made by the SPS on the provision of TVs must be phenomenal;

all of them had seen better days and were the same make and size. I estimated that each TV would pay for itself after a maximum of one year and after that it was pure profit all the way.

The NightSan operated like this. Only one con was allowed to be out in any Section at any one time. There was a call button, which you pressed when you needed to go. You were then shown either a red light, meaning that your request had been noted and that you were in the queue, or a green light, telling you that you could open your cell door and go and do your business. If you didn't get any light at all, it meant there were already too many people in the queue. It could only handle a maximum of eight requests at any one time. This meant that you had to plan your toilet breaks well in advance. Each time you left the cell, you were allowed a maximum of eight minutes. If there were eight guys in the queue and all of them took eight minutes each, and you were unlucky Mr Nine, you were waiting for over an hour to do your toilet business. Glenochil had a massive problem at that time of human waste being thrown out of cell windows onto exercise yards – the basis of the problem was the NightSan system.

Once, when I was in B Hall and was suffering a dose of the runs, I got up in the middle of the night and got out straight away with a green light, but because I took a minute or so longer than my allotted eight minutes – my guts were turning inside out – I was told by cell intercom that my NightSan facility had been withdrawn till morning. Trying to explain to a screw sitting in some control room that you're suffering from diarrhoea and really could do with having access to a toilet was one of the most bizarre experiences I went through inside. It made no difference – my NightSan was still withdrawn.

One of the landing screws came in to see me the afternoon of my arrival. He had a load of papers in his hand and sat down on the plastic seat, as I sat on the bed. He introduced himself and gave me a message from Steve, the screw from Throughcare in Saughton. I started to choke up as he told me that Steve had called him and briefed him on what type of guy I was. He also passed on a message from Steve wishing me good luck for the future. When I'd left Throughcare earlier that day, Steve had been on a course and I'd been unable to say my goodbyes and thanks to him. I later received a fantastic greetings card, signed by everyone in Throughcare, wishing me well. Both of these gestures touched me deeply.

The D Hall screw was an experienced guy, who knew his stuff, explained everything clearly and asked me if I understood the NightSan arrangements. He then started to go through my personal details and verified my name, date of birth, sentence, parole qualifying date, security category . . . 'STOP!' he said. 'I never even noticed that. I'm not used to checking the security category for new arrivals. Fuck me,' he said as he shuffled through my file, 'you're actually a low-cat! I've been doing this particular job for ages and I've never admitted a low-cat to this prison, other than downgrades from open conditions and they're immediately re-categorised on arrival here.' He was shaking his head as he continued to look through the papers in my file. There was a pause of about five or six seconds and then he said, 'Do you want to try telling me why you're here?'

I said that I had absolutely no idea.

CHAPTER FIFTEEN

D Hall in general, and that first Flat in particular, housed, amongst others, downgrades and a variety of troglodytes who didn't conform to the system but didn't cause a specific threat.

The laundry passman on our Section was a Glaswegian guy who charged cons a Mars bar or some other type of chocolate of similar value for the privilege of doing their laundry – a task he was paid for doing, by the jail. He popped his head around my cell door at the tea meal and delivered his well-practised sales pitch. 'Eh, no thanks, pal, I'll be doing my smalls myself.' He muttered something unintelligible on the way out, but I didn't care about him. All I was thinking about was making the phone call to my wife later that evening to tell her that I'd been moved to Glenochil. I hoped that she'd take it OK, but I was very apprehensive about making that call. I needn't have been; although she got upset, she quickly tried to turn it into a positive and encouraged me by saying that a change would be good as I needed to get away from the situation that was developing in Saughton with Croft.

I agreed with all that she said but felt shockingly betrayed by the system. I'd tried to work within its confines, both literally and metaphorically, and had been shafted. The landing screw's reaction on learning of my security category was all the evidence I needed to push me over the edge of reason. Sounds dramatic, I know, but the moment I put down that phone on my first night in Glenochil I changed as a person. My attitude became one of:

'Fuck the system!' I told myself over and over again, 'If the system thinks it can fuck with me, it's got another thing coming.'

I knew only five other guys in the place and, out of that five, only two of them reasonably well. I had no need to keep up any pretence with anyone; the only thing I had to keep uppermost in my mind was that I couldn't lose my low-cat – that was the key to progression out of the place. Mind you, I couldn't see that happening any time soon, and I was right.

I spent seven nights in D Hall and was then moved to a drug-free area on the top Flat of C Hall. Even in Glenochil, with the screws running as tight a regime as could be imagined, there were still drug-free Flats and, by extension, non-drug-free Flats, where guys who had been tested as positive at an MDT were stuck until they gave a series of negative samples.

My first weekend in C Hall was a hoot. Only kidding! At about 8 p.m., during the long lock-up from the Sunday at 5.15 p.m. through to the Monday morning, there was a load of shouting and bawling coming from the Flat below, which was a non-drug-free Flat. About 15 minutes later, with the shouting still going on, I noticed smoke passing my window on its way skywards. I got up and went over to the window, where I noticed a load of guys in B Hall opposite us, shouting and making gestures out of their windows. Some of them were throwing stuff onto the exercise yard. The smoke was getting thicker and I started to get worried. I had taken advice from one of the other cons on arrival in C Hall to get hold of a large plastic bottle and fill it with fresh water every day, as the first thing the screws did in the event of a smash-up was to turn the water off. I moved over to the sink, which was at the end of the bunker, and noticed that the floor was hot, and getting hotter.

Fuck me! There was a good-going fire immediately underneath me, and it seemed as if nothing was being done to sort the problem. Rapidly, the floor became an alien environment for me. It was far too hot to stand on. Ever tried to fish for your shoes from a bed, using a pillowcase with a jail polo shirt stuffed into it for ballast? No? You've never lived!

I later learned that the arsonist underneath me had let himself out on the NightSan and set light to his mattress and bedding. He also destroyed the Section toilet into the bargain – not an action that endeared him to his fellow Section cons. He was immediately shipped out to the protection Flat. The fire burned itself out in about 15 minutes and my floor started to cool down.

The screws' policy in these situations is that going in to tackle the arsonist or the fire is precisely their last option. It's only convicted criminals, after all, who are in any kind of mortal danger. All of the cells in Glenochil are self-contained concrete cubes and, as such, the potential for any one person's actions affecting another is strictly limited.

It was while in C Hall that I met the best screw I encountered during my time behind bars. I must have had dealings with dozens of the fuckers during my sentence, but Glenn Sutherland was a total gentleman from the get-go. He was a giant of a guy, standing about six-foot-two tall and carrying about seventeen stone easily. He must have been in his mid-30s and had been a screw for over ten years at that time. The first thing that struck me about him was that he was polite. Most screws in Glenochil either called you by your surname, or put 'Mister' in front of it in a vain attempt to sound as if they were treating you with respect, when, in fact, that was precisely the last thing they were doing.

I met Glenn during week one in C Hall, when I asked him for a visits form. In Glenochil, cons were allowed three one-hour-long visits per calendar month. He asked me to come into the office and sit down. The construction of each Flat in Glenochil is like a tuning fork set on its side. The handle of the fork and its two prongs are the three sections holding the cells and the joint in the centre of the fork is the desk area, also comprising a shower and toilet block. I was ultra-wary of sitting down with any screw in any of the desk areas in any of the prisons I spent time in – eyes were always watching, and, inside, two plus two often made seven, never mind five. Glenn reassured me and I sat down.

We chatted for about five minutes, mainly about how I was settling into the Hall and more generally into life in Glenochil. How were my visits going? How was my family coping? Could he call me by my first name? 'What?' He was a screw, he could call me exactly what he wanted, and some of them did.

Glenn was a diamond in what was a very, very deep coalmine, and I will never forget the kindness he showed to me. He helped to get me through a very difficult time in my sentence by showing compassion and consideration towards me. In my time in Glenochil, I never heard any con bad-mouthing Glenn in any way whatsoever. He was one of the screws weighed down with requests, as everyone knew that he would do his best for them. Equally, no con messed with him; he could handle himself, no doubt about that.

I went through a three-week induction at Glenochil, during which all the new cons did courses on health and hygiene, care of substances hazardous to health, basic first aid and, of course, the group education assessments, all of which were intermingled with the usual sessions from social workers, PTIs and the like. There were ten guys in my induction group, including all the Saughton boys who'd travelled up on the same minibus as me. All ten of us got maximum marks for the English and arithmetic tests – I wonder how often that happens? – telling the education people absolutely fuck all.

I'd settled well into my life in C Hall and had caught up with an old mucker from Saughton who was the Flat brewer. Jail hooch is legendary and is normally disgusting to the taste. Adam's particular brew was just like orange juice but had a hugely potent kick – one you could feel from the very first sip, and that was all you could take of it, a sip. Remember, I hadn't had a drink of any kind for well over six months. I wasn't a huge drinker on the out, but that first half-mug of hooch had me singing and dancing when I got back to my cell. The recipe for the brew was a couple of over-ripe bananas and five or six litres of orange juice concentrate. Adam had managed to get hold of a huge jam container and had mashed up the bananas and added the juice, carefully lifting the lid every few hours to allow the fermentation process to continue properly. After stirring it regularly, the hooch was available for drinking within five days. Some guys were at the really heavy stuff for upwards of a fortnight.

Screws were really wary of hooch – far more so than they were with drugs. Alcohol accentuates the aggressive tendencies in some people; the drugs used in jail tend not to do that, although there is the odd numptie who takes some speed, but he only ever takes it once. Jumping and dancing around a small ten by eight foot cell is not an advised activity. Consequently, the last place you would want alcohol available in any quantity is in a prison. I slipped past the desk that evening desperately trying not to giggle and managed to take a deep breath just as the screw was locking my door so that I could say 'goodnight' without slurring it. If he'd asked me to repeat it, I'd have been fucked.

Davie McNally was a well-known face on the top Flat of C Hall. He'd been up in open conditions at Castle Huntly, near Dundee, and had recently been sent back for failing an MDT. He acted as if it didn't bother him that he was back in maximum-security conditions, but that was always the case with the so-called 'hard men' – more likely it would be breaking his back. He had that exaggerated 'heavy swagger' associated with some of the mostly West Coast supposed hard men. His rep wasn't the heaviest I'd heard about, but nonetheless he wasn't a guy to take lightly. He had a reputation as a 'taxer'. Some guys paid up immediately and continued paying up, some guys went on to protection right away and some guys were beaten up for non-payment and then went on to protection. Either way, McNally got his way, but it was apparent that, as with all bullies anywhere, he only targeted those whom he thought he could control. I definitely wasn't in that group, but as he wasn't in my Section I assumed the chances of my having any contact with him were minimal. Wrong again!

It was a Saturday morning. We were opened up after the count and breakfast were over. There aren't many guys up and about at 9.30 on a Saturday in any prison anywhere, but I'd never been one to lie in.

My breakfast consisted of a bowl of a Frosties-like cereal and a roll with spread and a spoonful of cheap jam. There was a toaster and a microwave situated at the central desk area for the Flat, and there were also a few loaves of bread on top of the unit housing the toaster and microwave. On the shelf below, there were a couple of baskets, one holding portions of spread and the other portions of the same cheap jam that you spooned out at the Hall servery. I just fancied a couple of pieces of toast that particular Saturday morning and scooted along to the desk area with my plastic plate and knife tucked into my right mitt.

I lifted a couple of slices of brown bread out of the plastic and stuck them into the toaster, which was a six-slice industrial monster that had seen better days. You just had to ignore how stained and marked it was. I was lost in space, thinking about I don't know what, waiting for my toast, when McNally came alongside me and said something. I was so far away on some sunny beach somewhere that I didn't hear anything other than the words 'half-ounce'. I was immediately on my guard and could feel the adrenalin starting to flood through my bloodstream.

'What's that, mate?' I said, desperately trying to work out how I was going to deal with this bastard. McNally was about five foot nine inches tall, so I was looking down on him. He was too heavy for his height, probably carrying at least a stone and a half in excess weight, and he sported these ridiculous-looking circular specs that made him look like Heinrich fucking Himmler.

'You'll be geein' me a half-ounce o' snout every week from next week,' he said.

'I don't even smoke!' was my less-than-witty reply. I was desperately trying to work out what to do and that needed time. Still, that super-chilled feeling was starting to wash over me. I could feel it happening.

He spluttered a laugh and sort of snorted at my impudence. 'Ye ken whit I fuckin' mean!' he said as he moved along to the other end of the unit and prepared to bend down to get some of the spread and jam portions from the lower shelf.

This was it. I reached over and unplugged the toaster. He'd squatted down on his haunches to get a better look at the selection of stuff on that lower shelf and as he came back up he managed to raise his head just far enough above the counter so that I could slam the toaster square into his coupon. Interestingly, both my slices of half-toasted bread were violently ejected from their respective slots as the toaster made contact with McNally's beak. He went down in a heap; his nose was bust and there was blood starting to flow freely from it.

I leant over him and whispered into his right ear, 'I know exactly what you fuckin' mean.' I stood up, retrieved my plate and knife, stamped on his left wrist and then walked calmly back to my cell. I was strangely calm inside as well, something that disturbed me later, and still does now.

Both the screws in the desk area looked around at the noise but couldn't see McNally lying on the deck, as their window only went down so far. My seemingly relaxed demeanour lulled them into sitting in their chairs, drinking their coffees.

Later that morning, after he'd dragged himself back to his cell, trying in vain to mould his nose back into shape, a couple of guys he'd been taxing took the opportunity to get stuck into him. McNally took a tanking and was shipped out on to protection before lunch that day. Nobody knew it was me – other than McNally – and that's how it stayed. Until now.

CHAPTER SIXTEEN

It was my fifth week at Glenochil and I'd already spent one full week in what is known as the General Purposes Work Party, or GPP. The GPP occupied a huge shed off the short side of the L-shaped structure that was the jail. The other worksheds were off the same corridor.

The GPP used to be the work party reserved only for those prisoners under protection, however this had recently changed in anticipation of protections being moved out en masse to HMP Dumfries. The GPP produced garden fences for Wickes DIY stores, forklift palettes for a variety of customers and garden sheds, again for a variety of different customers. About 30 cons were employed in the GPP.

My first job was painting three-foot-high fence posts a vivid, bright-green colour. Surgical gloves were issued to protect my hands from the paint. They were a whole lot cheaper than proper protective gloves and they singularly failed to achieve their objective. The paint stank and seeped through the gloves, as it was thin and very runny. It made my hands itchy and I came out in blotches.

While I was working in the GPP, I met up with Brian King, whom I knew from Saughton. He was borderline manic depressive – always happy and laughing and joking in the company of others but he'd confessed to me on more than one occasion that he cried a lot of the time that he was dubbed up in his cell. He could be a bloody pest, depending on when exactly he burst into your cell for a chat or to pass on the latest scandal. Brian was doing a five-stretch for being 'concerned in the supply of class-A drugs'. In other words, he was a small-time dealer who had been caught a couple of times and was now landed with substantial jail time. He was twenty-five years old and had been in a relationship with his girlfriend, Jackie, for over three years. The light of his life was his two-year-old daughter, Jasmine. Brian would get ever more hyper in the lead-up to a family visit and then would be crestfallen on arrival back in the Hall, when the visit was over.

Another of the GPP workforce was Ronnie Stevens. He was a whole different ball game. During my first week, he was pointed out to me as someone to avoid. He was fat – hugely fat, in fact – weighing about twenty stone, to my eyes, all encased within a height of less than six foot. His back-up team comprised Tony McWilliams, nickname 'Mac', and a complete fuckwit called Davie Taylor, called 'DaTa' by his friends, who numbered precisely zero. Stevens was a bully, plain and simple. The other two were coat-tail hangers, no less dangerous but never willing to kick it off without Stevens' support. Mac and DaTa were skinny bastards and methadone junkies.

On the Thursday of my second week in the GPP, I could feel there was an atmosphere as soon as I arrived in the shed at around 8.20 a.m. My antennae were working and they identified something was up. I kept a lid on my concerns and went about my work in the usual fashion – head down and get on with it. I had progressed on to forklift-pallet building. It was a two-man job and my teammate was a young soldier, who'd been jailed for serious assault. We built the pallets standing either side of a workbench, using pre-cut blocks and planks of wood and battering in six-inch nails with a large Stanley claw hammer. As far as I know, we still hold the record for the highest number of pallets built in an hour – 12. Tea break was around 10 a.m. and all tools had to be checked back in before it began. Tea packs were issued at your place of work and they consisted of jail tea bags and sugar and whitener sachets. I was convinced the tea bags contained sawdust – they certainly didn't taste like tea. I took my own single-serving sachets of Nescafé coffee, which I purchased from the canteen. The first time I took them to work it caused a stir, as they set off the metal detectors on the route.

The problem with tea packs in the GPP was that the screws didn't issue individual packs, which they should have done. This created tension, as the contents formed part of the jail currency and the hardest and most intimidating cons accumulated the most, especially sugar sachets. Stevens and his crew dominated the bunfights that tea breaks turned into. The screws fucked off to their office at the other end of the shed, whilst about 30 of us were left sitting in a circle, scrambling over a few tea bags. I was sitting drinking my black Gucci coffee but saw things start to unravel.

DaTa asked in a loud voice, 'Who the fuck's been intae my tea pack?'

Silence.

Then again DaTa asked the question, whilst at the same time swinging round to face Brian King. Brian was around five foot nine and probably around eleven stone dripping wet. He wasn't particularly athletic and very seldom attended the gym. Brian started laughing, as was his reaction to most things.

DaTa immediately accused Brian of having stolen the contents of his tea pack. Brian stopped laughing at that stage and told him to 'Fuck off and get a grip'.

Had Brian sat where he was, I'm almost certain that he would have been safe. Instead, he got up and walked over to the sink to get rid of the dregs from his Styrofoam cup. He was halfway over to the sink when both Mac and DaTa moved over towards him. Brian fired his tea into the sink and then threw the cup into the bin that sat alongside and turned back only to be punched on the side of the head by Mac.

I was saying over and over to myself in that fraction of a second, 'Don't go down, don't go down.' He didn't go down; not at that stage, at any rate. No, he went down when the next punch hit him, a straight right from DaTa, which probably hurt DaTa more than Brian, if DaTa's immediate reaction was anything to go by. But Brian was off-balance. The blow hit him high on the left side of his forehead and he went over onto his right side. Other than standing up to get a better view, nobody moved – nobody, that is, other than Stevens, who moved in very quickly for a fat bastard, so that he could get in on the good bit.

Mac and DaTa had already kicked Brian once or twice when Stevens arrived to jump up and land both of his feet on the side of Brian's head. We all heard the double thump of Stevens' jail-issue shoes hitting his head, and then his head hitting the hard floor. Brian was out by this stage – at least I hoped he was. Stevens even looked round, as if he were seeking acclaim for the manner in which he'd jumped on Brian. He had a sick grin on his coupon.

He resumed the beating by stepping back and taking a full swing with his right foot and connecting it flush with Brian's face. Brian's nose was broken then, as well as him suffering the double cheekbone fracture, his skull having been cracked some time before Stevens' kick. It was a free-for-all of kicks and stamps for the three of them, using Brian as a kick-bag.

The whole thing lasted about 45 seconds, although it seemed like hours. The three of them stopped kicking Brian voluntarily and, as they moved away, I was able to see Brian's face. It was mush, covered in blood. His left eye was open, even though he was unconscious. He was bleeding from that eye, which made me think that he was either dead or dying. His nose was no longer visible and his hair was matted in blood. His head was skewed backwards slightly, which looked unnatural, contributing to my belief that he was dead.

The three screws in the shed eventually sussed from their distance that something was up and walked briskly down from their office, mugs of tea still in their hands. Us all standing had alerted them that there was something up. Their reaction on seeing Brian lying unconscious in an ever-widening pool of his own blood was total panic. One screw pressed his alarm and within ten seconds about a dozen screws came pouring into the shed, only to scream to a halt when they realised that exactly nothing was happening – it had already happened.

Stevens and his crew were sitting down, drinking the dregs of their teas, having already wiped their jail-issue shoes on the backs of the legs of their trousers to get rid of any incriminating bloodstains.

The screw manager then asked in a loud, sort-of-panicky voice, 'Who did this?'

Silence. Did he really expect any other response? I was in shock – total shock. I had stood by and let a harmless young guy be beaten to a pulp by three fucking scumbags. I could have taken a charge at the group during their kicking spree and knocked all of them over. I might have taken a hammering myself, but surely, certainly, Brian wouldn't have been in such a state. I honestly thought they'd killed him.

The jail nurse arrived after about five minutes, followed by the doctor a couple of minutes later. It was only then that an ambulance was called. Brian was still out cold and we were told not to move so that the investigation could start. The screw manager walked around inside the circle, asking what went on and calling us all animals. He reserved even greater abuse for those of us who he knew wouldn't come forward and tell him what had gone on. He stopped in front of Stevens and asked him directly if he knew what happened. Stevens said nothing, but had a smirk on his face, which upset the screw. Stevens knew that the GPP wasn't covered by CCTV.

Then the screw lost it and started shouting at Stevens only a couple of inches from his face. 'Don't fuck with me, sonny. You'll be in that fuckin' digger quicker than your feet can carry you.'

Stevens replied by asking why the screw had dug him out and told him that he should be careful of the accusations he was making. 'Do you want me to get my brief up?' The screw backed off. All this was going on whilst they were trying to get Brian into the recovery position.

My mind was racing. I was still in shock, although the guilt was starting to take over as the dominant emotion – guilt and rising anger – all of this starting to come to the forefront of my mind. The anger I felt about the way I'd been treated – the slopping out, the progression system, all of that – was battering around in my mind at a rate of knots. I kept shaking my head. I tried desperately not to look at Stevens or the other two but eventually my eyes were drawn to him as he sat, still leaning forward, his chest resting on his enormous gut. He still had that smug grin on his face as he took long drags on his roll-up. He was scanning round the group, saying nothing but he appeared to be checking for reactions.

Mac and DaTa were sitting a few spaces away from Stevens and, as time dragged on, they couldn't help themselves from chatting to each other. DaTa was almost in a state of hysteria, laughing and giggling. He shook as he spoke, his skinny frame moving from side to side. Mac ignored him to start with, but something DaTa said made him laugh and then he was into it as well. Stevens tolerated their gassing for about half a minute and then, out of the side of his mouth, said, 'Shut the fuck up!'

It was just after he'd said this that he noticed me looking at him. Our eyes locked for the first time ever and they must have been communicating exactly what I wanted to do to him. He looked uncomfortable for a couple of seconds, at least that's what I thought at the time. Like all accomplished bullies, he quickly put his mask back on and asked me if I had a problem. I looked away slowly and said nothing. At that point, the screws started to split us into groups of five or six. Stevens, Mac and DaTa weren't in the same group until Stevens pulled a guy from Mac and DaTa's group and swung him into the group he had been originally split into. The screws didn't notice and the guy who had been moved said fuck all. The fuckwits were now all in the same group, which allowed them to get their story straight.

My guilt was beginning to get the better of me and I was just sitting with my head bowed, staring at the floor. The ambulance crew arrived and began tending to Brian. An oxygen cylinder and mask were removed from a bag and we could see one of the paramedics talking to one of the screws, who then rushed round the various groups, telling us to put out all fags. Stevens took ages putting his out and only did so after taking at least a couple of long drags. His theatrical stamping and rubbing out of the roll-up almost did it for me. He seemed to be looking at me as he ground his foot on the stub, but perhaps my imagination was getting the better of me in that white-hot atmosphere. It was still only about 15 minutes since the attack.

The rage inside me was boiling up and yet I started to feel cold and was getting colder. It was strange, very strange. I had never felt like that before. I hated this guy so much. I wanted to do him real damage. Enough damage to ensure that he would never do this to anyone ever again. He had taken an absolute liberty with a harmless young guy who was probably dying right there in front of us. I vowed at that precise moment to right this particular wrong – Brian deserved that, at least.

In a funny sort of way, I think that Stevens knew this wasn't the end of it. He gave me an odd look and I was aware of his interest in me. Over the next few days, guys told me that he had been asking questions about me.

The jail had a weird atmosphere over the next week or so. There was the initial buzz about exactly what had happened and who was involved, along with the accompanying police inquiry, which was cursory, to say the least. I was interviewed and told them absolutely zero. I might have wanted to right a wrong, but I wanted to do it my way, without the potential for being plugged by one of Stevens' footsoldiers as a grass. I also had my family to consider; my being shipped out or compulsorily put on protection would have had serious repercussions for them.

Brian King was kept in Stirling Royal Infirmary for about four weeks before being shipped back to the jail – the Governor couldn't afford to have a member of staff full-time at his bedside for longer than a month. He had suffered a fractured skull, a double fracture of the left cheekbone and the left eye-socket, a broken nose, a broken left forearm and three broken ribs on his left side. He spent a further six weeks in the jail infirmary. We managed to get messages in to him via the surgery passman, and he appeared to be holding up whilst his injuries healed around the various titanium plates that had been inserted by the surgeons in Stirling.

The screws all knew who had done it, but without any evidence they were powerless. The police investigation petered out amid a lack of evidence and a degree of indifference. It was over. The jail was back to 'normal' within five days or so. There were more up-to-date, albeit minor, scandals, involving failed MDTs, returns from open conditions and the odd liberation.

I didn't sleep the night after the attack. I couldn't get the images out of my head. Thank goodness the next visit from my family wasn't for another six days; time to get my jail head back on and start thinking straight again.

Right. No, totally fucking wrong! Sleep just wouldn't come and I knew why. The anger in me was taking over and I started to plan reprisals.

CHAPTER SEVENTEEN

Two weeks after Brian's beating, I was still struggling to sleep. Vivid nightmares and memories of the attack haunted me amidst the noise, shouts and screams that punctuate jail nights. Listening to my music or watching TV was no distraction either. I was becoming consumed with what I'd witnessed.

My plans for exacting revenge on Stevens and the other two started off as a pipe dream but fairly rapidly began to crystallise into a more solid strategy. The physical aspect of it all didn't worry me unduly, so long as I was able to pick them off one by one; taking on all three of them at once would have led me down the route to Stirling Royal, just like Brian.

Stevens was a lard-bucket – guys his size can retain some physical speed, depending on their individual athletic ability; however, the one thing they don't have is the capability to keep fighting. Their aerobic capacity is low and they run out of gas quickly. If you can keep going with a fat guy, then you'll eventually get on top. I didn't anticipate keeping going with any of them – I wanted to get the first, second and third dig in, and hopefully a few more on top, before they even knew what had hit them.

I was in fair physical nick when I'd left Saughton; I'd done a good bit of cardiovascular (CV) work on treadmills and bikes, and also played a lot of table tennis, which is a great sport for honing reflexes. I set about constructing a fitness regime that would make me much stronger and fitter and, above all, faster. Speed is the key. Devastating force combines power with speed and I planned to improve both.

A former school-rugby master of mine made a point of explaining to all the teams coming through his hands that the game requires each player to have the capacity to get to where he is needed on the field and, once there, have the strength and capability to do what he is meant to do. I set about getting myself into a physical state that would allow me to carry out all that.

The PE facilities in Glenochil were excellent. The CV room had recently been refurbished and was equipped with new treadmills, bikes and rowing and step machines. The weights facility had also been moved into a larger room, with more free weights, as well as a variety of resistance equipment. The main gym was used for soft tennis, which is played on a badminton court with sponge balls and modified racquets. It's a fantastic game that can be played as singles or doubles. I couldn't possibly estimate the number of hours I played soft tennis during my time in various jails; it had to run into the many hundreds.

One of the PTIs was called Sandy. He had rowed at international level, so I asked him to devise a rowing plan for me. He was a screw who had obvious favourites amongst the cons, therefore was all too obvious in giving out negative vibes to the cons he disliked. Apart from that, he helped get me into the required physical shape.

I had moved job into Employability – they obviously thought I was above painting fences. This facility was a converted former workshed and was used for all the induction sessions, as well as specific courses, such as alcohol awareness and tobacco cessation. It brought me into contact with all the new arrivals into the jail and I quickly became the one the screws turned to when they needed to have a quiet word with a new inmate. It was a comfortable place to work and while I was there I met up with a great young guy whom I am still firm friends with today.

Pete Nisbet was a young lifer. At the time I met him, he was in his early twenties. He had been moved up to Glenochil from HM Young Offenders Institution Polmont on his 21st birthday. His index offence was murder. He had killed a guy while fuelled by drink and drugs. Stabbed him to death. He had given himself up to the police the morning after and had served almost four years of his twelve-year lifer recommendation when I first met him.

Pete and I hit it off immediately. He was a similar age to my younger daughter and I found connecting with Pete very easy. He was an intelligent, prison-wise young guy who realised that he was not worldly-wise. He loved his music and played guitar and sang in the jail band. We were both employed as passmen in Employability.

Most passman jobs in jail involve huge doses of cleaning and this one was no different. The floor area was massive and so hoovering was a one-hour job, which we rotated at the end of each day. The big draw for me in moving into Employability was that the jail had decided to house the new library there and the passmen were to be involved in setting up the catalogue and lending system, as well as doing what I thought were the usual librarian-type jobs. The existing library arrangements in what was a jail housing long-term prisoners were lamentable. This new facility was sure to be a hell of a lot better.

Pete and I started off cataloguing the books, but I was shocked that there were so few. George Cairns, Employability manager and former sheet-metal worker (I laughed like crazy when he told me, 'Believe it or not, I was a sheet-metal worker') explained the reason to me. He had only been given a budget of £500, he said, and so had gone to the local bookshop and spent it. I asked if it would be possible for the jail to write to bookstores, publishing houses, bookclubs, libraries, etc. to enquire whether they would consider donating some books to the jail. After a couple of days considering this request, George came back to tell me that we should really try and make do with the books we had. I took this to mean: 'Fuck off and don't bother me again 'cause thinking is just too hard.' I then tried another tack and asked if he minded my contacting the Governor to propose that I write to the various organisations, identifying myself as a prisoner in the jail. I have to say that Andy Dufresne's experiences in *The Shawshank Redemption* gave me plenty of encouragement in my quest to improve the jail library. She finally agreed and the letters were sent.

Then one morning on arriving in Employability at around 8.20 a.m., I got hooked by the manager of the workshed next door, who asked me what he was to do with the eight boxes of books that had been delivered to the jail. I was astonished and my first question was, 'Who are they from?' He snarled back that he didn't know and didn't care, but that I should get them out of his fucking shed 'tout fuckin' suite'.

Pete had slipped past me into Employability whilst I'd been getting it in the neck from this nice officer. 'Come on, son, we've got some books to pick up!' I shouted at him. Little did we know as we were walking through the boatshed into the back storeroom that we were going to take four days to get through what turned out to be eight tea chests of books that had arrived from the local council. All of them had been deemed 'not fit for use' in local libraries and so they had kindly responded to my letter by sending countless hundreds of books to the jail. What a feeling it was! It meant that Pete and I were connected to the outside world for a short time – crazy, but true. Someone other than our friends and family had been in contact. It was fantastic.

All the while, my plans for revenge continued to develop. I had been moved to B Hall, which brought me into contact with Mac. It was the top hall in Glenochil and was the last port of call before being shipped out to less secure conditions. I was now entitled to two additional visits per month and as each Section had a shower in its toilet block, I could take a super-quick shower in the allotted eight-minute time allocation under the NightSan arrangements. That helped enormously, as the summer of 2003 was long and sometimes very hot.

Mac was a strange guy, who suffered massive mood swings – typical of an addict. He was about six foot tall and weighed in at approximately eleven stone, maybe underweight by a stone or so. Covered in tattoos, he retained a dark, swarthy complexion, totally at odds with the 'jail pale' norm, as well as the time of year – April.

Liver problems might have been the reason. My one abiding memory of Mac is his teeth – rotten, and a variety of shades of brown and black. One side effect of methadone is the way it rots teeth unless they are properly cared for. It looked as though Mac hadn't been to see the jail dentist – ever. I looked forward to knocking a few of those rotten fuckers right down his skinny tattooed throat.

With Mac now in the same Hall as me, the order for picking these bastards off was obvious. I needed to leave Stevens till last, so that made Mac first and DaTa second. I didn't realise until I was well into the entire escapade how important this order would be. Getting into Mac dominated my thoughts and I set about devising a scheme to carry it out. I shared my thoughts with Pete. I trusted him completely. I don't know why because I'd only known him for a couple of months and I'd never trusted anyone in the system up until that time. I just got the feeling that we shared the same values and a couple of deep conversations in Employability persuaded me that he would be up for helping me to exact revenge on these bastards.

Another guy I knew from Saughton was Stevie Quinn. He was serving an eight-year sentence for serious assault after attacking a guy in a bar and had been transferred up to Glenochil about three months prior to me. Stevie said that he had jumped in to defend his brother, who had been attacked by a couple of guys. The mess he had left both guys in meant that he would get a heavy term. He was a big guy with a fearsome temper. Stevie had recently been moved on to the pantry. This meant that he was one of three cons who served food from the servery in the rec hall on the ground floor of the Hall.

There were always two screws on duty during 'feeding', the term the screws used for mealtimes. One of the screws was behind the servery, with the three cons manning the pantry, whilst the other was always positioned at the front of the queue. Most mealtimes there was at least one niggle over portion size or menu choices. At mealtimes, every inmate carried down his plastic plate and bowl and his menu sheet, which indicated the con's selection from the previous week. Normally, the main problem with menus occurred when new guys arrived in the various Halls. Their menus didn't travel with them, so they always had to choose from what was left on the hotplate. Another regular problem arose when guys forgot to bring their menu down to the pantry. Depending on which screw was standing at the front of the queue, you could either be given your original choice or made to go and stand at the back and wait until the end.

The potential for giving Mac a few digs had to be in the queue for meals. I was certain that I could carry out an attack without him even knowing what had hit him if I could engineer a 'smother' – in jail parlance, a distraction or diversion, call it what you like, but it allows something illegal to take place without the knowledge of the screws. All I had to do was pick the right mealtime and get Stevie to create a smother that would last at least ten seconds – that's all I needed.

My fitness regime was going great and I had managed to get myself hooked up to eight gym sessions per week, with Sundays set aside for my body to recover. It was a bit like being back playing rugby again; some Sundays I would wake up feeling as if I'd been hit by a bus, but it was always a nice, sort of satisfying pain. In-cell exercise, especially during the long weekend lock-ups, was doubly beneficial in that it was developing my strength as well as tiring me out for sleep. Press-ups, both elevated and normal, were easy to do, as were sit-ups and crunches.

I had managed to get Stevie to get me a couple of five-litre red-plastic jam drums from the pantry. If you've never scooped ultra-cheap jam from one of these deep drums, believe me, you've never lived. I needed the lids as well, so that after filling the drum with water I could secure the top, then I connected two together by gaffer-taping an old brush handle to two metal loop handles – a ten-kilo barbell materialised! Not a great weight, but better than nothing. It was good for carefully lifting into squats and bicep curls and for a jail form of bench-pressing. OK, so the screws occasionally emptied the water out of each of the drums during the regular cell spins, meaning that they had to be refilled from the main toilet block, as they were too deep to fill from the cell's sink, but other than that the improvised barbell worked great.

. . .

A month had passed since Brian's beating, and Stevens and the others had started to regain their profiles. Surprise, surprise, nothing had come of the police investigation and so they felt safe again. I felt very strong physically, and mentally I had reconciled myself to the fact that this was the way to go – no ifs, no buts, and I couldn't afford any maybes.

I had struggled to think through the consequences of my intended actions on the remainder of my sentence and what effect they might have for my family. A move to open conditions would be postponed at best and parole might prove more difficult. As I was doing a four-year sentence, I knew I only got one shot at parole, so it would be like getting a further eight-month sentence if I missed out – all of it probably to be served in maximum security. These thoughts constantly flashed through my mind but were ultimately subsumed by those images of Brian lying prone and taking the kicks and blows. In a perverse sort of way, it also helped that my weekly visits were of only one hour's duration. Had they been longer, or more frequent, then my mind might have wandered on to the more specific threat of how the remainder of my sentence would be affected by any actions I took and how those precious to me might react.

I knew now how to get Mac and I had also worked out how to cover my actions. I had pinched a couple of pairs of surgical gloves from the cleaning cupboard in Employability – stuffed them inside my pants and hoped I wasn't randomly picked for a strip-search on my way back along the route to B Hall. Fistfights leave telltale marks, grazes and scratches on knuckles and one of the first things the screws did after a roll-about was to check hands and knuckles. A double covering of the stretchy plastic would be sufficient to avoid detection, if I was lucky. All that remained was to pick my moment.

I thought carefully about which mealtime I should target Mac. I decided on Friday teatime, the reason being that it seemed a bit more relaxed than other mealtimes, which I'm certain was due to the fact that the screws on the backshift and working through until 9.30 p.m. on Fridays invariably had the weekend off. This would allow me the best opportunity to get Mac and have a decent chance of not being spotted or fingered for it. I needed Stevie to challenge Mac on his menu choice, creating a situation where Mac would be shunted to the back of the queue. I then planned to join the queue last, right behind Mac, and do the deed. Stevie was up for it.

That Friday was like any other in Glenochil. Canteen was distributed after lunch and the round of square-ups lasted for over an hour, followed by a more relaxed period when everyone enjoyed their chocolate bars, coffee, biscuits or whatever else they'd ordered. The tea meal was always earlier on Fridays, for some unknown reason, and always less popular, probably because some of the guys were so full of chocolate and other munchies. When tea was called by the screw on the Flat, I put on both pairs of the surgical gloves carefully – a difficult process – and then took my specs and wristwatch off and put them in the cupboard under the sink in my cell. I waited a few minutes, so that the queue would be formed. I got down to the pantry and stood outside the door for a few seconds, which allowed me to see the queue winding through the rec hall. Fortunately, Mac was about 15 guys from the end of the queue and by that time about six back from the servery. I only needed to wait a few more seconds and Mac would be exactly where I needed him to be. Fuck, I was scared. Not scared enough not to go ahead with the plan, but just scared of things like what the consequences of my actions would be, what might happen if Mac sussed it before I got to him or a screw got in the way. What is it that they say about fear? It adds caution to courage. I fucking hoped so.

I made small-talk with Stevie, who was handing out the yoghurts as if it were just another mealtime, although I could feel the nerves in my voice. Mac walked up to the servery, his curry and rice were put on his plastic plate, and then he asked Stevie for his yoghurt. Stevie asked for his menu. The screw at the head of the queue was leaning forward from the waist, resting on the stainless steel of the counter.

I heard something like, 'I dinnae need a fuckin' menu!'

The screw stood straight up and told him, 'Put your curry back and get to the end. We'll sort it out once everybody's been served.'

Mac eyeballed the screw for a couple of seconds and then turned and trudged to the back. Here was my chance. I quickly entered the rec hall and walked swiftly across to join the queue behind Mac, with both my hands firmly in my pockets, concealing the gloves, knowing that I had to be the last person for tea service that evening.

As the queue snaked towards the wall housing the servery, I could feel myself getting colder and more and more focused on the back of Mac's head. He wasn't talking to the guy in front of him and had only given me a cursory glance as I'd joined the queue. He was a total fucking scumbag. I could feel myself tensing up just before I tapped him on the shoulder. He half turned, enough for me to head-butt him an absolute beauty, connecting just above his right eyebrow. He actually staggered only slightly away from me and I only took a half-step forward with my left leg whilst swinging an enormous right hook that hit him flush on the mouth, probably saving him some heavy dental bills in the future. I didn't have time to admire my handiwork as before he hit the deck I was peeling off the gloves and slipping them into the bin that was hooked up to the servery wall. Stevie told me later that it was just like switching off a light.

I did hear his head hit the floor with a sort of ping, but he was out cold long before that. The screw seemed to take ages – probably only five seconds – to actually suss that Mac was down and needed attention. Looking down on him, he seemed very peaceful, even though he was bleeding from above his right eye and from his mouth. The lump above his eye was getting bigger by the second. What worked in my favour was that the three guys ahead of Mac in the queue turned and moved towards him before the screw got to the scene. I managed to squeeze part way along the wall, so as to get myself into a position where I wasn't the closest person to Mac as he lay on the ground. The screw immediately pressed his alarm and within fifteen seconds there were about six screws in the rec hall, including the one who had got there quickest from behind the servery.

The Hall manager – Two Pips – asked what had happened. I continued to act as if I had nothing to do with it. He was busy asking the nuggets who had crowded around Mac as I'd slid along the wall towards the servery.

Taking my menu out of the back pocket of my jeans, I asked whether I could get my meal. Stevie slid a tray of pasta onto my plastic plate and put a strawberry yoghurt alongside. I glanced back and heard Two Pips say to the other screws to get Mac on to protection, where the nurse would see him. The guy was still out cold, but I could see him breathing slowly and deeply. I went back upstairs to eat my meal.

Only Stevie, and of course Mac, knew it was me.

CHAPTER EIGHTEEN

The two flights of stairs to the second Flat in B Hall felt like a climb up Everest. My head was spinning with thoughts of the digger, or being stuck in protection or plugged by one of Stevens' crew in retaliation for my actions. All these thoughts were stirring round in the adrenalin pool that was flooding my system and causing me to lose strength in my legs – those same strong legs that had powered me through my life with relative ease. I had never felt as weak as that before. I didn't feel dizzy, just weak. When I reached the first Flat landing, I stopped or slowed down – I can't recall exactly which it was. One of the screws on that Flat was standing in the desk area and looked over to me. He had been left behind when the alarm had gone off and was frantically looking around, making sure that nothing else was going to kick off whilst he was on his own. His glance was no more than that.

I managed to take a couple of deep breaths on the first-floor landing and then started the climb up to the second Flat. The strength was coming back into my legs and at the same time I could feel a throbbing pain in the middle finger of my right hand. I was carrying my plate with the foil container of pasta and my strawberry yoghurt in that hand and I was determined to keep it where it was, just in case anybody noticed the hand damage I was certain I'd sustained.

The solitary screw on the second Flat was waiting on me to come back up so he could lock the gate to the stairs – standard practice when an alarm went off. He was getting impatient, and when he saw me turning onto the last set of stairs after the half-landing, he gave me the hurry-up. Fortunately, my legs were back to at least 50 per cent strength and I managed to put on a spurt for him. He locked the gate behind me and followed me along to my cell, locking the door behind me again. I took another couple of deep breaths and laid the plate and its contents on the bunker by the TV. It was only then that I was able to inspect the damage to my right hand.

The last knuckle on the middle finger was starting to swell at an alarming rate. I had injured that particular joint playing rugby years earlier, when I had suffered a compression injury to it. This was different, however, and the joint looked strange as, with great difficulty, I tried to straighten it out. I immediately went over to the sink and started to run the cold tap. The water ran cold quite quickly and I placed my right hand under the stream. It stung under the flow, but the throbbing started to dissipate a bit whilst I straightened the joint using my left thumb and forefinger.

As I was standing at the sink, I looked up and into the mirror above the sink. (I had managed to get hold of a decent mirror from one of the guys who had recently been libbed.) There was a mark in the left of my forehead, where I had made contact with Mac's right eyebrow. I felt it carefully, determined not to increase the possibility of redness developing. I couldn't feel a bump, and if it hadn't started by now, the likelihood was that it wasn't going to. If the only problem was with my right hand, then I'd got off lightly.

I heard the spyhole going and then heard keys in the lock of my door. I quickly turned around to face the door and picked up my plate in my right hand. Fuck, it hurt! It seemed as if all the weight of the plate was bearing down on the injured joint.

'Not started eating yet?' was the screw's comment as he entered. 'Always wash my hands first,' was my retort.

He then went on to tell me that the Hall manager wanted to see me at 8 p.m. that night so that he could get my take on events in the rec hall. I said that I hadn't even been facing Mac when he had gone down. 'He must have been hit by a fuckin' ghost then,' the screw responded.

'I heard the place was haunted,' I came back.

He left with a sort of knowing look on his face, but I was certain he knew fuck all. Screws tend to act as if they know everything about everything that's happening in the jail, but it's mostly an act. They knew absolutely fuck all about this and after the initial scandal things would die down, just like they had after the attack on Brian. At least I hoped like hell they would.

Of course the scandal would die down quickly, from an official standpoint anyway – but it might take a little longer for the repercussions from the cons to fade, depending on how things panned out.

I peeled back the lid of the foil container holding my pasta. It had probably been in there for about an hour by now and was looking decidedly the worse for it. I picked at the tiny pieces of ham with my plastic fork, which I was holding in my left hand. My appetite had gone almost completely after a few small forkfuls, so I decided to ditch the pasta and cut straight to the yoghurt. I managed to finish it off and then felt waves of fatigue wash over me. I needed to lie down.

I binned the pasta container and the empty yoghurt carton, took a long drink of cold water and then lay down on my bed. My head was spinning. I was desperately trying to think rationally, whilst keeping the pressure on the middle finger of my right hand. I was going to have to cadge a couple of paracetamol tablets from someone so that I could get to sleep. No chance of asking any of the screws for them – paracetamol tablets are strictly controlled and always recorded in case of a potential overdose – just in case they put two and two together and came up with exactly four.

I must have dozed off, I don't know how. The feeling of fatigue surely overcame the pain in my right hand. I woke when the spyhole went again at opening-up for evening recreation. I felt amazingly good. The snooze had brought back the strength in my legs. I'd rediscovered my appetite and knew that I had to eat. A couple of Yorkie bars might help, I thought, so I opened the drawer, took them out and wolfed them. I decided I would keep a low profile for the start of rec and then move around as normally as I felt I could. The Channel 4 news was just starting, so it must have been around seven o'clock.

We'd been opened up for around 25 minutes when I decided to get into the queue for the phone. One phone between forty-two cons means a queue, and a long one at that, especially on Fridays. The guys who phoned out – and not all did, by any means – had received the phonecards they'd ordered in their canteen, so Friday evenings were always busy on the single phone. After going around about seven guys, I finally located the end of the queue. It would give me a slot in around half an hour to 45 minutes. The phones were automatically closed down at 9.10 p.m., Monday to Friday, so I had plenty of time to call my wife.

I went back to my cell and started to try and watch Jon Snow and the team delivering what I consider to be the best news programme on TV. I was concentrating on one of the reports when Stevie came breezing into my cell and slowly pushed the door to behind him. He asked if I was all right and I tried to sound convincing. Then came one of those moments that only come along very rarely in your life; that is, if they ever do. Stevie told me that Mac had still been out cold when the nurse arrived. After the alarm had gone off, the pantry passmen had been told to clean and clear up as quickly as they could, but he had dallied until after Mac had been carried up to the top Flat and into protection.

Stevie reckoned I had punched out at least five of his teeth, although some of them were only stumps. The nurse had been heard saying that he would need at least five stitches above his right eye and so the prison doctor had to be called out. Then Stevie dropped the bombshell – he was grinning all over his face and calling me all the lucky bastards under the sun as he said that all protections were being moved out to HMP Dumfries the following day, including Mac. The chances of Mac getting word to Stevens before he was shipped out were minimal, probably insignificant in the overall scheme of things. This meant that I had one thing that was precious to me, and that was time. Time to get myself over the attack and whatever consequences, if any, were coming my way. Time to plan the next strike: against that little shithouse DaTa. I'd see just how fucking brave that little shit would be face to face, with no Mac or Stevens to give him back-up. Time for Stevens to think about what had happened and ponder why one of his oppos would get whacked and shipped out. Time for him to worry . . . I stopped myself there before I got carried away. That was one thing I couldn't afford to do.

Time was rattling on and Stevie and I had been chinwagging for ages, although it seemed like no time. A bang on the cell door and a shout that it was my turn for the phone made us break for the night. I checked my watch; it was almost 7.55 p.m. as I made my way to the phone box, which was located on the top Section of the second Flat. The phone was free and I quickly got in, sat down and slid a phonecard into the slot. I dialled my home number and started to chat to my wife, who had picked up quickly. I completely forgot about the appointment with the Hall manager and was busy listening to all her chat when I spied him standing in the desk area chatting to one of the landing screws. I could see the screw point at me, probably saying that I was on the phone. The Hall manager turned his back towards me and I lost concentration on exactly what my wife was telling me. She obviously realised that my non-verbals were in the wrong place and in the wrong tone, and she asked me if there was anything up. I heard her question OK and just as I was reassuring her that everything was fine, the Hall manager turned round, walked through the gate and started down the stairs.

I spent another couple of minutes on the phone, then said my goodbyes and put the phone back on its cradle. Stepping out of the booth, I called for Adam, who was next in the queue. He came skipping along a few seconds later and said, 'Thanks, mate.' Adam was a decent guy I knew from Saughton. He was involved in a bitter dispute with the SPS over the withdrawal of his cross-border visits to his young son. I was to become his 'advocate' at a later stage in the process.

I scooted down the nine steps to the middle Section and as I passed the desk area I was waiting on a shout from one of the two screws to go down and see the Hall manager. Nothing came, so I continued along to my cell, number 19, about two-thirds of the way along the middle Section on the left.

It was now 8.10 p.m. I sat there trying to watch TV, still waiting on a knock that would send me downstairs to face the music. I attempted to settle down in front of the telly and concentrate, but the throbbing in my right hand seemed to be getting worse, if anything. I jumped up to check my forehead in the mirror and the mark was no more visible than earlier. I just sat there waiting on the call from the screws, but it never came. Lock-up was at 9.15 p.m. and I'd never been happier to see the screw pop his head round my cell door, say goodnight and then turn his key in the lock.

The way the screws' shift patterns worked meant that the Hall manager wouldn't be back on duty until Monday morning at the earliest – you little beauty! The greater the delay into any investigation, the better my chances of remaining undetected.

Stevie had managed to dig me up a couple of 500 mg paracetamol tablets, but I was determined not to take them until I was ready for sleep. I tried again to watch TV, then I picked up the book I was reading and tried to get into it, but laid it down quickly, and then for ages I just stood and stared out of my window at the Ochil Hills in the distance, with the last vestiges of daylight tickling their peaks. Christ, how I wished I was out somewhere on those hills right then, breathing fresh air and able to walk where I wanted, when I wanted, feeling the warmth of the last rays of sunshine on my face. What I would have given for that right at that moment.

Thinking about that sense of freedom led me to consider the various phone-ins I'd listened to on BBC Radio 5 Live (my favourite radio station) over the years. Crime and punishment, and the Criminal Justice System in general, are never allowed to stray very far from the nation's consciousness. The media fan the flames and the politicians are ultra-keen to jump up and speak on all the issues relating to crime in all its various forms. The term 'holiday camp' is frequently used, as is the argument that cons are allowed TVs, PlayStations, etc.

I need to say this now. Just imagine yourself locked up somewhere luxurious, say Buckingham Palace. You are able to enjoy all of the creature comforts available within that establishment and can go anywhere inside the building, order and eat what you want, when you want, from a range of five-star menus, use any and all of the equipment and other facilities available, but – and it's a massive fucking BUT – you just can't leave the place. Worse, you are there with others whom you would not want to be with any time, anywhere. Your family can visit you for one hour only every week and you can phone them for about five minutes every day. I wonder how long it would take for the 'hang 'em and flog 'em' brigade to start reconsidering their position on the holiday-camp issue.

The real punishment in being sent to prison is your withdrawal from society, and specifically your family and friends. This should be the only punishment for the vast majority of criminals. The conditions in which you are held should reflect the sophistication of the society that has imprisoned you. It should always be humane and adopt a forward-thinking approach designed to help reduce the potential for re-offending. Any other system is doomed to failure.

CHAPTER NINETEEN

Two weeks after my attack on Mac, everything about my life inside had reverted to 'normal'. I was totally focused on my exercise programme and my rowing times were coming down with Sandy's help. Stevie came into my cell most nights for a blether and a cup of Gucci coffee, and one night he came up with a proposal that tickled my fancy. He said that the Hall manager in A Hall was the leading light in some local charity that raised funds for kids suffering from leukaemia. The screw manager was running a raffle and was punting the tickets at £1 a piece around the jail. The key to Stevie's proposal was this: the organiser guaranteed that there would be a specific prize allocated to the prisoner population for which every con who bought a ticket would automatically be entered.

'None of the tight fuckers in here are going to buy a ticket at £1 a shot, are they?' Stevie said. I couldn't do anything other than agree. 'Let's buy a fiver's worth each, giving us ten chances of winning the prize. We'll probably have a 50–50 chance of winning it.'

'What's the prize?' I asked.

He started laughing, almost hysterically, and through his gasps told me, 'A grand Indian banquet valued at £20!' I started laughing as well and soon Stevie was dancing crazily around the very tight floor space in my cell.

'Let's do it. We've both got plenty of cash in our PPCs. Hopefully, we'll win it,' I said.

'I'll get the forms sorted for the deductions from our PPC and get the tickets,' Stevie decided.

'When's it being drawn?' I asked.

'This Saturday.'

Not long to wait – it was Tuesday night.

I'd honestly forgotten about the raffle by the time Saturday came around, but that afternoon I heard Stevie coming up the stairs from the rec hall long before I could see him. He was shouting at the top of his voice, reciting dishes from Indian menus. Once he'd got to the kulfi, he started again with the pakoras and samosas. I jumped up from my chair to catch him striding down the Section towards me, with a huge swagger and a smile as wide as the Clyde. 'Ya fuckin' beauty! We won it, mate!'

We both danced up and down in the Section for a couple of minutes and then things got serious: Stevie produced the menu.

The screw manager had brought the restaurant menu along to the raffle draw to give to the winner for consideration; we had until Monday evening to choose our banquet selections. The meal itself would be delivered personally by the screw manager on the Tuesday evening at around 7.30 p.m.

That meal was one of the highlights of my time inside. Stevie had managed to get hold of a small table, at which we sat either side in my cell. One of the decent Flat screws had managed to get us a couple of cloth napkins and we were waiting with the napkins tucked into our necklines as our prize was presented to us. Both of us had foregone the tea meal and were starving. All the cons in B Hall, and most of the rest in the other Halls, knew we'd won the meal – all of them were green around the gills. We promised ourselves that we would take our time over all of it and I've never eaten a meal quite so slowly, savouring every mouthful. It took us almost an hour to finish it. Stevie insisted on swinging the plastic bag holding all the empty containers up and down the Section after we were finished – the entire Flat stank of Indian food. All the other guys took it in good part.

All my other problems were forgotten for this short period; these blinks of time are invaluable, as they reconnect you with what you consider to be normality – the only things that kept us pinned exactly where we were, were the plastic plates and cutlery. Oh well, we were in the tin pail after all.

I'd started to sense that there was suspicion amongst some screws that I'd been involved in the Mac incident, and by that time it was well known throughout the prison that Davie McNally's broken nose was my handiwork. Stevie insisted on calling me 'Pop Tart' because of the toaster's involvement in the deed, but only ever to my face and always accompanied by more of his raucous but very infectious laughter. Both the screws I worked alongside in Employability were decent blokes. Andy Hepburn and Tommy Dawson were both in their 40s and were experienced screws. Hepburn was a bit more cerebral than Dawson; he was always trying to analyse the actions and attitudes of cons going through Employability, either for induction or other courses. Completely out of the blue, as I was cleaning the toilet block one afternoon, Hepburn wandered in, unzipped his trousers to take a piss and said, 'I hear that DaTa is coming over to join you in B Hall.' I glanced over at him, wanting to look at him but realising that I couldn't, as he was taking a piss. It might be OK to sneak a glance at another guy's dick when you're standing alongside him in the shunkie, but it's another entirely to conduct a conversation with a guy who's pissing while you're looking at him.

I wondered if he was going to warn me off any further action and just said, 'It doesn't concern me where that little bastard is, in this or any other jail.'

Hepburn was zipping himself up by now and I got out of the toilet block pronto.

I told Pete as soon as it was practicable that DaTa was about to be shifted to B Hall. 'Don't dive in. Plan the whole thing, just like Mac, and you'll be OK,' he said.

The only thing was, I didn't really trust myself to keep my hands off that annoying little fuckwit while he strode around the place as if he owned it. If he'd suffered from any apprehension after Mac's fate, he'd got rid of it very quickly. I'd just have to wait until an opportunity came up.

• • •

My reputation for being a 'jail lawyer' had preceded me from Saughton and soon I was drafting complaints for all and sundry. All the guys in Glenochil were subject to the parole process. One of the stages in that process is the opportunity to have a self-representation put before the Parole Board when it considers your case. That self-representation has to be made in writing and cannot be delivered in person. Again, the system effectively fucked the majority of cons, who were unable to write a self-rep or felt that they could not put into suitable words and terms exactly what they wanted to say in their favour. I provided the opportunity for them to say what they wanted to say in their own words, whilst ensuring that all of their feelings were properly expressed.

The success rate of my complaints matched the levels achieved in Saughton. There was no reason why they shouldn't, when you think about it. I was well versed in the prison rules by that time and acted as a first sift for complaints made by cons against decisions made by staff in the prison. There were plenty of cons whose complaints I deemed not worthy of submitting because in my opinion they had zero chance of success. Some decided to go ahead anyway – I always told them that they could do whatever they wanted after hearing my opinion. All it meant was that the success rate of complaints in which I was involved was phenomenal. Out of the first 18 complaints I helped to submit, 17 of them were successful – it was a marginal decision on my behalf whether to proceed with the other one in the first instance.

Prison rules are there to protect the staff and the prisoners. If prison staff do not operate by the rules, prisoners have the wholly legitimate right to formally complain and have that complaint properly assessed and heard. If prisoners do not abide by the rules, punishments are swift and severe and are dished out by the kangaroo courts that masquerade as Orderly Rooms, where your appearance is mandatory but the evidence is almost always tainted.

The screws say one thing, the con says the opposite, the Governor hearing the case decides that he believes his staff and consequently you're fucked!

It was a sunny and very warm Friday in June 2003 and, as with all other prisons, Glenochil had shut down at lunchtime that day. Canteen had been handed out and the guys had started to go through the square-up drill that accompanied every canteen day. Square-up always meant that for about half an hour there were loads of guys scuttling around the Hall, visiting other cons to whom they owed a Mars bar, a half-ounce of Golden Virginia or a packet of skins. I was in my cell reading something or other. My cell faced west and during that warm summer it got unbelievably hot. There were no curtains on the window, and of course it didn't open very far to allow any ventilation. The sun started to get into it around 2 p.m. and was still battering in after 10 p.m. One Sunday night, I was writing a letter to my mum (she wrote to me at least once a week during my time inside and I can't thank her enough for that) and it was so warm in the cell that I was sitting down wearing only a pair of sports shorts and the sweat was dripping off my chin.

Anyway, back to that Friday afternoon. It was around 3.30 p.m. when I heard my name being shouted by one of the Flat screws from the desk area. They didn't walk the short distance along to your cell, they just shouted at the tops of their voices – it all made for a tranquil atmosphere.

'Bridges!' it came again, before I could get to my door.

'Yup,' I said, as I looked around my door along the Section and towards the screw. 'You've got a visitor,' he shouted back and beckoned me towards him.

I was dressed in a T-shirt, shorts and flip-flops – standard swag for a Friday afternoon in a roasting cell. I pulled my cell door to and walked along to the desk area. The screw motioned up to the top Section and towards a small office opposite the phone. 'He's in there,' he said.

I was determined not to play this fucking stupid game and just walked up the nine stairs and turned towards the small office without asking who it was I'd been summoned to see. The door was slightly open and so I knocked and waited for a call to enter. 'Come in!' I ventured inside, not knowing who had spoken.

I recognised the guy, dressed in a brown suit, white shirt and patterned tie. He showed me to the seat opposite him at the small circular table – the same one Stevie and I had dined off so spectacularly only that week.

'Mr Bridges, I'm Derek McGill, one of the governors here. You're causing me trouble and I don't like that.'

I said fuck all. I sat forward in my chair and could feel the sweat building up between my bare legs and the plastic. I moved the chair slightly round to the right, so that I was partly side on to him and could stretch my legs out a bit more. I still said nothing.

'You did hear me, didn't you?' he asked.

'Yes,' I replied.

'Why don't you tell me what trouble you're causing for me?'

'I figure that you've walked all the way to this Hall to tell me yourself what I've done to upset you, so the last thing I want to do is piss on your cornflakes.' I looked straight into his yaks whilst I spoke and once I was finished kept the look going for a second or two, just long enough to gauge his reaction. It didn't look good. I looked down at the floor and he started going at it.

'I don't know how to put this, Mr Bridges, but the problems you are causing me are all to do with the complaints you are encouraging other cons to put in. You should be warned that life could be made very difficult for you during your stay with us – I'm guessing you don't want to end up in the digger.'

I heard every word he said but was determined to keep looking down whilst I formulated a suitable response. After a few seconds, I pulled the right leg of my shorts open a bit further, and he asked me what I was doing.

'I'm showing you the evidence that my bowels are still intact!'

This response seemed to knock his previous composure, and I took my chance.

'For the record,' I continued, 'I draft complaints for cons who come to me with what I consider to be valid grievances. You should know that I turn away loads of guys whose complaints are either ill-founded or vexatious in either tone or content.'

That almost fucking blew him away. He just sat there looking at me. It was as if no one had spoken to him like that ever before – apart from his mum, that is.

'Can I call you Sean?' he said, after a few seconds' pause.

I wasn't in the mood to allow him back in just yet. 'Call me what you want,' I replied, as I resumed looking at the floor.

'I've been in the Prison Service for many, many years,' he said.

Here we go, the sympathy pitch: the bit where he plays good cop after his futile attempt at playing bad cop. I'll fucking kill this right now, I decided.

'I'm 49 years old and see the block of life that we all run around. You having been in the Prison Service for a long time qualifies you, in my opinion, to be turning left at the first corner of that block. I'm on my third or fourth lap of the block. Do you understand that? I'm not some fuckwit con who you can threaten and manipulate at will. I don't care what you've got planned or planted for me. I'm not changing what I'm doing, as I see it as providing a valuable service for guys who are at their most vulnerable.'

That did kill it. He was stunned. He gradually recovered his composure, although it was a slow process, but we eventually got round to talking about the fatally flawed Prisoner Supervision System. The governor seemed to agree that it failed cons like me but was unable to offer any alternative. He asked how would I like to prepare a paper for him on how progression should and could work. The meeting had gone from black to brilliant white.

I duly prepared a paper during my free time in Employability and in the evenings in which I devised a system for progression that was fairer for every con, as it was based squarely on time served, linked to behaviour and how long each con had held his low-cat status. It was adopted by the SPS in November 2003, some two months after I'd left Glenochil.

As I got up to leave the meeting at around 4.30 p.m., he offered his hand and I shook it. He was good to me after that interesting first meeting and was instrumental in having me moved to open conditions a few months later. I am grateful to him for that.

One thing I did as soon as I came out of that office, other than field questions from other cons about what the fuck had been going on, was to speak to my personal officer, Pat Maxwell. Every con is allocated a personal officer in each jail they are in. They are always residential staff and are meant to look after your interests at all times. They are someone to go to if you need to get something done. As with all screws, it was a total fucking lottery whether you got a diamond or a lump of fucking coal. Pat was a big, round Englishman from the south-east – Brighton, I think – and he was always decent with me. He hadn't been at Glenochil for very long; he'd transferred in from the English Prison Service and so was still finding his feet. I recited my conversation with the governor word for word, and Pat's reaction was exactly what I was looking for, as he reassured me that he'd watch my back.

The postscript to this caper was that the following Thursday while I was playing soft tennis during a PT session I was shouted over by one of the PTIs. He was standing beside two security screws and told me that I was wanted for a cell spin. I quickly got changed and was then escorted back to B Hall. As we arrived on the second Flat, I was relieved to see that Pat Maxwell was on duty. There was another screw standing outside my cell, holding the toolbox they needed to dismantle the entire contents. Before Pat opened the cell door, one of the security screws asked me if I had anything that I should tell them about. I laughed and said nothing. He asked me again and I just shook my head, still laughing. I don't know if I was laughing through misplaced confidence or was actually shitting myself at what they might find.

The door was opened. One of the screws brought out my plastic seat and put it down in the corridor, inviting me to take a seat. They could be a while, he said. I sat there for over two hours as they systematically dismantled and removed everything in the cell, including the bed, wardrobe and bunker. The plumbing was disconnected, leaving a pool of water from the U-bend snaking across the floor.

All the time I was sitting there, I was crapping it about what was going to happen. But they found nothing and after they had finished, I was just left to tidy the place up. One of the security screws told me that they had been acting on information received. I replied that they needed to be more careful which of their informants they believed.

CHAPTER TWENTY

Jail time is a series of layers of routine – weekly routines laid over daily routines laid over hourly routines. The regime in Glenochil is so tight that the routines seem endless and yet it becomes more and more comfortable to exist in them. It's your life.

The daily routine always started with a count, open-up and breakfast, which meant a trip down two flights of stairs and then back up to your cell carrying a bowl of cereal and a roll. I used to dump the food in my cell and then fire in for a shower. Get back to the cell, get dressed and then I had my breakfast. The shout of 'Sheds!' – meaning worksheds – went up around 8.15 a.m. Everyone then made their way down to the main door of the Hall. All cons had to be rubbed down by a screw before joining the route. The route in Glenochil was nicknamed 'the Russian Front'. There were two reasons for that: the first because it was almost 350 yards long and shaped in a huge 'L'; the second because there was so much violence perpetrated on it during the early '90s, when the jail was out of control. All four residential Halls fed onto the long leg of the L, whilst education, gym and the worksheds fed off the short leg.

The route was a corridor about 15 feet wide. When it was moving, cons were restricted to a narrow width inside a yellow-painted line three feet from one of the walls – single file only and hands out of your pockets. Thank God those jail jeans fitted me!

Some violence occurred on the route, but most of the planned stuff was dished out in the worksheds, the reason being that the level of supervision in the sheds was, how can I say, just a wee bit more relaxed. Smothers were easy to plan on the route and were essential if you planned an attack in one of the sheds, as there were a couple of metal detectors to negotiate; the detectors were identical to those found in airports. The rubdown as you left the Hall was a joke – all rubdowns were. I never, ever, saw anyone being pulled up by a screw who'd found something on a con during one. If you could get a weapon into your scants, you could get it on to the route. If you could get it past both metal detectors, you could get it into the shed. If you could get it into the shed, bingo!

Smothers were easily created at metal detectors by a guy stopping to tie his laces, say, just in front of the frame of the detector. That always caused a pile-up – there were 500 guys moving at the same time and the screws around the detector were sufficiently distracted to allow the weapon to be handed around the frame of the detector. I saw it happen plenty of times and it always looked remarkably easy. The screws who stood on the route, making sure that all the cons behaved themselves, looked as if they'd rather be cleaning their cookers than standing where they were. Their lack of vigilance contributed to the problems with weapons being taken to and used in sheds.

Cons made weapons out of anything and everything. Blades were easily made out of a toothbrush and a disposable razor. A Bic razor could be smashed up and the foil blades carefully extracted from the debris. Then you took a toothbrush and melted the handle end with a lighter. When it was nice and softened, you pushed in the foil blade, being very careful to leave the sharp side sticking out, before leaving it to set hard. This proved to be a highly effective weapon for slashing someone.

Shanks or chibs could be made from anything you could sharpen – a plastic knife sharpened to a point meant that an attacker could get at least one plug into his target. The problem with plastic shanks was they broke easily. Instead you'd get all your mates tooled up so that three or four guys could stab one poor bastard. I saw one guy being stabbed about a dozen times by four different guys one morning on the way to work. It took less than three seconds. The guy had only felt thumps until he walked on a few yards and realised he was bleeding from numerous stab wounds. He lived, principally because home-made weapons invariably never went in too far. Some consolation for those who have been stabbed, I suppose.

All prisons are full of characters: some you like, some you hate and some you're just plain petrified of. Life inside is a microcosm of life outside with one gigantic difference – everything is magnified. A month in a prison relationship is like a year outside. That works both ways, whether that relationship is good or bad. The main problem is that there's no escape from a bad one.

The cell immediately opposite mine in B Hall was occupied by a guy called Colin Laidlaw. Colin was a proud Geordie, in spite of his Scottish-sounding name. He was doing an eight-stretch for illegal possession of weapons, namely a huge amount of guns, rifles and automatic fuckers. He looked like a thin Mister Magoo, with his balding head and wire glasses. I met him when I arrived in B Hall and got to know him reasonably well over the next couple of months before he was liberated. He had consciously refused to countenance transfer to open conditions, as he didn't trust himself to come back from the weekend home leave, which was granted every four weeks. It was a happy day when Colin learned that he'd been granted full parole; he was scared that his refusal to move to open would jeopardise his chances at that crucial first assessment stage.

Nothing was moving one quiet Sunday morning as Colin stood just inside my door and we ended up in conversation about bombs and explosives. Don't ask me how we got around to that subject, but it was obvious very quickly that Colin knew loads about it. He spent the next half-hour or so explaining to me in minute detail how anyone could make an effective explosive device from stuff you could buy from B&Q. After that first half an hour, I thought I would move the chat on from a subject I couldn't offer any input into and asked him about his home life, now that he was getting out in about six weeks' time. He then told me a story I'll never forget.

Colin stayed in a small cottage in a small village just south-west of the city of Durham. His story centred on his first brush with the law about seven years previously. It had been a Saturday night and he'd been in his local pub for most of the evening and was well pissed by the time he was walking home. As some drunk people do, he went inside, picked up a shotgun from its position above the fire and then went out to shoot rabbits or anything else that moved. All of this at just after midnight, in the pitch-black. His Jack Russell called Tommy followed him out of the door on his shooting spree, a decision the terrier would come to regret.

Colin fired off a few rounds from his double-barrelled shotgun – he gave me all the technical details of the gun, but I can't remember them. He didn't kill anything and only succeeded in waking up his neighbours, who contacted the police. The bizzies arrived and duly arrested him. Colin was taken to the police station, Tommy was taken to the dogs' home. He was remanded in custody pending trial, pled guilty and was sentenced to a year in prison. He served six months inside, as did Tommy in the dogs' home. The funny bit of the story came next.

A few weeks after he got out, the same thing happened again. Colin got pissed, went back to his cottage and reached for the shotgun, ready for another midnight shooting spree. This time, however, Tommy reckoned that discretion was the better part of valour and, as Colin stood checking the shotgun, Tommy bolted under the sofa and lay there looking out at Colin with a 'no fucking way' look on his face. I almost collapsed with laughter. It turned out that Tommy's actions had stopped Colin in his tracks. On telling his mum about the incident, her response was: 'That dog's got more sense than you!'

■ ■ ■

As I said before, it is the drugs dealers who get hit with heavy sentences and I met loads of them in Glenochil. They all had similar stories to tell. One recounted by a number of them concerned the cash they were caught with. I can best describe it by relating an account I heard from a guy who was serving six years for intent to supply. He was caught red-handed with a small quantity of drugs on him.

He had been under surveillance for some weeks and was stopped in his car by two unmarked police vehicles. There were three cops involved in his arrest and when they searched his car, they found a large quantity of cash in a holdall in the boot. When he was back at the station being charged at the desk, the sergeant blabbed on about drugs, etc. and then said that he had been detained with £48,000 in cash in a holdall in his car. He knew exactly how much had been in the holdall – well, you would, wouldn't you? See, major dealers are very seldom users, ensuring that their grasp on their business is ultra-tight. He knew that there was just over £57,000 in the bag.

The cops have got it all tied up. Does the accused really want the cops to charge them with the correct amount, knowing full well that the more you're caught with the longer the likely sentence? Say fuck all. Not a bad payday for three cops, eh? A nice three grand each! I heard similar stories throughout my sentence.

Also on my Section was a guy called Donnie Hunter. Hunter was a young 22-year-old lifer who would never get out. He'd killed two guys in horrific circumstances over a drug-territory dispute; one of them had been his cousin and he'd stored his head on the mantelpiece for weeks after he'd killed him, just as a warning, you understand, to anyone else considering crossing him. He was always OK with me, and I used to give him a hand with his maths homework. It was a Monday lunchtime and I was sorting out his algebra for him when he suddenly told me that the second guy he'd killed was causing him problems.

'What do you mean?' I asked him.

'Well, see, after I tied him to a chair and set him alight, I threw him over a bridge.'

I said fuck all. I could feel myself holding my breath.

'The problem I've goat wi' a' that is that he never went "Aaaaaahhhhh!" when he fell,' he said.

What he had told me stood me up, but I managed to get his algebra sorted. What the fuck was I doing in here with guys like him? I was a first offender, convicted of a fraud, a white-collar crime, and I was sharing accommodation with guys like Hunter – and he was only one of the bampots in the place. My hatred for Croft and his ridiculous population management system was kept firmly on the front burner.

■ ■ ■

The reality of life alongside recently sentenced lifers with long tariffs is one of constant vigilance at a level that's absolutely exhausting – you never know what's going to happen when. In those first few years, due to the fact that they are at the start of exceptionally long sentences, they are effectively allowed carte blanche. They all know that whatever they do, when it comes to their parole assessment those actions will be written off as a reaction to having been handed down a long sentence. They are effectively saying: 'Whatever he did was part of settling into his sentence.' What about the poor bastards that suffered the damage dished out by some of these nuggets? When was the last time you read or heard about an assault happening in a prison – never, I'd bet! They happen all the time but are never reported or, more likely, never reach court. Brian King's serious assault would have been headline news if it had happened on a street somewhere.

CHAPTER TWENTY-ONE

By June 2003, my appeal had dragged all the way through to the first sift and had been summarily knocked back. Deep down, I knew that it was going nowhere but desperately hoped for the contrary. I really appreciated the fact that Dick Whyte and my new QC, one of the most senior legal figures in Scotland, both took the trouble to visit me in person to break the bad news. Apparently the sifting judges had decided that the matters highlighted in our appeal had not influenced the judge in sentencing and that the sentence was not excessive. Dick was very disappointed that the appeal hadn't got through the sift and I felt it was an injustice, because mistakes had been made. I left that meeting knowing that I'd done ten months of my sentence and if this was all this rotten fucking system could throw at me, well, I knew that I could just get through the rest of it.

I needed to get my plans for DaTa sorted out. He was on the first Flat in B Hall, having moved over a week or so previously. I hadn't seen much of him since he came over, which was just as well for me, and him. He was in the same Section as an old con called Jackie. He was well into his 60s and was doing a seven-stretch for drugs. He wasn't able to work in the sheds in Glenochil, all of which required heavy physical work, so Jackie was given a passman job with special responsibility for operating the hall DVD/video player. The TVs in cells had the five terrestrial channels, as well as a video channel – no Sky TV at that time. Jackie's responsibility was to load a different DVD or video each night, from the strictly limited selection available, and switch the player on just before lock-up. The player itself was kept in the screws' office in the desk area of the first Flat.

One of the guys in the Hall was a 'gangster' from Glasgow and was involved in the security and doors rackets. He conducted himself in an open, conciliatory fashion in spite of his 'heavy rep' tag. He had a line for DVDs that were made to look like music CDs. His first batch, which he'd had sent in to him, contained a couple of hardcore porn DVDs masquerading as a couple of volumes of *Now That's What I Call Music*. Jackie was brought into the loop as the operator of the DVD player and couldn't contain his excitement going round the Hall at about 9 p.m. one night, urging everyone to watch the video at lock-up. Shouts of 'What's the movie?' sang round the place, but Jackie's response was always a 'Just wait and see. Ye'll enjoy it, I think.'

I'd done Jackie a favour by writing his request to be allowed off heavy work in the sheds, so he popped his head around my door to tell me about the porn. After lock-up that night, at 9.15 p.m., once the screws had carried out their final checks and the count, I'd bet every TV was hooked up to the video channel. The movie started as promised and was the full hardcore version of some American title, which escapes me now. Please forgive me that lapse.

By 9.30 p.m., you could hear a pin drop in the Hall. Ordinarily, there were always shouts and chatter going on immediately after lock-up and someone was always out on NightSan as soon as it was switched on, which was normally about five minutes after lock-up. I'd like to think that all the guys were enjoying the movie as much as I was. It was 25 minutes in and was moving in all the right directions.

The place was so quiet I could hear guys in A Hall, 40 yards across the exercise yard, talking to each other. Then I heard a door open. Some nutter was out on the NightSan – he couldn't have got the message from Jackie. It was the mad laundry passman! He proceeded to walk round our Section, lifting up each viewing flap in turn and shouting at the top of his voice that he wouldn't be washing any white sports socks for the next couple of days. He wouldn't be able to tell where they'd been or what had been in them. It was fucking hilarious! I didn't really appreciate exactly how funny it was until later that night once things had settled down, so to speak – or, more accurately, once the movie had run its course.

We got treated to porn about once a week, but it didn't last for long. Sex in prisons is something that's never talked about outside and, to be honest, is very seldom talked about in an open way inside. It's never included in any induction session.

I once lost a crown eating particularly tough pakoras one teatime and set about finding it in the main Section bin, where I thought it might have found its way. The bin was a huge fucker kept at the desk-area end of the Section. There had been a curry meal that evening and most guys had taken it – the food at Glenochil was regularly of a much higher quality than at Saughton. I asked the Flat screws if I could dump the contents of the bin out to look for my crown; they told me to use the floor space in the shower block, which was tiled and could be washed down easily. I carefully ripped up a black bin liner, laid it down on the tiles and started to tip the stuff onto the floor. I never found my crown, but I did find a wedding ring and a used condom – one that had been tied at the open end and I was absolutely certain – yes, definitely most certain – had been used.

There were a couple of gay guys on the Flat below me and they spent loads of time in each other's company. They must have had sex at some time. As for the rest of us, we had to be content with strapping on the furry glove, or more likely the white sports sock.

One thing that was noticeable, though, was the way certain female members of staff, both screw and civilian, dressed and smelt when on duty. There was one particularly attractive brunette screw in Glenochil and she wore the tightest trousers she could get into; she must have known the effect it was having on the guys and seemed to patently enjoy it.

There were a couple of flings between cons and female staff during my time in Glenochil, but nothing more than that. I suppose for some women being surrounded by young, and not so young, sex-starved men generates a major turn-on. I know that the smell of some of their fragrances was something that momentarily took me out of the place.

■ ■ ■

Man's best-laid plans and all that. It's true what Burns said about planning and I was to experience it at first hand with the DaTa situation. Jackie's scam with the porn had been rumbled courtesy of some grassing bastard who'd needed a trade-off with the screws and had scuppered a once-a-week treat for the rest of us. Jackie had been placed on report and had asked me to help him to prepare his defence – a completely pointless exercise, as he had no defence. And it really wouldn't have mattered even if he did – he would be found guilty, guaranteed.

Jackie had been rumbled on a Saturday and so his Orderly Room appearance was scheduled for the following Monday. It was the Sunday and I was sitting in his cell on the first Flat, debating with him what strategy he should employ in the Orderly Room. My suggestion of 'Guilty, sir, and I'm really sorry' wasn't going down too well. Then an alarm went off.

Alarms were fairly frequent occurrences in the closed prisons I was in. The thing that was unusual about this one was that it had gone off at the weekend, normally a quiet time for the alarm. Jackie jumped up and shot to his door, immediately looking down the Section to the desk area.

'Oh, oh! There's something going on in the middle Section. There's screws flying in from everywhere!' he said. He walked slowly out of the cell and I got up and followed him. By the time I actually got into the Section corridor, Jackie was well on his way down to the desk area. I slowly followed him down the Section and, completely by chance, just as I was passing DaTa's cell, the little fucker popped his head around his door and knocked against my left shoulder. It was too good a chance. The decision was made for me, especially when he growled at me to be more careful and started to rub the back of his head. I did stall momentarily and then swivelled round and grabbed him by the neck of his jail-issue polo shirt. He didn't know what the fuck was happening, as I propelled him backwards into his cell and kept the momentum going until he hit the wall just under the window. He ended up part-standing, part-sitting, as I was holding him tightly against the wall over his chair. The look on his face was one of terror. He was in the process of asking me what the fuck I thought I was doing and if I knew who he was, when all the memories of what he had done to Brian came flooding back and that cold feeling started to flood through my veins.

I threw him onto his bed and he started to try and get out of the cell. No fucking chance. I took a couple of steps towards the door and pushed it to. By this time, he was pulling himself up into a sitting position. I let go a short right hand, which caught him on the side of the head. He was bubbling before he hit the deck. He got up slowly and obviously thought that was it.

He sat down again on the bed and I gave him another dig, this time with the left duke, which connected with his beak and knocked him backwards, ensuring that he banged his head off the wall with a dull 'ping'. He was snivelling through the snot and blood from his nose and had obviously had enough. Only thing was, I hadn't. That cold feeling was still there.

I knelt on the bed beside him to tell him that all this shit was for Brian King and that he should make sure that Stevens knew that he was next up. Telling him to inform Stevens about my plans brought me out of the zone and I leant my right elbow in the middle of his bony chest to push myself up. He doubled-up as my elbow sought out the softer parts of his chest and stomach. I got to my feet, left his cell and made my way back up to the second Flat and my own Section. The shenanigans in the middle Section of the first Flat were still going on as I passed. It was some argument over a game of cards that had turned sour. A lock-up inevitably followed an alarm and I managed to get myself well calmed down before we were opened up again.

I had new problems, though, and I'd need to think them through carefully.

CHAPTER TWENTY-TWO

Stevens knew what had happened to DaTa before Sunday was out. So did most of the jail. I didn't care, or rather I didn't fear people knowing it was me; it was the most enjoyable bit of the whole caper, letting that fuckwit Stevens wait for the hammering he was going to get.

There was one unexpected development later that week. It came in the shape of a violent, predatory homosexual who specialised in preying on young guys who had just been shipped in from the Young Offenders: to celebrate your 21st birthday, you got shipped to Glenochil and were then seen as fresh meat for this fat, ugly, dangerous bastard. Harry was a major drug dealer who allegedly had fortunes stashed away and had been handed down his life sentence because of the 'three strikes and you're most definitely out!' rule.

His methods of recruitment of likely 'bum boys' was to ingratiate himself with them by offering them protection as soon as they arrived in the prison. This was quickly followed by getting them new gear sent in – the boys had their choice of trainers, jeans, shirts, etc. Before they knew it, they were hooked, and the next thing he was forcing himself on them. He had one of the screws in A Hall in his pocket, so he was guaranteed some private time with his chosen target. Some of the poor young guys just capitulated and went along with all of it – they appeared to accept their lot and chose, or rather were advised, not to ask anyone for help. After I left Glenochil, I heard that one of the young boys had stabbed him twenty-three times in a shower encounter. I've never wished for someone to die more in my life – unfortunately, he survived. I felt real sorrow and concern for all of them but couldn't get involved in any of it.

During the months of May through till September, the prison allowed us two one-hour blocks of outside exercise on weekdays only. That summer had long, very hot spells and I always took exercise – it had started for me in Saughton and I loved being out in the open air. It was the Thursday after I'd whacked DaTa and I was striding around the exercise yard, which A and B Halls shared. Harry was on the lifer Flat in A Hall – another so-called drug-free environment. He never did much walking around, just sat on the ground facing the sun, surrounded by his harem of young boys. I was well into my stride and knew that in just short of a full hour I could squeeze in just over 60 laps at 93 paces per lap – I did say numbers have always fascinated me. I often walked with guys I knew or, more often during a single session, with several guys I knew – they linked up for a few laps, chatted away and then moved on. I was focused on maximising the exercise potential and enjoying the warmth of the sunshine.

I was on my 23rd lap of the yard when he spoke to me. I only heard something like 'I sort things out in this jail'. I never turned round, just kept walking. I was asking myself: 'Did I imagine that?' As I continued around the lap I decided not to even acknowledge what he'd said, that is if he'd said anything at all. I got around to where he and his harem were sitting; I knew he was watching me coming around, but I didn't make eye contact.

'Did you hear me?' He'd definitely spoken to me this time and what I'd picked up on the previous lap was probably right.

I've got less than a minute to decide what to say. Fuck, that's not long.

The last thing I wanted to happen was to be fighting on two fronts – certainly not with two fat fucks at the same time. Everybody in prison knows when alliances have been formed and who the relevant parties are. I would have known if Stevens and Harry had formed some sort of unholy alliance – wouldn't I? Maybe he was just reinforcing his status in front of his harem. Maybe he'd agreed a protection arrangement with Stevens. Maybe DaTa already had that type of arrangement with Harry. No, I'd have heard about that by now.

I finished the lap quicker than I'd hoped. 'What did you say?' I said to him as I shot past.

'I fuckin' sort things out in this jail!' he said in a voice that was increasing in volume as I walked away from him. The fact that two screws were standing on the opposite side of the yard and could possibly hear what he said made no apparent difference to him.

My next lap seemed to be even quicker than the previous one. Well, here goes. 'Not this time, Harry – stick out of this!'

No response – I was ten yards past him in no time and I'd heard nothing by way of reply. My next lap passed without comment and I tried to look his way in a fashion that showed I wasn't scared but also didn't want to escalate any of this – all at the same time, with short-lived glances.

The next lap came round and he said in a quieter voice, 'I've got my rep to consider!'

I said fuck all. This was getting crazy and comical and I shrugged off a snigger as I set off on my next lap. The entire conversation, regardless of where it was going, could be over and done with in ten seconds. Instead it had already gone on for three minutes and counting. 'This is personal – don't get in the way!' was my next offering.

My next lap was filled with trepidation: that's either killed it, I thought, or it's a war, and I didn't want that just at that moment. I floated along those last dozen strides as I swung around the corner of the yard to start walking down the side where he was sitting.

'OK,' he said.

I walked on, still floating; had he said OK to me or to one of his bum boys?

Next lap: 'I said OK!' he came out with, in a slightly louder voice.

Next lap: 'Thanks,' I said – I'm always polite, even to violent, predatory homosexuals.

Getting Stevens turned out to be dead easy. Stevens, like Harry, was also in A Hall but not on a drug-free Flat – no surprise there, then. The work that Pete and I had put into setting up the library had been worthwhile – more and more cons were using it – the only problem was that the strict regime in the jail meant that there were very few opportunities for cons to get along and browse the titles. One of the screws suggested that a library trolley should be taken around the Halls so that everybody could get a sample of what the library had to offer. Both Pete and I would get the old 'yellow passes' to allow us free movement throughout the jail.

It took a couple of weeks for the Engineer's shed to make a trolley for us. The worksheds in Glenochil were mostly useless. There was a boat shed that made fibre-glass boats. It was a hellish place to work and was classed as a downgrade work placement – the fumes of the solvents could be smelled throughout the prison. There was a joinery shed, the GPP and the Engineers, which made trolleys for Royal Mail so that posties could transport their bundles of mail more comfortably. Wages in the Engineers were of astronaut proportions. With bonuses, guys could earn over £40 per week, which, when compared to an average wage of less than a tenner, meant that there was always a huge waiting list to get into that shed. The boat shed made money by selling its produce – the two screws who ran it were brothers and I had my suspicions that they were at it. The only other fibre-glass boat-building operation in Scotland was a family-owned business north of Dundee. Good prospects, then, for all the cons who'd spent years honing their boat-building skills, eh! Loads of wood also went out the back of the joiners' shed, and garden sheds and fencing were sold for a nominal charge to screws and their friends. It was a lively place, which guaranteed cheap, cheap prices, what with all that cheap labour. Only thing was that the same cheap labour was costing the taxpayer over £35,000 per year.

Whilst I'm on my high horse, prisons make fortunes on phone

calls made by prisoners. Politicians and prison staff make great noises about how family contact is a vital ingredient in tackling the problems associated with the causes of recidivism – then they charge cons over the odds to maintain that contact. When I was serving my time, there were no cheap rates for calls made from prison telephones. Evenings and weekend calls were charged at the full rate. A £2 phonecard used to get me just over 15 minutes and all my calls were made at the so-called 'cheap rate'. Christmas 2002 saw BT announce that anyone could make a call from their coin boxes at the rate of one pence per minute, meaning that a phonecard would get you 200 minutes. Just before that particular Christmas, the phone in our Section was damaged by some bam using a shaved card. This practice involved carefully shaving the magnetic strip of the card so that it gave the shaver double the units. The card would be pushed in just far enough for the strip to be recognised and once the card had run out, it was pushed further in, allowing the strip to be picked up by the reader a second time. All very well, you might think, but the downside was that the card unit recognised that it had been fucked and immediately shut down once the second set of units had expired or the shaved card had been withdrawn. The BT engineer who came to fix our phone unit that Christmas told me that all prison phone units were on the standard tariff. This is scandalous and needs to be addressed – an example of the typical hypocrisy trotted out regularly in relation to criminal justice.

We got our trolley and although it was fairly rudimentary, it did the job. Our yellow passes came through, although because I'd had words with the Hall manager in B Hall over my progression prospects, it had been more difficult for Hepburn to convince the security manager to allow me a pass, as there was an entry on my security file.

The Hall manager was a small guy who was suffering from Napoleon complex. You know the type – vertically challenged guy who tries to make up for his lack of inches by being super-assertive, super-smart and super-confident, all the while only succeeding in showing everybody what a super prick he is. It was agreed after discussion that we'd take the trolley around the jail on Friday afternoons. Perfect! It meant that both Pete and I would be working at a time when the jail was effectively shut down, which was great. The relaxed atmosphere that followed the square-up period on Fridays was also ideal for confronting Stevens.

The week leading up to that fateful Friday was quiet. The weather was still very warm and that seemed to have a dumbing-down effect on everyone. I was still loving my exercise regime and the soft tennis. I also played a few games of six-a-side football, which always provided plenty of laughs. It all sounds great, eh? My feelings of guilt and responsibility were still very much at the front of my mind and hadn't dissipated in any way. My wife and girls visited every week – I lived for their visits.

Stevens had clocked me a couple of times on the route, once when he was in the company of DaTa, and there was one thing for certain: he didn't look quite as cocky as he had when he was jumping up and down on Brian's head. I knew exactly where his cell was in A Hall. Pete had recently moved over to the lifer Flat on the top of A Hall and Stevens' cell was almost immediately underneath Pete's.

After the lunch meal that Friday, Hepburn came to collect Pete and me from our respective Halls. We filled up the trolley with a selection of books and set off round the jail to punt our wares. We were unaccompanied as we travelled along an empty route – an eerie experience. We were forced to stop at each locked gate and wait for a passing screw to open it up for us. A Hall was at the end of that long, long corridor and it took us over half an hour to travel about 250 yards and negotiate four locked sets of gates.

We had to wait at the main door to A Hall for another few minutes before a residential screw opened it for us and, as we waited, I could feel my nerves starting to get the better of me. Pete asked if I was OK and I nodded, not trusting myself to give him a spoken response that sounded reasonable. Stevens was a big guy and he was getting bigger in my mind as the seconds ticked away. Sure, he was a big guy, but he was a fucking lard-bucket and couldn't go the distance with me. I was as fit and fast as I'd ever been, even when I'd been playing top-class rugby. My recent sessions in the gym had included time on the heavy bag with coaching provided by a former Scottish ABA champion. If I got this right, it would be all over in no time. My confidence started to return, albeit slowly, as we were walking up the stairs, carrying the trolley between us.

Pete and I decided to leave the middle Section till last, as we knew that Stevens' cell was midway along that Section on the right-hand side. We scooted along the top Section and took our time on the bottom Section, as we both met guys we knew and stopped to shoot the breeze with them. We got back to the desk area and Pete said that we'd need to go round the Section with the trolley first and that there was no way that I could be seen by Stevens until I went into his cell. I asked the screw if I could use the Flat toilet and he nodded. Pete meantime pushed the trolley along the middle Section, with no takers – not many readers in this Hall. I came out of the toilet just as Pete was returning to the desk area. He stalled before he reached the end of the middle Section and I walked towards him. He nodded and whispered, 'The cunt's in his peter! He's lying on his bed reading a mag.'

This was it! I took a deep breath and started along the Section towards his cell. I wasn't in the zone yet and that bothered me. Maybe I'd changed back into the person I was before I'd been sentenced. Maybe I was no longer capable of carrying out this attack, which I'd dreamt about for months – maybe, but then again, maybe not.

I got to Stevens' door. I could see him through the hinged side of the door, lying in his scratcher, reading a magazine of sorts. His boom box was blasting out some noisy shit – fantastic. Oh, and he was eating a Picnic bar, or it might have been two, both at the same time. Perfect, the fat fuck didn't know I was there. 'Here it comes,' I thought. I could feel that feeling washing over me again as I thought about Brian lying in the infirmary, his face and body in bits, whilst

Stevens stuffed his face with chocolate bars. I had no plan but to keep hitting the bastard. That changed as I burst into his cell.

I shoved the door open but kept hold of it, so that it didn't bang on his bed and rebound against me – the doors weighed a ton and this one would have fired me back out of the cell quicker than I'd come into it if I'd given it half a chance. I quickly unplugged his TV as I passed it. The aerial connection came out when I lifted the telly up off the bunker. Stevens was struggling to get upright, but he said nothing – his problems were only just starting. I battered him over the head with the telly just as he'd managed to get his feet over the side of the bed. I'd kept hold of the telly and battered him with it again. I was standing by the side of his bed and his telly felt like a cocktail stick in my hand – I must have hit him with it half a dozen times. I couldn't hear anything other than his fucking music and he certainly wasn't saying much. He adopted a foetal position, facing the wall, as I slammed the telly into his head and shoulder area. I placed the telly on the chair by his bed and started punching the fucker until Pete said something from the door of the cell.

'Let's go, big man! He's had enough.'

I had no idea how long I'd been hitting him – maybe only half a minute or so, but I'm guessing. He said it again and suddenly I stopped – I was covered in sweat but just turned on my right foot and walked out of the cell. We said nothing to each other as we walked along to the desk area.

We managed to get back to Employability in less than half the time we took to make the outward journey. Just as well, as my legs were beginning to go as we got to the bottom of the stairs, although their strength had returned by the time we got back.

Stevens went on voluntary protection later that same Friday. I never saw him again.

EPILOGUE

The mood and temper of the public in regard to the treatment of crime and criminals is one of the most unfailing tests of the civilisation of any country. A calm and dispassionate recognition of the rights of the accused against the state, and even of convicted criminals against the state, a constant heart-searching by all charged with the duty of punishment, a desire and eagerness to rehabilitate in the world of industry all those who have paid their dues in the hard coinage of punishment, tireless efforts towards the discovery of curative and regenerating processes, and an unfaltering faith that there is a treasure, if only you can find it, in the heart of every person – these are the symbols which in the treatment of crime and criminals mark and measure the stored up strength of a nation, and are the sign and proof of the living virtue in it.

Winston Churchill, Home Secretary,
Speech to the Commons, 1910

It took me another three and a half months to get out of Glenochil and into open conditions. I spent 12 nights in HMP Castle Huntly, near Dundee, and probably got 48 hours' sleep in total over those 12 nights. I was sharing in a five-man dorm with four smackheads. Every night they started smoking the gear around 10.30 p.m., once they were certain the screws had fucked off for the night. They'd smoke, chat and watch the telly through until about 2.30 a.m. and then an alarm would go off at 5.30 a.m. so that they could all flush the shit out of their bodies. I managed to engineer a transfer to HMP Noranside, which is near Forfar and in the middle of nowhere. It's a former tuberculosis hospital, complete with small mortuary, and is home to one of the largest rookeries in Europe. My reception there came from the senior residential screw in the jail. He was the most disliked screw among any of the con populations I'd been part of – and there were good reasons for that. He was a bastard and actually seemed to enjoy making cons' lives a misery.

The time you spend in open conditions during your sentence should be filled with positivity, when every aspect of your life inside is being targeted at the future and how you are likely to cope with life on the out. Nothing could be further from the truth, as far as the Open Estate is concerned. Work opportunities in each of the two jails are lamentable, as are the placement opportunities outside the jails on a day-release basis – that is, unless you enjoy working in a charity shop. The screws, particularly those at Noranside, should not be working in the service in my opinion, never mind in the Open Estate. It has to be the most difficult job in the Prison Service, but the guys who were in those jobs when I was there were dinosaurs who took apparent delight in bamming guys up for no reason other than that it seemed to be their favourite sport.

Home leaves comprising three nights from Friday to Sunday inclusive were taken every four weeks. I loved them, but going back to the jail was torture. Counting down the days until your next home leave was even worse. I'd never been a day-counter until that time – there were guys in Saughton who had five-bar gates on their walls!

I managed to get myself on to an HNC course in e-commerce at Angus College in Arbroath. The course was full time and meant that I was out of the jail from around 8.05 a.m. through until 5.30 p.m., Monday to Friday. I loved being at the college and met some fantastic people there amongst the students and staff. I was one of six guys attending the college from Noranside, and both students and staff all knew who we were but never ever judged us. The canteen staff and the girls in the college library were particularly kind to me and I have visited them to thank them for their kindness since being released on parole.

My first meeting with the senior residential screw was a classic moment. He asked me if I was the guy who'd transferred in from the Castle. I said that I was and his response was, 'Well, if you fuckin' hated it there, you're going to hate it even more here. Oh, and by the way, I'll no' be standin' for any o' your fuckin' nonsense either!'

I said nothing. The parameters of my relationship with him were set at that time. I hated the man for what he was and probably still is. The guys who attended the college won a long fight with the SPS over one of his decisions on our home leaves – we were all awarded £1,000 each in compensation. I wrote to him to tell him of our award. I've kept a copy of that letter – I needed to.

■ ■ ■

On 19 August, I was released on parole. The build-up to my being granted parole was stressful, as it is for every con, and those stress levels were heightened by what I felt was the incompetence of the prison social workers, who are intimately involved with all the parole applications. They seemed to continually fuck up on simple things, either through laziness or indifference or a combination of both, I don't know. The roles of prison social workers, especially those who are operating in the Open Estate, should be reviewed immediately.

I had to report to my nominated supervising officer, another social worker, on the first day I was released. He was very kind and understanding with me and very quickly I'd been moved from weekly to fortnightly and then to monthly visits. After my first year of the licence, I was moved on to quarterly visits and completed the licence period without any significant problems – certainly none in connection with re-offending or with the original crime. The problems I encountered were from trying to settle back into home life – a home life that whilst having a structure was nowhere near as rigid as any jail routine.

I also had huge amounts of anger in me and there were a couple of incidents where that flared up – but again I was nowhere near being in violation of my licence restrictions.

The understanding and love given to me by my wife are difficult to describe in words. Both of our daughters are fantastic human beings who are making valuable contributions to society and hopefully we've given them both the wings to fly but also the ability to recognise when to set down roots – they are, and always will be, the twinkles in my eyes.